RED FLAGS AND RED TAPE
The Making of a Labour Bureaucracy

Labour bureaucracy has long been a subject of interest to sociologists and industrial-relations specialists, but it has rarely been examined by labour historians. In *Red Flags and Red Tape* Mark Leier aims to understand how and why bureaucracy came to dominate an organization that was established to promote greater democracy for the working class. The formative years of the Vancouver Trades and Labour Council, from 1889 to 1910, provide the basis for his study of the interplay between bureaucracy, class, and ideology.

Leier sets himself three tasks: to outline the theoretical debates on the labour bureaucracy; to investigate the early history of the VTLC in order to show how and why bureaucratic structures evolve over time; and to examine the ideology and personnel of the labour council in order to understand the complex relationship between bureaucrats of the left and the right and their ideologies. He closely examines the ideology of the bureaucrats (including their attitudes towards gender and race), and how it compares with that of the council's members. He concludes that bureaucrats are defined by their power over a movement rather than by their ideology. Finally, since the VTLC was, at different times, dominated by labourists and socialists, Leier explores why different leaders held different or even antagonistic views.

Leier concludes that the pressure of trade unionism and the class position of labour officials led to increased bureaucracy and conservatism, even among the socialists of the labour council, and that, as the Vancouver Trades and Labour Council matured, increased red tape isolated the officials from the membership.

MARK LEIER is an assistant professor in the Department of History at Simon Fraser University.

MARK LEIER

Red Flags and Red Tape
The Making of a
Labour Bureaucracy

UNIVERSITY OF TORONTO PRESS
Toronto Buffalo London

© University of Toronto Press Incorporated 1995
Toronto Buffalo London   LKP
Printed in Canada

ISBN 0-8020-0661-2 (cloth)
ISBN 0-8020-7615-7 (paper)

Printed on acid-free paper

Canadian Cataloguing in Publication Data

Leier, James Mark.
    Red flags and red tape

    Includes bibliographical references and index.
    ISBN 0-8020-0661-2 (bound). – ISBN 0-8020-7615-7 (pbk.)

    1. Vancouver Trades and Labour Council – History.
    2. Trade-unions – British Columbia – Vancouver –
    Officials and employees. 3. Trade-unions – British
    Columbia – Vancouver – History. 4. Trade-union
    democracy – British Columbia – Vancouver.
    5. Bureaucracy – British Columbia – Vancouver – Case
    studies. I. Title.

    HD6529.V35L4 1995   331.88'09711'33   C95-931356-7

This book has been published with the help of a grant from the Social Science
Federation of Canada, using funds provided by the Social Sciences and Humanities
Research Council of Canada.

University of Toronto Press acknowledges the financial assistance to its publishing
program of the Canada Council and the Ontario Arts Council.

FOR ANNETTE

Contents

ACKNOWLEDGMENTS ix

Introduction 3

1
Bureaucracy and the Labour Movement:
Some Theoretical Concerns 13

2
The Vancouver Trades and
Labour Council: Early Structure and the Beginning of
Bureaucracy 43

3
The Development of Institutions and
Formal Bureaucracy 71

4
Labourism, Bureaucracy, and the Labour
Aristocracy 92

5
Culture and Community 108

6
Relations of Race and Gender 125

7
The Clash with Socialism:
Intellectuals versus Artisans 143

8
Continuity, Change, and Resolution 158

Conclusion 180

NOTES 185
REFERENCES 221
ILLUSTRATION CREDITS 238
INDEX 239

Acknowledgments

I would like to thank several people for their assistance with this book. Anne Yandle and George Brandak of the Special Collections Division of the University of British Columbia, and Sue Baptie and Donna MacKinnon of the Vancouver City Archives were always courteous and skilful in meeting my sometimes confused requests for material. Robert A. J. McDonald of the History Department of the University of British Columbia graciously shared his knowledge and research on early Vancouver and its labour leaders.

Sean Cadigan of Memorial University provided friendship and suggestions during the course of this project. His delight with arcane points of Marxist philosophy and his warm humour are both deeply appreciated. Mark Warrior's experience as a shop-floor unionist and as an officer of the United Fishermen and Allied Workers' Union was particularly valuable as a healthy antidote to the cynicism that dominates much left-wing thought on the labour movement. The late anarchist writer Sam Dolgoff made many useful comments on early drafts of the chapter on the theory of bureaucracy.

The research and writing of this study were supported by a doctoral fellowship from the Social Sciences and Humanities Research Council of Canada. Photographic reproductions were made possible by a grant from Simon Fraser University. Versions of some of the material in this work have appeared in the *International Review of Social History,* the *Journal of History and Politics,* and the *Canadian Historical Review.* I am grateful to the editors of these journals for permission to reprint this material. Irene Whitfield and Joan MacDonald translated my illegible handwriting, sloppy typewriting, and last-minute changes into copy that could be read. Their patience, skill, and good humour in the face of unreasonable demands are keenly appreciated.

Gregory S. Kealey supervised the original thesis from which this book is derived, and I drew often on his fount of knowledge and moral support. Linda Kealey and Andy den Otter acted as the other members of the supervisory committee and offered much valuable advice, often from points of view very different from my own. The suggestions and arguments of these three scholars contributed greatly to the study. So too did the critiques of Stuart Pierson, David Frank, and David Montgomery.

My parents, Jim and Margaret, and my brother, Ben, have been especially supportive during this project. I would also like to thank Heather Way, Bill and Pam Bennett, Ray and Gale DeFaveri, Drew DeFaveri, Sheena Collins, and Donna and Nolan Kelly.

My deepest gratitude, however, is owed to Annette DeFaveri. Without her encouragement, help, and support, this work could not have been done.

The first meetings of the Vancouver Trades and Labour Council were held in a rented room in the Sullivan Building (left mid-ground, across the street from the Manitoba Hotel).

Unable to gain support and money to build its own hall, the VTLC purchased the Methodist church at the northwest corner of Dunsmuir and Homer streets in 1899.

In 1909, the council created a joint stock company to finance the building of a new labour temple. The building illustrated the strong presence of the labour movement in Vancouver, but the formation of the company meant that control over the hall would pass from the membership to a small board of directors.

Union bakers don the uniform of their trade and decorate special loaves for Labour Day, 1892.

The Amalgamated Carpenters and Joiners march east on Cordova Street on Labour Day, 1894. They are wearing work aprons and are marching behind a small horse-drawn float made by union members to celebrate their skill and pride of craft.

The Bricklayers and Masons' International Union float, Labour Day, probably 1898. By then employers were also entering floats in the Labour Day parade, as demonstrated by the B.C. Iron Works float (*right*).

Printers' picnic, circa 1894–5, at Gibson's Landing. Picnics were another way in which workers expressed solidarity. George Bartley, VTLC officer and historian, is standing on the dock, second from the right.

Deadman's Island, 1898. The decision to log the small island split the labour council as no other issue had. Trade unionists differed on the relative importance of jobs and recreational space, depending on their craft and politics.

The flat land at the left of the photograph is Deadman's Island after the last tree was felled in 1909.

RED FLAGS AND RED TAPE

Introduction

Why is there no socialism in North America? Since it was first posed by
Werner Sombart in 1906, this question has continued to underscore the writing of labour history. Though it has been approached in many different ways,
no single answer has been generally accepted. Some have insisted that the
question is irrelevant, that there is no reason why a socialist consciousness
should have evolved. Other historians, particularly those of the left, have not
accepted this answer, and have challenged it with a variety of responses. Following Sombart himself, some maintain that socialism foundered on the
shoals of prosperity in the new world. Other historians suggest that we must
redefine socialism and look for it in different places. Granting that a formal,
political socialist party has not taken root, they have found resistance to capitalism among immigrant ethnic groups, in shop-floor struggles for control
over the work process, and in working-class communities. Much of the
labour history written in the 1970s and 1980s similarly argued that class consciousness, if not an intellectualized socialist ideology, could be found in the
informal culture of workers. Patterns of behaviour, mores, even recreational
activities, separated workers from their employers and provided a rough
unity for protest and confrontation organized along lines of class.[1]

Still other historians reject all or parts of these explanations, arguing instead
that a militant and radical working class has always existed and has regularly
risen up to attack the capitalist order. This resistance, it is maintained, was just
as regularly defeated, sometimes by the state, but more often by the betrayal
of the working class by its leaders. In this scenario, it is union leaders who are
responsible for the failure of socialism and it is the role of the labour bureaucracy that answers the question Why no socialism in North America?[2]

This explanation has a certain appeal. Bureaucracy in all its forms is a universal target of anger and distrust, and any explanation that depends on it is

guaranteed a favourable first hearing. It is, for the left in general, a relatively hopeful answer, for it implies that the historical failure of socialism need not be repeated in the future. If the working class is ever ready to rise up, all that is to be done is to replace the labour bureaucrats with a revolutionary cadre.

But, however tempting such explanations may be, it is not so clear that the labour bureaucracy is the principal reason for the failure of socialism. If the labour bureaucrats are cast in the role of King Canute ordering back the sea of working-class revolt, it must still be asked why the rank and file have rarely resisted them. Blaming the labour bureaucrats also poses a philosophical question for historians, perhaps especially so for Marxists and other materialists. If the working class is perennially ready for revolution but is always thwarted by the actions of union officials, structural explanations for the failure of socialism are unnecessary, even irrelevant. The failure of socialism is then simply a failure of nerve on the part of the leaders. This in turn, however, implies that history is largely an issue of free will and free choice, for if only the labour bureaucrats had chosen to fan the flames of discontent, the revolutionary masses would have succeeded. If this argument is accepted, the only lesson history holds is that the working class is not very good at choosing its leaders. As a general principle for historical understanding or political action, this is not very useful.[3]

Other analyses of the role of the labour bureaucracy have refined the debate considerably. Indeed, recent work has so refined the issue that some historians argue that there is no split between the leaders and the led, that the very concept of a labour bureaucracy is a *non sequitur*.[4] The choice, apparently, is between a labour bureaucracy that is responsible for everything and a labour bureaucracy that is responsible for nothing.

This book is an attempt to find a middle ground. It uses one labour organization, the Vancouver Trades and Labour Council (VTLC), as a case study for examining the interplay between bureaucracy, class, and ideology. In doing so, it undertakes three different tasks: first, to examine the theoretical debates on the labour bureaucracy; second, to investigate the early history of the VTLC in order to show how and why bureaucratic structures evolved over time; and third, to examine the ideology and personnel of the labour council to try to understand the complex relationship between bureaucrats of the left and the right and their ideologies.

The VTLC has been chosen as the object of study for several reasons. First, the militant history of British Columbia labour makes the debate over the role of the bureaucracy particularly invigorating, even if western exceptionalism is no longer a useful way to view the region's union movement.[5] More practically, most records of early Vancouver unions have not survived. Those that have are usually not very detailed, and often have large gaps that cannot be filled from other sources. In any case, few records of local unions provide evidence for the development of bureaucracy. Discussions and debates were rarely recorded, as secretaries were concerned with recording motions, and perhaps with providing a record that would minimize dissent in the interests of solidarity and maintaining the status quo. All too often the only clue to controversy and argument before a vote is the laconic observation 'much discussion ensued.' The records of the council, however have largely survived. Gaps in the record may be filled by using the daily press, which gave the council considerably more coverage than it did individual unions, even publishing its minutes verbatim. No other labour organization received such continuous and complete newspaper coverage, and, as a result, no individual union can be examined in such detail. The council also published its own newspapers: the *Independent*, from 1900 to 1904; the *BC Trades Unionist and Label Bulletin*, from 1907 to 1909; and the *Western Wage Earner*, from 1909 to 1911. These newspapers, endorsed, funded, and controlled by the council, were official organs, and are extremely valuable sources that are not available for other unions. They provide information on the council's policy, debates, members, and activities, and they give some insight into the worldview of the council's leaders. Thus, the VTLC is much more accessible than are individual unions.

The labour council was also much more representative of the city's labour movement than any individual union. Throughout the 1880s and 1890s, when labour and bureaucracy began to develop in the city, there were about 1,600 trade union members spread across fifteen to twenty unions. Examining an individual union, or even a handful of them, sources permitting, draws upon a very small sample. But as a loose federation, the VTLC was made up of delegates from most of the city's unions and represented a significant cross-section of activists and leaders. Delegates were often officials in their own unions, and an examination of the VTLC includes virtually all of the officers who would be counted in a study of any individual or group of labour organizations.

This study focuses on the impact of bureaucracy on ideology, and for that reason the VTLC is a more appropriate body to study than a union. The labour council was created to put forward the political and social concerns of the city's union movement, and it was the council, not individual unions, that created and directed labour's position on matters ranging from industrial relations to park space. Individual unions contributed, but it was in joint meetings with other unions in the labour council that they developed and articulated their ideology. When Vancouver labour spoke, it spoke through the VTLC. Only by studying the council and the unions that made it up can we identify and assess labour's ideology in this period.

Finally, the city labour council was chosen over a provincial or federal body because I believe that it is at the local, community level where clues to the bureaucracy's creation and behaviour are most likely to be found. No one would deny that the federal government is, to some degree, a bureaucracy; considering the scope and size of that government, it is difficult to conceive of administration without bureaucracy. Municipal governments, by contrast, are not usually assumed to be inherently bureaucratic. But bureaucracy is perhaps most insidious when it is closest, for that is when it is hardest to see. In addition, larger bodies, such as the Dominion Trades and Labour Congress (DTLC), met only once a year, passed resolutions of a general nature, and had no real power in this period. Affiliated bodies, including on occasion the VTLC, simply ignored directives and policies from the Dominion Congress with which they disagreed, to no ill effect. Nor was the DTLC an important player in developing ideology and strategy, for politics and industrial struggles took place at the local level of regions and unions. For these reasons, the city-wide council is the most useful model for examining bureaucracy.

The period of this study – 1889 to 1910 – is not arbitrary. It is important to understand the early years of the council, for it was during that period that the leadership first decided on its priorities and procedures. Although many argue that collective bargaining, formal contracts, and the intervention of the state are the key to the development of bureaucracy, it is my belief that the roots of the problem may be found earlier. Indeed, they may be traced to the first meetings of the labour council. Although the early leaders did not create the present-day labour bureaucracy, they set the movement on its course, and it is the earliest period that suggests how and why they did so, even if the bureaucracy they created is a pale thing by comparison with those of today. The study ends in 1910 for several reasons. In that year labour leaders created the British Columbia Federation of Labour (BCFL), a province-wide organization. At this time the BCFL replaced the Vancouver Trades and Labour Council as the most important and most representative labour body in the province. Many VTLC activists then devoted their energies to the new organization, and the council declined in importance. An examination of the VTLC past 1910 would thus produce diminishing returns, and an expansion of the work to include the BCFL would require another volume. In addition, by 1910 the city's socialist movement had split into the Socialist Party of Canada and the more reformist Social Democratic Party. Identifying and examining the left in the labour council after that point becomes more difficult, as the waters are muddied by the schism. I have examined the labour council from 1910 to 1914 in a previous book, and have chosen not to cover the same ground twice.[6] Finally, the council's minutes for the war years are incomplete, with minutes missing for the years 1916–19. Such a gap in this crucial period makes it difficult to understand the council from the beginning of the war in 1914 on. In contrast, the years 1889 to 1910 provide a clearly defined, reasonably complete, and relatively discrete periodization in which to discuss the issue at hand.

It may, however, be argued that a labour council is not the best place to look for a study of union bureaucracy. The council was not a rank-and-file organization. It was instead a forum exclusively for union officers. Serving as a delegate to the VTLC meant that one was part of the labour bureaucracy, with the power to decide and influence the direction and policies of the labour movement of the city. By definition, a study of the VTLC eliminates the union membership and thus cannot examine the conflict between the leadership and the rank and file. While this is accurate, it is not relevant. If the rank and file does, on occasion, fight its leadership, more often it does not. To focus on the sharp, short moments of rank-and-file insurgency is to distort our understanding of the relationship between leaders and led, for it ignores the more prevalent patterns of agreement, acquiescence, or apathy. Furthermore, most studies of union dissidents focus on either fights between competing elites or on wildcat strikes. Struggles between two factions of leaders, however, even if one is conservative and one radical, are not the same as rank-and-file insurgency. Nor is the examination of wildcat strikes a clear and positive way to understand the ideology of the rank and file. Far from being a protest against the bureaucracy, most wildcat strikes are engineered and encouraged by the leadership itself. It is true that spontaneous walk-outs do occur, and it is also true that the union leaders are legally required to tell workers to go back to work under the terms of the collective agreement. Nonetheless, the great majority of wildcat strikes are called by the leadership to enforce the company's compliance with the terms of the contract, to hasten the processing of grievances, or to spur on negotiations. Indeed, in my own experience as a trade union member and shop steward in the construction industry, I was involved in two wildcat strikes, both called by the business agent and undertaken with extreme reluctance by the rank and file. Some studies even suggest that it is the leadership, not the rank and file, that is more likely to advocate illegal work stoppages and to dislike playing by the rules of modern industrial relations.[7]

Because of the issues considered and the theoretical framework adopted in this study, it may be a little difficult to place the book in the contemporary historiography of labour history. Although the labour bureaucracy has long been a subject of interest to sociologists and industrial-relations specialists, it has rarely been examined by labour historians.[8] The effects of the labour bureaucracy in Canada, especially in the post–Second World War era, have been noted by Bryan D. Palmer and Craig Heron in their survey texts, and by Ian McKay in his study of Halifax carpenters, but the creation of the bureaucracy, its causes, structures, and development, have not been studied in any detail.[9] However, bureaucrats did not take over the labour movement in 1935 or 1945. At their founding convention in 1905, the Industrial Workers of the World, or Wobblies, denounced 'labour fakirs' and 'pie-cards' as enemies of the working class. Thus, despite the necessity of examining the beginnings of the labour movement to understand bureaucracy, labour historians have virtually ignored earlier periods.

This examination differs from others in the field in one other key aspect. As discussed in Chapter 1, most work on the labour bureaucracy defines bureaucrats by ideology. That is to say, one person's leader is another's bureaucrat, depending on the politics of the unionist and the writer. I suggest that it is not useful to analyse bureaucracy and bureaucrats primarily as being ideologically at odds with the membership. Indeed, most theorists today argue that it is difficult to differentiate between leaders and led. After tracing the development of this theoretical impasse, I do argue that it is possible to draw a clear line between the bureaucracy and the rank and file. This line, however, is that of power, not ideology.[10]

Until recently, it was possible, and sufficient, to slot a book on North American labour history into one of two schools. In the United States, the custom was to refer to the 'old' labour history and the 'new,' while in Canada, the debate was between the 'first' and 'second' generations. The old labour historians, or the first generation, wrote histories of labour unions, political parties, important strikes, and famous union leaders. Much of this work was rooted in a liberal or social democratic analysis that assumed that North American workers did not really share a common experience of class. Radicalism was usually seen as a response to bad conditions or the result of personal deviance. The fight between labour and capital was most often rendered as a fight over the spoils of capitalism rather than as a challenge to the system itself. By the 1970s, however, this labour history was challenged by a new crop of younger scholars. Part of the revolutionary ferment of the universities in the 1960s and 1970s, this second generation was not content to write more histories of institutions and great men. Its members set out to make the issue of class and class conflict the centrepiece of their work, and they insisted that historians pay attention to all the varied parts of the lives of working people. Culture, the work process, family life, recreation, religion, virtually every aspect of day-to-day experience, was to be put under scrutiny so we might understand workers not just as union activists or politicians, but as complete human beings.[11]

Although the debate was argued fiercely and partisans drew rigid lines in articles, forewords, and conferences, it soon became clear that a kind of synthesis could take place. Indeed, both schools drew upon the strengths of the other, as 'old' labour historians acknowledged that it was necessary to examine other parts of working-class life to explain unionism and protest, and 'new' historians found it necessary to write about working-class institutions and leaders. By the 1980s labour historians were talking about the need for a 'new institutionalism,' that is, a re-examination of unions and political parties that drew upon the insights and theoretical work of the second generation.[12]

It may be that this study fits best under that heading, for certainly it is an examination of an institution. It is not, however, an uncritical study or one that attempts to play down class conflict and socialism. Rather, it focuses on those historical divisions that helped fragment the working class, in particular the role of bureaucracy and bureaucrats. Lizabeth Cohen, borrowing from J.H. Hexter, has suggested that labour historians may be placed into two further subsets, 'lumpers' and 'splitters.' That is, while some historians, including Cohen and many of the second generation, have looked for similarities and homogeneity – the things that have bound workers together – others have examined the things that have kept workers apart. My own preference, by temperament and experience, is to examine the divisions in the working class. Unlike most of the second generation, I was not part of the student revolts of the 1960s and 1970s. My interest in labour history came from my experience as a worker and shop steward in the mid-1970s and early 1980s. It was clear to me that workers did share a common culture, from the clothes we wore to our choices in recreational activities. Indeed, working-class culture was so obvious as to be unremarkable. More importantly, if this culture did bind us together in some ways, it did not do so in a way that enabled us to organize against the boss. If working-class culture was a necessary condition of organization, it was not a sufficient condition. What was noticeable and needed examination were the forces that kept workers from uniting. Thus, my research has leaned towards 'splitting' rather than 'lumping.'[13]

Unlike many 'splitters,' however, I do not believe that the differences between workers make the category of class less valid. I agree with Cohen when she insists that 'lumping must come first for splitting to have value,' and it is obvious that both perspectives are necessary to understand the history of labour and the working class. It is, of course, meaningless to examine splits in the working class without the prior assumption that classes exist.

Nor should this book be used to support those historians who charge that the failure of most workers to endorse socialism or revolution is proof that class is irrelevant. This liberal argument is usually based on a simplistic reading of E.P. Thompson's remark that 'class is class consciousness,' and goes something like this: If class were the primary concern of most workers, they would have formed and joined radical unions and political parties. Since most workers did not join revolutionary organizations, they could not have affected by class or been engaged in class struggle. Therefore, class is an ahistorical notion forced onto the past by left-wing historians with an ideological axe to grind. This argument, however, is wrong, and wrong in several ways. First, the daily experience of class ranges far beyond trade unions and politics. The class one belongs to determines, to a large degree, where one will live, what one will eat and wear, and how well one will be educated. It determines whether one punches a time clock or clips bond coupons to provide the necessities of life; class determines whether one is more likely to die from a lack of vitamins or a surfeit of *pâté de fois gras*. In this way, class is class experience, rather than an intellectual or political commitment. Thompson and other Marxist historians have insisted that it is this common experience that provides links between workers and separates them from employers, regardless of the ideologies they may hold. Second, no Marxist historian would commit the mistake of assuming that class experience is guaranteed to produce ideological unity or militancy. People may well draw different conclusions based on common and individual experiences. In his work on the labour aristocracy and the lumpen-proletariat, for example, Marx demonstrated that different sections of the working class could well have different political beliefs. What does remain constant, and what class analysis does illuminate, is the continuous struggle between workers and capitalists. Often this struggle is not perceived by workers – or capitalists – as class struggle. But as Ralph Miliband points out, 'The nature of the struggles in which people are engaged is not determined by the perception which they have of it.' Thousands of Canadians have gone off to war believing they were fighting for democracy, but few historians would claim this was sufficient explanation for the two world wars. Similarly, acts of individual protest, such as booking off sick to go to the beach, may be seen as examples of class struggle, even though the worker in question may believe that Karl was one of the Marx Brothers. In particular reference to the question of the labour bureaucracy, it is certainly true that many early labour leaders in Canada supported the Liberal and Conservative parties and rejected socialism. But we need to remember that even the most conservative union leaders were still leaders of organizations that were created to fight employers. Their actions as bureaucrats have no meaning outside the boundaries of class and class struggle. Even class collaboration was a tactic used to try to improve the conditions of workers. That many labour bureaucrats sought to leave the working class by becoming paid officals or starting a business is further proof that class formed the basis of their existence, for if class were irrelevant, why would these workers seek to leave one class for another? Class experience and class struggle help explain conservatism as well as radicalism, class collaboration as well as class conflict, for the fight between labour and capital takes many forms. Class analysis is the fundamental tool for understanding why and how the struggle takes different forms at different times by different workers. This book tries to throw some light on some of the reasons certain sections of the working class adopted the positions they did.[14]

Finally, in suggesting that the working class has not been successful in overcoming the obstacles placed in its path, I am not siding with the liberals and social democrats who heave a sigh of relief and say 'and a lucky thing, too!' I have approached the issue in the spirit of the anarchist Michael Bakunin, who appreciated that if it were historically true and perhaps even inevitable that the Roman civilization would supplant the Greek, it did not follow that the Romans were morally superior. It is possible to write the history of events without insisting that the outcome was inevitable and progressive. By writing about factions and divisions, I do not mean to imply that therefore the working class was unimportant or wrong or has been preordained to remain under the yoke of capitalism. Nor should it be concluded that because parts of this study are critical of the socialist movement that I have sided against socialism. On the contrary, I believe that socialists should be highly critical of their own movement, on the principle that all saints, especially one's own, should be considered guilty until proven innocent. Only by facing up to its conflicts and problems can socialist thought progress.

The first chapter of this book examines the theory of the labour bureaucracy to provide a new definition of it. If, as I argue, bureaucrats are defined by their power over the movement, it is necessary to understand how and why the bureaucracy created the policies, institutions, and regulations that separated it from the rank and file. Few trade unions start from a golden age of participatory democracy, but most develop into bureaucracies over time. Studying such developments as the evolution of paid positions, tighter control over finances, and the rotation of leaders shows how the relationship between the leadership and the rank and file changed. Chapters 2 and 3 outline these structural changes in the Vancouver Trades and Labour Council.

If there is no permanent and inevitable ideological split between leaders and led, we can no longer attribute the officers' ideology solely to their position in the labour bureaucracy. Although becoming a leader does have an impact on one's world-view, it does not necessarily force one to be a labourist or a socialist; nor does it necessarily place one in ideological opposition to the rank and file. This means that other explanations for the particular ideology of the leaders must be found. It also suggests that the chief difference in the ideology of the leadership will be in its own definition of its relationship to the membership. That is, it is possible that the bureaucracy may be in substantial agreement with the rank and file on questions of wages, militancy, state ownership, arbitration, and the like. It may, however, differ greatly on issues such as the allocation of union dues, the subsidizing of a labour press, and the role of dissidents. For these reasons, examining the ideology of the bureaucrats and suggesting the reasons why it was adopted assumes a new importance. If one defines ideology rather broadly to mean something more like world-view, it is necessary to look closely at the bureaucrats' attitudes towards gender and race as well. Chapters 4, 5, and 6 examine these issues.

Because the Vancouver Trades and Labour Council was, at different times, dominated by labourists and socialists, it is necessary to understand why different leaders held such variant and, on occasion, antagonistic views. Chapters 7 and 8 use theoretical and empirical arguments to locate the different wings of the bureaucracy and to provide some explanations for the differences. They also suggest the similarities between the two, both at the level of ideology and at the level of the bureaucratic impulse, for if ideology divided the bureaucrats, their positions helped unite them.

This study provides few answers to the issue of bureaucracy in the labour movement, save to stress that it is a complex phenomenon that is not easily summed up in a few generalizations. Still, I hope that an examination of bureaucracy, class, and ideology in this labour council will help us ask, and ultimately answer, better questions about these issues. In focusing on one division in the working class, I do not mean to assert that this was the only division, or even necessarily the most important one. Nor is it my wish to insist that the working class has always been fragmented and divided against itself. On many occasions, however, it has been so fractured, and one fault line that opened was between those who were and those who were not members of the labour bureaucracy. I hope to illuminate this aspect and, in doing so, to add another small piece to our picture of workers and unions in the late nineteenth and early twentieth centuries. By extension, surely if the left is to recover from its defeats in the 1980s and 1990s, some continuing examination of the nature of bureaucracy in all its guises will be necessary.

1

Bureaucracy and the Labour Movement: Some Theoretical Concerns

On 5 November 1916, 260 members of the Industrial Workers of the World left Seattle, Washington, aboard the ferry *Verona*. They were bound for the logging town of Everett, to take part in a free-speech fight that was entering its fourth month. As the ferry docked, the men were met by a crowd of deputies and vigilantes determined to stop the landing. Sheriff McRae shouted out to the Wobblies crowding the gangway, 'Who is your leader?' In a chorus of voices the answer came: 'We are all leaders.' As they pushed towards the shore, they were met with rifle fire from the sheriff's gang. At least five were killed; many more were wounded.[1]

The 1986 convention of the International Brotherhood of Teamsters was held in the glittering rooms of Caesar's Palace in Las Vegas, Nevada. The highlight of the proceedings was the opening night entrance of Teamster president Jackie Presser. Presser, reputed to weigh over three hundred pounds, was brought to the convention floor in a chariot pulled by four burly Teamsters dressed as Roman centurions. The imperial procession set the tone for the rest of the convention. The delegates overwhelmingly supported Presser and his staff, even though he had been indicted earlier in the week on charges of embezzlement and racketeering. The delegates, many appointed by Presser himself, defeated virtually every motion put forward by the opposition Teamsters for a Democratic Union (TDU). The defeated proposals included a motion to lower the president's salary from $550,000 to $125,000 and another that would have allowed local union members to elect convention delegates. The TDU candidate for the presidency, C. Sam Theodus, was forced to endure a public roll-call vote that lasted for three hours after he conceded the election. One after another 1,729 delegates stood up and loudly announced their support for Presser. Only twenty-four voted for Theodus. The convention ended on a macabre note as delegates paid fealty to former

Teamster boss Jimmy Hoffa, missing since 1975, by upholding a constitutional amendment that made him 'general president emeritus for life,' just in case he showed up again.[2]

The Teamsters illustrate vividly what union democracy is not. What then is the labour bureaucracy? Its historiography is part of several debates among historians, industrial relations experts, sociologists, and labour activists, and it is wrapped up in definitions of democracy and socialism, the relation of socialism to democracy, the nature of the working class, and the role of leadership. Opinions range from those of Robert Michels, who holds that bureaucracy and oligarchy follow inevitably from organization, to those of Jonathan Zeitlin, who suggests that it may be impossible to define or identify the labour bureaucracy and labour bureaucrats.[3] Debate on the significance and role of the labour bureaucracy swings between the position of Selig Perlman, who views it as one of the signs of a mature labour movement, to that of Gregory Zinoviev, who maintains that labour bureaucrats are 'the emissaries of bourgeois society in the camp of the proletariat.'[4]

Defining the word 'bureaucracy' is a delicate task, in part because the term has a tainted flavour to it. People are unlikely to give their job description as 'bureaucrat,' and even if they jokingly refer to it as such, they still tend to take offence if they are called bureaucrats by others. The word came into the English language with both a neutral, descriptive meaning and a negative one. It is derived from the French 'bureau,' originally the felt covering on a writing desk. Later, by extension, it came to mean first the desk itself and then an office. By 1720 it was used in English to denote an office for the transaction of public business. 'Bureaucracy' was coined by adding the suffix '-cracy,' meaning 'rule' or 'power.' Thus, the *Oxford English Dictionary* describes it as 'government by bureaux, usually officialism'; it may be rendered as 'rule by office-holders.' John Stuart Mill used the word in 1837, writing about 'that vast network of administrative tyranny ... that system of *bureaucracy*, which leaves no free agent in all France, except the man at Paris who pulls the wires.' R.R. Madden wrote in 1843 concerning 'this "bureaucracy" [which] was an inveterate evil of Ireland, in the early part of Earl Grey's administration.' Later Mill, in his *Political Economy*, refers to 'the inexpediency of concentrating in a dominant bureaucracy ... all the power of organized action in the community.' Carlyle, in 1850, mentions the 'Continental nuisance called Bureaucracy,' while Mill uses the word again in 1860. Mill's remark defines the term with some precision: 'The work of government has been in the hands of governors by profession; which is the essence and meaning of bureaucracy.' The word is used to denote a particular form of government, one that is not democratic and in which positions are held by career officials. The negative sense of the word is plain in most of these usages, and bureaucracy is not considered a technique fit for Englishmen, who were thought to embody strong notions of local control, popular sovereignty, and a distaste for the professional government agent.[5]

The systematic sociology of bureaucracy began with Max Weber. He outlined an 'ideal-type' of modern bureaucratic structure based on the model of the state bureaucracy of Prussia. This ideal-type included fixed and official jurisdictional areas, generally ordered by rules and administrative decisions; a firmly ordered system of super- and subordination; management based on written documents; full-time commitment to the job; and a system of general rules for the management of the office. The modern bureaucrats held office as a vocation and career; they were not amateurs helping out or civic-minded citizens taking on a shift in the government. Because the occupation required a relatively high degree of education and specific training, it conferred upon the bureaucrat a 'distinct social esteem as compared with the governed.' The 'pure' form of bureaucrat was appointed, not elected, and the position was held for life. These procedures were to make the bureaucrat independent of pressure from interest groups or superiors and to ensure that decisions were correct rather than expedient.[6]

The labour bureaucracy differs in some important ways from Max Weber's 'ideal-type' of bureaucracy. For example, unlike Weber's state model, most union officials are elected, either by the rank and file or by delegates. An important section of union officials is not paid. This section may range from shop stewards to presidents. Their positions may not require formal training, although usually some instruction is given, and increasingly in the latter half of the twentieth century, some officials, such as business agents, are university educated. While many of the positions are full-time careers, some are not. Unlike Weber's bureaucrats, union officers may be the highest authority in the organization, and usually they can make as well as implement policy. Finally, labour leaders usually have limited resources with which to enforce their decisions, and they are relatively more accountable to those they administer than are government officials. But Weber's ideal-type was an attempt to describe characteristics of the German state bureaucracy; it was not a definition of all types of bureaucrat. These differences reflect the different objectives and causes of the state and labour, and while they should be noted, they do not render the concept of a labour bureaucracy inappropriate. It may be suggested that instead of bureaucracy, this discussion is really about leadership, and to a limited extent, I agree. Indeed, the terms are used interchangeably in this study. It should be made clear that when I refer to union leaders, I do not mean individuals who are put forward on an ad hoc, informal basis to speak for their fellow workers. I am speaking of those who hold official positions in the union and who help create and implement official policy. To return to the origins of the word, union bureaucrats are office-holders who are empowered to make decisions that are binding on others; bureaucracy is the rule or control of others by those office-holders.[7]

In Weber's view, bureaucracies were created to rationalize administrative decisions: rule by experts was faster, more precise, and allowed for greater predictability, as decisions would be made objectively, in accordance with the regulations and criteria established by those employing the bureaucracy. As modern society and business became more complicated and specialized, the need for bureaucracy became greater and greater. Bureaucracy streamlined decision-making and allowed the tight control of vast enterprises. In government and business, the 'bureaucratic structure goes hand in hand with the concentration of the material means of management in the hands of the master.'[8]

Weber was not much interested in the political implications of bureaucracy. While he was concerned that elected leaders should maintain control over their bureaucrats, he held that the management of society by small groups was 'a basic fact of life.' Democracy and bureaucracy were not opposites, for 'democratic rule basically consisted in the formally free election of leaders.' As Weber put it, 'Any idea of abolishing the domination of man over man by any socialist social system whatsoever or by any sophisticated form of "democracy" whatsoever is utopian.' He concluded that the increasing bureaucratization of the German labour movement and the Social Democratic Party of Germany (SPD) was 'primarily a positive development,' for it meant that the SPD's revolutionary ideology would evolve into a 'constructive reformist policy which would bring about ... real improvements to the lot of the working class.'[9]

Others, however, were more critical. Robert Michels, a contemporary and friend of Weber's, was acutely aware of the power of bureaucracy and its basic opposition to democracy and socialism. Unlike Weber, Michels believed that the desirability of the socialist revolution was self-evident. Active in the SPD, he was bitterly disillusioned by the 1906 party congress in Mannheim. There the executive decisively turned the party from revolution to reformism and parliamentary struggle. The congress also demonstrated the strength of the trade union bureaucrats who favoured the reform strategy. Union officials used their power and control of the party machinery to push through resolutions for reform and created mechanisms that ensured that the party executive would be controlled by bureaucrats, not party delegates. This was a clear move away from democracy, defined by Michels as 'the self-government of the masses in conformity with the decisions of popular assemblies ... The officials, executive organs of the general will, play merely a subordinate part, are always dependent upon the collectivity, and can be deprived of their office at any moment.' Where Weber saw Mannheim as a positive step towards realism and reform, Michels saw it as a betrayal of socialism and democracy. His subsequent analysis of bureaucracy in the labour movement, still the starting point in the debate, tried to answer the question, 'Why do socialist parties degenerate into oligarchy and reformism?'[10]

According to Michels, bureaucracy came to dominate the left for many of the same reasons that Weber gave for its growth in the state and in private capital. The labour movement and its party were a 'fighting party'; to succeed, they had to obey the laws of tactics, the first of which is 'facility of mobilization.' To move as a coordinated body, policies and campaigns had to be formulated from the top and imposed on the membership. The very success of the labour movement and the SPD implied a need for bureaucracy, for with increased numbers, participation of the entire membership in decision-making became more difficult, and some form of delegation and representation was necessary to carry on business efficiently. The organizations were forced to confront issues of greater complexity, and decisions carried greater consequences; a mistake in tactics could cost an election or important reforms, even the security of the organization itself. When officials' duties became of greater consequence, when a mistake could prove fatal to the organization, it was imprudent to entrust the future to leaders selected by purely democratic means. As a result of this pragmatic, sensible move, however, labour organizations would be forced to choose leaders who had expertise, and would be forced to keep them in place even if popular sentiment were against them.[11]

This special education and selection process created an elite, and a 'continuous enlargement of the gulf which divides the leaders from the masses.' The division of labour based on technical specialization and a monopoly of knowledge became rule by a handful of experts. Not by conscious conspiracy, but through an evolution of rational decisions designed to further the ends of the party and labour, 'the leaders, who were at first no more than the executive organs of the collective will, soon emancipate themselves from the mass and become independent of its control.' Size, complexity, efficiency, and the self-interested action of officials themselves meant that even labour parties would become bureaucratic; as Michels put it, 'organization implies the tendency to oligarchy.'[12]

Michels argued that the tendency towards oligarchy would also be a tendency towards reformism. Regardless of their intentions, people put in positions of power would become more conservative. As their tasks became more complicated and numerous, they would lose sight of principles as they concentrated on practical tasks. As paid party or union bureaucrats, workers would be in a different position from the masses they were supposed to represent. Guaranteed a job and a healthy wage, freed from the exploitation of the workplace, assured of a certain status, they leave the proletariat and join the petit bourgeoisie. The material and class interests of the bureaucrats change, and so too does their view of revolution: 'What interest for them now the dogma of the social revolution? Their own social revolution has already been effected.' This process of adaptation as the result of changed social class could work in subtle ways. As the labour bureaucrats met and worked with their counterparts in the state and private enterprise, they would tend to emulate their erstwhile opponents, if only to establish a common culture to allow negotiations to proceed. Since the members of the bourgeoisie represented the dominant culture, the labour bureaucrats would feel more pressure to 'level up' than the members of the bourgeoisie would feel to 'level down.' Soon the working-class leaders also discovered that if they preached class war and were uncompromising, little could be accomplished at the negotiating table. If, however, they preached peace and class harmony, they would be saluted by their number on the opposite side of the table as labour diplomats. All of these different forces – social, political, economic, and psychological – virtually guaranteed that the labour and SPD leadership would become conservative.[13]

Michels had no hope that bureaucracy could be successfully opposed. Any elite that tried to make the bureaucracy accountable to the masses would soon fall victim to the same forces that corrupted the original leaders. With time, even the creation of challenging elites would be difficult, as the entrenched bureaucratic positions would attract those who aspired to be bureaucrats, and reformist politics would attract reformists. Ultimately, even appeals to union democracy would be little more than cynical ploys of careerists to remain in or to obtain power.

Neither could the masses hope to end their domination by elites. The 'law of inertia' would tend to maintain the status quo, as would the weight of tradition. The continued success of the organization would require stability and continuity, while the need for expertise in leaders would limit the number of candidates from the ranks. Those who did seek positions and change, especially those with skill and ability, would soon desert the masses. They would either be co-opted into the leadership cadre or would actively strive to enter it as a better avenue for their talents than the shop floor. The leaders themselves, grown accustomed to their privileged positions, and, equally important, convinced of their value as leaders, would fight any challenges from the shop floor with all the weapons at their disposal: prestige, knowledge, gratitude for past service, control of procedures, committees, and funding, and patronage. Most importantly, the masses would be unable to fight on their own behalf. In Michels's view, the masses were incompetent and cowardly. At best, the masses acting without leaders would be 'comparable to a savage and shapeless negro army, which is unable to withstand a single well-disciplined and well-drilled battalion of European soldiers.' The masses were largely uninterested in the problems outside their personal lives, and would in any case be unable to understand them. Save for the few leaders who rose to power from a Darwinian natural selection, the working class had 'an immense need for direction and guidance.' Indeed, Michels comes close to arguing that they would prefer bureaucracy to freedom.[14] Socialism could not solve the dilemma either. While it might be possible to create a mechanism for distributing wealth more equitably, socialism was much more than that. It was also an ideology of democracy. Any socialist government would soon face the same paradox that haunted the SPD. To function effectively, the government would have to organize into a hierarchy. The hierarchy would by definition be distinct from the rank and file; it would therefore have its own interests to defend, and these interests would not be the same as the interests of the masses. Conflict between the rulers and the ruled would be inevitable, and again the people would be unable to counter the power of the bureaucracy.[15]

Because he could see no way to avoid rule by bureaucracy, Michels cast his observations as a sociological law, the so-called iron law of oligarchy: 'It is organization which gives birth to the dominion of the elected over the electors, of the mandataries over the mandators, of the delegates over the delegators. Who says organization, says oligarchy.'[16]

Michels's work contains most of the elements of the debate over the labour bureaucracy. Much of the historiography is, explicitly or implicitly, an argument with specific parts of his analysis. The necessity of working-class revolution; the domination of elites; the tendency of leaders to bureaucracy and conservatism; the relationship, both real and ideal, of the masses and the leadership; the autonomy and awareness of the masses: each of these parts of Michels's analysis has been contested.[17] Selig Perlman, for example, in *A Theory of the Labor Movement*, simply holds that Michels's critique of bureaucracy is irrelevant. Echoing Weber and expanding on the work of United States labour historian John Commons, Perlman first responded that radicalism was not a natural response of labour to capitalism; it was instead an alien ideology foisted on the working class by intellectuals. There was a 'natural divergence' between revolution and the 'mentality' of trade unions;

left to their own devices, workers would evolve their own ideology that was neither revolutionary nor Marxist. The Mannheim congress that delighted Weber and disillusioned Michels was, to Perlman, a positive sign that 'the trade unions had emancipated themselves from the hegemony of the intellectual revolutionists.' Having cast off the agitators, the German workers' movement could look after its own interests and move to establish its own economic reforms.[18]

Central to Perlman's view was his belief that capitalism was not at bottom an exploitative economic class relation, but merely a social organization 'presided over by a class with an "effective will to power." ' The interests of capital and labour were not opposed; in fact, they had to work together to increase productivity and the well-being of all. To support his notion that capital and labour were in a symbiotic, not a parasitic, relationship, Perlman argued that capitalists and workers were selected by a kind of pyschological social Darwinism. Those who feared taking risks, he wrote, preferred to become workers, while the high rollers with a 'sufficiently agile mind' became capitalists.[19] Since the inequities of capitalism were rooted in human nature and not in social organization, revolution was unnecessary, even unnatural. There was no fundamental conflict between the classes that required a struggle to the death. While the labour movement was a 'campaign against the absolute rights of private property,' its natural goal was not the abolition of private property but the implementation of workplace rules that would reduce its sting. Workers were concerned with equality of opportunity and freedom from discrimination; they were not interested in managing industry or society. Given that labour and capital were both necessary to modern industry, the proper, advanced trade-union ideology was not 'a dogmatic anti-capitalist philosophy, but more and more ... a pragmatic faith in industrial government through a cooperation of equally indispensable "functional" classes.'[20] Good labour leaders, therefore, were ones who realized that reformism and corporatism were the proper lessons to be drawn out from the struggles of the working class. Michels argued that the business unionism of Samuel Gompers and the American Federation of Labor was proof that they had betrayed the working class. Perlman countered that business unionism succeeded because it had grasped the essential nature of the working class.[21]

Democracy in the union was no more an issue for Perlman than was revolution. Implicit in his view is a belief that some people have more ability to rule than others, and though they should rule benevolently and without corruption, their power over others is not undemocratic. To challenge Michels, Perlman argued that democracy must be representative, not participatory; that capitalism was not a system of exploitation and thus revolution was unnecessary; therefore, the question, 'Why do revolutionary parties degen-erate into bureaucracy and conservatism?' is irrelevant. Oligarchy and con-servatism are integral parts of modern society and must be accepted.

This analysis can be attacked on several grounds. Most importantly, Perl-man's assertion that capitalism is not an exploitative social relationship is false, and it is based more on wishful thinking than on objective study. This is not the place to provide a *Readers' Digest* version of *Capital*, but it must be pointed out that the wealth and power of the capitalist did not spring from psychological ability and a simple 'will to power.' The ownership of the means of production was not granted, even by default, by workers who real-ized that they were not high rollers or financial schemers. Producers were separated from the means of production violently; in Marx's graphic phrase, capitalist relations came into the world 'dripping from head to foot, from every pore, with blood and dirt.'[22] Ownership of the means of production confers great power on the owner, not the least of which is the 'right' to appropriate the surplus value produced by workers. Profit is wealth created by workers that is taken from them; this is the basis of capitalism. Exploita-tion is the very foundation of capitalism. Furthermore, even if Perlman's psychological explanation is accepted, we need to ask if it is precisely the capitalist environment itself that creates such differences in abilities and character.

Perlman's reading of the working class is also too one-sided. For it is by no means clear that Perlman's perception of workers as timid and reformist is more objective or more accurate than a left-wing one. A strike for higher wages may indicate a simple economism that views labour's role as a struggle for 'more'; it may also indicate a powerful belief in the need for a radical redistribution of wealth. Much depends on the eye of the beholder. The lack of an explicit socialist ideology in the working class may also be explained in a number of ways. It may show the existence of a home-made worker ideol-ogy of reform, as Perlman argues. It may, however, show the power of a con-servative union bureaucracy or the ability of the ruling class to shape and mould public opinion. It may also indicate a cautious pragmatism in the face of superior odds. Even in the conservative 1980s, for example, when labour was on the retreat, sociologists have found convincing evidence of class con-sciousness among workers in the United States, but they also found workers extremely reluctant to voice these views, in part because of the fear of retali-ation from employers and government.[23] Perlman's generalizations about the working class, made without specific reference to particular issues and actions, are hardly as self-evident as he suggests. Furthermore, his history is highly selective. Perlman was writing in the 1920s, a period of relative labour quiescence. The late 1910s, however, saw a very different labour movement, one in which socialism and syndicalism were on the agenda. The decade following Perlman's work was also one in which radicalism was part of the working class's program. The successes of the Industrial Workers of the World, the Socialist Party of America, and the Communist Party suggest that reformism is only a part of working-class ideology, and that it too may require an injection from outside labour's ranks.

The kind of struggles Perlman observed also coloured his analysis. His brand of institutional history was progressive in its day, but more recent work has outlined working-class action at different levels and for different issues. Struggles for control and decision-making power were not part of Perlman's institutional history, but they suggest a different kind of consciousness than he was willing to ascribe to the labour movement. Challenges to the state, in the form of mass strikes, political action, even armed resistance, and challenges to capital, ranging from occupations of factories to sabotage, indicate that a more militant and radical ideology existed in the working class.[24] This is not to say that the American working class was always a class-conscious force that actively fought for socialism. It is to say that at different times and in different places, different strategies and visions evolved. Perlman's generalizations are simply inadequate and unconvincing. It is by no means clear that a reformist labour bureaucracy is necessarily an accurate reflection of the working class. Thus, Perlman actually supports Michels's observations of the labour bureaucracy; he merely differs on the moral and political conclusions that are to be drawn.

Seymour Martin Lipset represents a second anti-Marxist position in the labour bureaucracy debate. He explicitly challenges Michels's view that the development of bureaucracy is inevitable by providing a counter-example of a democratic union. In *Union Democracy*, written in the 1950s, Lipset maintains that the International Typographical Union (ITU) 'does not fit the pattern' of elite control outlined by Michels.[25]

Lipset, however, can only make this claim by changing the terms of the debate. First, in best Cold War fashion, he argues that oligarchy is the same as one-party rule. Second, he suggests that the only important conflict over power is between incumbent officials and an organized opposition that seeks to take their place. Michels, however, held that the essential contradiction was between officials and the masses. Arguing that the conflict is between incumbents and would-be leaders, Lipset defines democracy as a choice of leaders. Combining this with the definition of oligarchy as one-party rule, Lipset suggests that the two-party system of the American government is the democratic model that would satisfy Michels. He then finds a union with a two-party structure – the ITU – and argues that it has successfully avoided bureaucracy.[26]

In fact, Lipset has only provided a model of rotating elites. Nowhere does he demonstrate that the ITU membership has real control over its leaders beyond a formal choice between competing bureaucracies. His assumption that the American two-party system is the best model of democracy is little more than Cold War sleight of hand. He does not show that the two-party system is democratic, or more democratic than a one-party, multiparty, or a no-party system; this position is only asserted. We are left with a circular argument: the two-party system is democratic because democracy is a two-party system. The tautology tells more about the hidden assumptions of liberalism in the 1950s than about union bureaucracy.

Lipset's work does offer other insights into the labour bureaucracy, however. In constructing a two-party model, he suggests that there is a tension between leaders and led, that there may be a substantial difference between the interests of those in power and those outside. In addition, the period in which he was writing saw Communist unionists being purged from bureaucratic positions in the labour movement. Lipset concluded, like Michels, that there was a connection between bureaucracy and radicalism, but that it moved in the opposite direction. Radicals, he suggested, tended to assume bureaucratic positions to preserve and spread their ideology among an unwilling membership. Only by seizing leadership positions could radicals fend off rank-and-file opposition to their politics.[27]

The important part of this observation is not Lipset's belief that radicals had to force their views onto a resisting working class, a notion he shares with Perlman. Rather, it is the observation that radicals could seize power and maintain it through the control of the bureaucracy. Conservatism was not an inevitable part of leadership, as Michels asserted. This suggests that in studying the bureaucracy, it is helpful to separate ideology from process; it suggests that there is no necessary causal connection between the two. In short, conservatism and radicalism are opposites, as are democracy and bureaucracy. Combinations of these two sets are possible: a bureaucracy may be radical or conservative, as might a democracy; a radical might be democratic or bureaucratic, as might a conservative.

The liberal analysis of the labour bureaucracy has tried to resolve the problems presented by Michels from a very different starting point. Using an a priori assumption, it is denied that radicalism is a legitimate concern of the working class. Reformism is instead the proper course to take. To win reforms, leaders must be able to compromise and negotiate; this means they must have the power to act as they see fit in a given circumstance. As most people cannot look after their own interests, in Perlman's view, and the demands of efficiency require a limited representative form of administration, in Lipset's view, real democracy is impossible. It is therefore meaningless to talk about a separation of interests between leaders and led based on power, as no other system is possible. Democracy must be defined as some sort of rule by elites combined with certain guarantees of elections; the exercise of power over the masses does not constitute bureaucracy. This attack does not refute Michels, for in changing the definition so radically the liberals have destroyed democracy in order to save it as a useful category.[28]

Marxists have approached the problem of bureaucracy in a different way. Lenin and other Bolsheviks made a distinction between leaders who serve the interests of the working class by advocating revolution and those who betray it by abandoning socialism. The former are legitimate and their power does not constitute bureaucracy, for they act in the name of the working class; the latter are bureaucrats who abuse their power. The leaders of the SPD and the German labour movement, of the British trade unionists, and the American business unionists could therefore be denounced in terms similar to those of Michels's. By defining bureaucracy by ideology, not power over the rank and file, the Bolsheviks could denounce these leaders as bureaucrats because they did not take up a revolutionary line. A materialist explanation was given for their treason. Karl Radek noted in 1916 that the 'top layer' of the German and British working class was relatively well paid and secure. This 'labour aristocracy' was represented and protected by the labour bureaucracy at the expense of the rest of the working class and exploited workers in other nations. As the result of their relative wealth and security, 'socialism became a far-off ideal or simply an empty slogan. Their daily work was limited to a struggle for minor gains. They judge politics on how it affects this struggle. They resist every attempt at constructing a mass movement that would enable the broad masses of the working class to secure political rights and improvements in living conditions. They protest against such "revolutionary romanticism," claiming that such actions are impossible ... For this reason the entire labor bureaucracy supported the revisionist policy of rapprochement with the bourgeoisie.'[29]

Conservatism and bureaucracy, then, had their roots in the material condition of the period and not in the power and privilege of the bureaucratic positions themselves, as Michels argued. It was their position as a wealthier 'caste' that determined the consciousness of bureaucrats, and this consciousness determined their label of bureaucrat.[30] While agreeing that the privileged position of the bureaucrats could lead to conservatism, however, Lenin argued that not every leader would succumb. To prevent reformism, working-class organizations had to be controlled by the leaders of the revolutionary party. Like Perlman, Lenin believed that socialism was not a natural outgrowth of working-class experience. The working class has to be led and pushed onto the proper road. In *What Is to Be Done?*, Lenin outlined his view of the working class and the necessity of a vanguard party. His observations led him to his oft-quoted dictum that revolutionary consciousness would have to be brought to the working class from without, for despite its embryonic groping, the working class 'is able to develop only trade union consciousness, i.e., the conviction that it is necessary to combine in unions, fight the employers, and strive to compel the government to pass this or that necessary labour law, etc.'[31] Because the ideology of the ruling class was largely in place, with deep roots and powerful means of dissemination, the 'spontaneous development of the working-class movement leads precisely to its subordination to bourgeois ideology.'[32] This meant that revolutionary intellectuals, usually of bourgeois origin, would have to take socialism to the working class. The party, a smaller organization restricted to those with the proper consciousness, would act as the legitimate leaders of the working class. Bukharin outlined the relationship of the party to the working class in a corporatist metaphor that demonstrates the Bolshevik commitment to exerting power over the working class when he wrote that 'we naturally expect to find the entire class led by that section of it that is most advanced, best schooled, most united: the party. The party is not the class; in fact, it may be but a small part of the class, as the head is but a small part of the body ... The party is simply the thing that best expresses the interests of the class.'[33] Incorrect ideology, then, not power over the rank and file, was the definition of bureaucracy, and there was no real contradiction between oligarchy and democracy, so long as the right hand was on the tiller. Control of the masses by a small elite was vital to ensure that the working class learned and adhered to the proper revolutionary path. Democracy would come later, when the 'incompetence of the masses will disappear' as the result of training and education.[34]

This analysis of bureaucracy is useful as an explanation of the material base of conservatism. But in defining labour leaders as bureaucrats by their ideology it ignores the criterion of power as the defining characteristic of bureaucracy. The Bolshevik analysis, like the liberal one, argues that some elite is inevitable; it just changes the definition of what a 'good' elite should do. It leads to a moral justification of Bolshevik control of the labour movement that is best appreciated for its sophistry, not its clarity. For by denying that power defined bureaucracy, the Bolsheviks could try to deflect criticism of their party as a bureaucracy that controlled the working class. Insisting that power came only from ownership of the means of production, Bukharin could argue that a classless society existed in Russia after the Bolshevik revolution, for a ruling stratum or elite could not develop in a socialist society: 'Communist society is a society with highly developed, increased productive forces. Consequently, it can have no economic basis for the creation of its peculiar ruling class. For – even assuming the power of the administrators to be stable, as does Michels – this power will be the power of the specialist over machines, not over men. How could they, in fact, realize this power with regard to men? Michels neglects the fundamental decisive fact that each administratively dominant position has hitherto been an envelope for economic exploitation.'

In short, 'the society of the future will not involve private property, or the formation of such private property, and it is precisely this private property that constitutes this basis of the class.'[35] It is clear that Bukharin's vision of the socialist society does not do away with managers; in his words, 'We know that the classes themselves have risen organically ... from the division of labor, from the organizational functions that had become technically necessary for the further evolution of society. Obviously, in the society of the future, such organizational work will also be necessary.'[36] According to Bukharin, because these organizers do not own the means of production and do not personally profit from them, they do not form a class and thus do not rule. But this is really a case of special pleading. For the central issue is not the formal, ritual ownership of the factories or of land. It is the issue of control over production and expropriation of surplus value. Orthodox Marxists are quite willing to grant the truth of this when applied to capitalists, but deny it when applied to themselves. Managers of corporations in capitalist societies may not own the means of production either; indeed, they are often productive workers who sell their labour power. Their control of the administration of capital and labour, however, surely puts them in the capitalist class. The administration of large capital, even if managed in the name of the people, gives the administrator power.[37] The administrators may not form part of a new class – Marxists are not agreed on the name for this phenomenon – but they do stand in a position of power and authority over the workers in the factory. These managers must govern, and it is by no means certain that their notions of efficiency and proper production coincide with the interests of the masses. Still less can the party assume that it acts in the interests of the working class in a way different from the bureaucracy of the labour movement.[38] Power over others, stemming from alleged authority as expert or interpreter of the working class and presumed laws of history, or from control of the state, or from physical force, or from control over the means of production, is still antithetical to democracy. When this power is held by officials who are not responsible to the masses, it is called bureaucracy. The Bolshevik analysis of the labour bureaucracy refuses to recognize this, and it tries to avoid it by insisting on an economistic interpretation of power and the identification of bureaucracy with ideology rather than process.[39] Similarly, its analysis of the labour bureaucracy ignores the issue of the power of left-wing leaders over the rank and file.

Thus, liberals and the old left agreed that hierarchy is necessary, though they disagreed over the ideology that leaders should espouse. Unlike the liberals, however, these early Marxist writers were caught in a dilemma. They could not denounce the principle of leadership, for they were committed to a specific political agenda that could be realized only by a united working class moving in a carefully defined direction. They did not wish to argue that the 'workers are always right,' for workers often opposed the left. Therefore, they argued for a certain kind of leadership, one that moves towards a specific objective. Since this direction is not always the same as that in which the rank and file is heading, these writers faced a constant dilemma. They argued for the autonomy of the working class when the class supported their program, and against autonomy when it did not. The leadership was defined as 'good' or 'bad' according to how closely it conformed to what the left considered the 'proper political agenda.

Other left-wing writers have approached the problem of the labour bureaucracy in different ways. In the late 1940s, C. Wright Mills noted that the labour movement faced a paradox. Trade unions, whether the leader knew it or not, 'and often he seems not to know,' were fundamentally at odds with capital. The fight for the closed shop was a fight against freedom of contract; fights for improvements in conditions and control encroached upon the alleged rights of management; fights for higher wages attacked the 'uncontrolled sway of property.' But instead of acting as a force that was opposed to capital, union leaders were, sometimes tacitly, sometimes openly, seeking to cooperate with it. In return for some reforms – union recognition, dues check-offs, grievance procedures, explicit work rules, stability, and higher wages – unions were conceding too much ground to employers. Signing the collective agreement meant that workplace protests could no longer be made by the workers themselves. Slow-downs, deputations, wildcats, study sessions, in fact any work stoppage or disruption, was now illegal during the life of a collective agreement. Protest could only be made through the grievance procedure. Arbitration was interpreted by lawyers and industrial relations experts who were committed to the status quo of capitalism and capitalist law. While the union's rights and obligations were clearly defined, every contract, whether it contained a management's rights clause or not, gave the employer all residual and non-specified rights. Only those actions by the company that actually violated a specific clause of the contract could be grieved. If workers protested against actions that were not clear violations of the agreement, or if they protested in ways other than the grievance procedure, the union was held legally responsible. To avoid lawsuits, fines, and even jail, union leaders had to act as policemen, making sure that the workers obeyed the letter and spirit of the contract. Now the union, not management, had to prevent and end illegal work stoppages. Ironically, the very processes and procedures that unions had fought for severely limited their struggle against the employer. Worse, the leaders and members could be pitted against each other by the boss and the law. The labour leaders, in seeking to protect their members and the union, had embarked on a course that was contrary to the best interests of the membership. Some leaders had openly sought such a course; others had drifted into it. In any case, the 'new men of power' had to move to the left and democratize the union, industry, and society. Only in this way could the interests of the working class be fulfilled.[40]

By the 1960s and 1970s it was clear to a new generation of activists and radicals that these 'new men of power' had not lived up to the responsibility Mills had charged them with. Identifying the bureaucracy as the top level of old-time union leaders, writers focused on the violations of union constitutions, the subversion of the electoral process, and the corruption symbolized by Jimmy Hoffa. These accounts were largely journalistic; the early literature set out little analysis beyond painting wealthy union leaders as sell-outs and crooks.[41] Later work, reflecting the rise of the New Left, offered more complex analyses that took Mills as a starting point, and looked for structural, rather than personal, reasons for the bureaucratic union leadership.

Stan Weir's work is typical of this school. Weir argued that the unions of the CIO were led into what he called 'institutionalized bargaining' by naive or corrupt union officials. Institutional bargaining came about when all the corporations in a given industry agreed together to recognize the union and begin collective bargaining. Until all agreed to recognize the union, individual companies were not forced to bargain in good faith, and could try to fight the unions. But a militant and radical rank and file created chaos: wildcat strikes, sit-downs, and slow-downs plagued industry. At that point, employers recognized that the refusal to meet with the unions was costing too much; at the same time, their prolonged and often violent rejection of organization meant that the corporations had lost their recognized authority to control and discipline the workforce. They needed a substitute authority and believed they could use the union leadership to maintain order on the shop floor. Now eager to accept unions, the companies agreed to sit down and bargain, confident that they could institutionalize the union leadership and incorporate it into the smooth running of the company. Once the contract was signed, the union leadership had to be concerned with the employers' well-being. This meant backing off during contract negotiations and working towards industry-wide agreements so no single company could gain a competitive edge. Most importantly, it meant making sure the militant workforce went along with the new conservatism. This put the leadership in direct conflict with the rank and file and meant it would have to assume bureaucratic control if it were to remain in power.[42]

Although this line of reasoning, often called the 'incorporation thesis,' has a great deal of validity, it is somewhat overstated. Borrowing heavily from the work of Gabriel Kolko and James Weinstein on the development of corporate liberalism, it sees every reform and advance as the result of a conscious scheme on the part of corporate leadership working with governments and unions to create stability and growth that all agree is desirable. Reforms and advances are seen not as the result of class conflict, but as the result of the collaboration of elites.[43] Certainly capital is often very flexible, and it has shown a remarkable ability to adapt pressures for change to forms that are less dangerous to it. However, this flexibility is not the same as cunning or conspiracy; it is more a bowing to the inevitable. It is clear that the industries organized by the CIO in the 1930s and 1940s did not have a united vision of institutionalizing the unions. The Ford company, for example, resisted unionization for three years after the other manufacturers had capitulated; likewise, 'Little Steel' fought the Steelworkers to a standstill even though 'Big Steel' settled. Furthermore, the farsightedness attributed to capital is questionable. The inability of the companies to unite in the face of the union onslaught suggests that they do not always have the foresight or interest to develop joint plans that include the sophisticated notion of corporatism. And it is by no means self-evident that corporate leaders, government officials, and labour leaders were in substantial agreement over the desirability of tripartism. Earlier and later periods of repression suggest that capital is rarely united and that its strategies are short-term responses to immediate problems rather than carefully laid ambushes. Furthermore, most of the 'solutions' to labour conflict were in fact put in place by the liberal state, not capital. Indeed, capital has fought, and continues to fight, the Rand formula, social welfare legislation, and the state's guarantees of union rights. Moreover, the postwar consensus and the reforms of the 1940s and 1950s have been under attack in the 1980s and 1990s, as corporations and the state have collaborated to roll back wages, break unions, and create social conditions that favour corporations, not workers.[44]

The portrayal of the union is similarly too rigid in this analysis. Weir identifies bureaucracy as an upper stratum of leadership that differs from the rank and file by class interest and ideology. Bureaucrats are defined by their policy, not their relationship to democratic control by the rank and file. Good leaders are those who assume the working class is radical; bureaucrats are bad leaders who assume the working class is, or ought to be, conservative. Weir's underlying assumption is that the rank and file is always more militant than the leadership. This is a dubious assertion. Jonathan Zeitlin, for example, has noted that while there are many cases where leaders restrained a militant membership, there are an equal number of cases where militant leaders had to drag along reluctant, more conservative rank-and-file members. John Bodnar has collected a volume of oral testimony that shows persuasively that many CIO rank-and-filers were not interested in revolution. They favoured a pragmatic bread-and-butter unionism and supported Communist organizers and leaders because they were better tacticians, not because they talked about revolution.[45] In the 1940s and 1950s a 'white' cadre was able to muster considerable rank-and-file support to oust the 'red' leadership of the IWA, the Boilermakers Union, and the UAW in Canada and the United States. Whatever the merits of either faction, and even allowing for a great deal of skulduggery by the 'whites,' the purges are a clear example of a less-radical membership repudiating a left leadership. Where the 'reds' held on, as in the Mine Mill and Smelter Workers' Union and the United Electrical Workers, it was their skills as unionists, not their political views, that kept them in power. Canadian Communist Jack Scott made this clear, declaring to mineworkers who questioned his beliefs, 'My politics are none of your business, unless my politics affect my union activities.'[46] In attributing the label *bureaucracy* to a top level of union leaders who actively oppose the real interests of the working class, Weir does not go far beyond an analysis that views the bureaucrats as simple traitors or 'sell-outs.' The other side of this argument is that the rank and file is powerless to fight against measures and leaders it recognizes as being against its best interests. This may be true in some cases, especially where union 'machines' restrict rank-and-file votes for leaders and contracts, but in many instances, it is not obvious that workers either acquiesce or see their interests as opposed to the policy of the leadership.

James Hinton and Richard Price have put forward arguments similar to Weir's for the British union movement. Unlike Weir, they see the move to bureaucracy occurring in the late nineteenth century, as the managerial push to deskill the work process led rank-and-file workers to find new ways to fight for job control. They were hampered in their struggle, however, by the union leadership, which sought refuge in centralized conciliation boards, larger bargaining units, national agreements, and centralized unions. The rank and file, Hinton and Price argue, fought the bureaucratizing efforts of union leaders as they fought for job control.[47] Recent work has contradicted important elements of their theory. In his examination of British railway unions, Tony Adams has found that there is no evidence to 'suggest that the "rank and file" or indeed union activists on the railways opposed centralized conciliation schemes.' The executive of the National Union of Railwaymen was pressured into centralized bargaining by the regional district councils, while it was left-wing activists outside the union bureaucracy who pushed for centralized bargaining to give the union greater clout and weaken sectional interests in favour of industrial and class consciousness. Far from union leaders, the state, and business being in agreement over the virtues of institutionalized bargaining, Adams argues that the rail companies opposed it, and were forced into nationwide bargaining by the unions and the state. Similarly, Jonathan Zeitlin has argued that in the Amalgamated Society of Engineers, centralization was promoted by a 'socialist-led "rank-and-file" campaign,' while local autonomy was defended by levels of the official hierarchy and by 'formal representative bodies within the union itself, rather than by "informal" groups on the shop floor.' Their research has led both Adams and Zeitlin to conclude that it is impossible to separate the trade union officials from the rank and file on the basis of ideology, as both the right and the left have adopted policies that made accommodations with capital and strengthened union officials at the expense of the rank and file.[48] Zeitlin in particular has insisted that what some have called bureaucracy is simply a reflection of the fact that 'externally, trade unions are torn between the demands of opposition and accommodation; internally, between those of centralisation and mobilisation.' Ultimately, Zeitlin concludes, the notion of a split between rank and file and leadership is 'fundamentally unsatisfactory and should be abandoned outright.'[49] If this is an overstatement, the net effect of this refined analysis of the labour bureaucracy has been, in the words of Eric Hobsbawm, to destroy the theory of the labour bureaucracy as a 'conflict between a theoretically militant rank and file and the theoretically conservative union leadership.'[50]

Richard Hyman has tried to accommodate some of this new work while still maintaining that union leaders tend to act as policemen and tend to incorporate unions into capitalist society. To present a united front and coordinate effective action, Hyman suggests, unions must exert some control over the membership. To achieve their collective ends, the members must be able to apply some pressure to reluctant fellow workers; at the very least, the union must be able to decide and act on policies established for the good of all. Hyman calls for a reformulation of Michels: 'who says organization says, firstly discipline, secondly routinisation.' From the union's beginning, then, there is a tension between leaders and led, between the use of 'power for the members' and 'power over the members.' Outside of a revolutionary situation, unions must, by the very nature of the bargaining process, come to some kind of accommodation with capital. In addition, the work process itself creates conflicts on the shop floor that cannot be resolved by the grievance procedure or sophisticated managerial techniques. The day-to-day alienation and exploitation of the workers means they will periodically strike back spontaneously, sometimes united and organized with specific grievances, sometimes not. The union, however, must intervene to quell the illegal action and uphold the contract. This may mean repressing militants; it may mean coercing conservatives. Other pressures, more subtle than a desire to sell out, come to bear on union leaders. They have a responsibility to make sure the union survives, and this may encourage conservatism. It is especially liable to 'induce resistance to objectives or forms of action which unduly antagonize employers or the state and thus risk violent confrontation.' Because union officers must come to terms with employers at the bargaining table and during grievance procedures, they have an ongoing relationship with their counterparts across the table. It is often useful to encourage a certain stability in the relationship, and thus there is a built-in tendency to go along with the 'rules of the game.' Finally, leadership positions were, at least in part, created to put experts at the head of the union, for the best interests of the collectivity. To expand and maintain their positions, leaders come to define trade union activity in ways that emphasize expertise and hierarchy: they tend to stress 'professional competence' rather than mass action to resolve problems and advance the union cause. This has been reinforced by the state's use of complex legislation, government labour boards, and legal arbitration, all of which require specialists and experts. These forces may intensify and reinforce each other; together, they pressure leaders to move towards reformism and bureaucratic control over the membership. In this view, the problems attributed to the labour bureaucracy are often problems inherent in trade unionism in capitalist society. Hyman goes so far as to suggest, in language similar to that of incorporation thesis critics such as Zeitlin and Adams, that

there is an important sense in which the problem of 'bureaucracy' denotes not so much a distinct stratum of personnel as a relationship which permeates the whole practice of trade unionism. 'Bureaucracy' is in large measure a question of the differential distribution of expertise and activism: of the dependence of the mass of union membership on the initiative and strategic experience of a relatively small cadre of leadership – both 'official' and 'unofficial' ... But ... [this] constitutes a problem even in the case of a cadre of militant lay activists sensitive to the need to encourage the autonomy and initiative of the membership. Hence the predicament of [even] the stewards [who are] ... 'torn between the forces of representation and bureaucratization.'[51]

Thus, Hyman, writing from the left, comes close to agreeing with Zeitlin that there is no fundamental split between leaders and led in the labour movement. He has also made an important distinction between rank-and-file activity and the left-wing opposition of factions acting in the name of the rank and file. The model of competing elites is a more accurate description of this factional opposition than the dichotomy of leaders versus members.

In continually revising the definition of the labour bureaucracy, however, even those who wish to preserve the distinction have done away with much of its explanatory power. If bureaucracy is only a 'tendency' or a 'tension' that ebbs and flows, how are we to define bureaucrats? Because leaders cannot simply assert their authority, but, in the words of Zeitlin, must continually 're-establish their claim on the active loyalty of the members,' is there any structured conflict between officials and rank and file? The debate appears to have been refined out of existence, and we need to ask if it is useful then to think of the labour bureaucracy as a hierarchy distinct from those it was created to serve. I believe it is, but several points must be re-thought.

First, the labour bureaucracy cannot be identified by ideology or certain policies of reform or conservatism. Leaders may be left or right, as may members. Nor can militancy be the defining characteristic. Hyman has argued persuasively that a tendency towards less militant action does affect the leadership, but it is not inevitable. Nor is conservatism always contrary to the wishes of the rank and file, although it may be contrary to the wishes of a political faction.[52]

Second, Zeitlin's contention that the leadership is democratic because it must continually seek support and loyalty is false. Obtaining consent from the ruled is not the same as democracy. Even dictators must get some consent from those they rule, but this does not mean the collectivity exerts meaningful control over the government. Furthermore, examples of local leaders fighting centralization are not really comments on democracy and bureaucracy; they are more akin to the struggles of feudal barons against the king. Zeitlin's argument that leaders must woo their voters is essentially a return to the liberal vision of democracy as formal elections and responsible leadership rather than control by the people.

Third, the bureaucracy cannot be defined solely as the agent for incorporating unions into capitalism and diluting working-class protest. While unions are usually agents only for reform, this is an issue separate from bureaucracy. Some leaders have moved quickly and openly to reach an accommodation with capital; others have done so reluctantly, or, in the absence of a militant rank and file, by default. Hyman has argued rightly that this is a problem inherent in trade unionism, and it cannot be pinned squarely on the bureaucrats. The rank and file has not always acted as the implacable foe of incorporation, and its conservatism – a tendency as marked as its radicalism – has sometimes pushed leaders to use the contract as the only means of guaranteeing rights and union protection.

Finally, the line to be drawn between bureaucrats and the rank and file, or leaders and members, must be that of power, that is, the ability to make others do what they would not have done otherwise.[53] By seeing bureaucracy as a question of who has power over whom, rather than a conflict over ideology, it is possible to demonstrate that reports of the death of the labour bureaucrats have been greatly exaggerated.

If the bureaucracy does have a consistent ideology and program, it is more profound and subtle than most incorporation theorists have argued. It lies in the bureaucrats' belief that the working class must be managed, that the masses cannot determine their own struggles. This deep-rooted position is common in the work of every theorist of the labour bureaucracy, from Adams to Hyman to Michels to Zeitlin. However, the bureaucracy can only be defined by its relationship to the rank and file. The distinguishing characteristic of the labour bureaucrats is not their ideology but their power over the membership. It is this power, whether obtained by force, manipulation, expertise, or consent, and institutionalized in formal offices, that defines the labour bureaucrat, no matter for what ends the power is used. The power may be overt and entrenched in constitutions, complete with the right to suspend and purge opposition, or it may be limited to the right to decide and implement policy. But insofar as leaders are able not only to suggest courses of action but to determine them, they have power over the membership. If their offices are protected from immediate and effective control by the membership, they have an entrenched position of power and may be said to be bureaucrats.

Is it realistic to argue that labour leaders exercise power? Compared with politicians or bosses, the labour bureaucrat is a weak creature. The union official exercises power over only a fragment of a worker's life, and may call upon union members to do only a small range of things. The labour leader has no great fortune or police force to enforce compliance, and the sanctions that can be applied to those who disobey are strictly limited. Furthermore, most union leaders are elected under rules more democratic than those used in government elections, and, of course, no corporate enterprise even pretends to be democratic. When we speak of the power of the labour leader, then, we do well to remember that it is a weak thing compared with that of capital and the state. This is especially true of the early days of the labour movement examined in this study. Nevertheless, the labour leader has always had more than the simple ability to act or the right to act on the instruction of another; the bureaucrat has had some power over others. We may define power as the ability to make decisions that are binding on another, the ability to implement decisions and policy that affect others without their express consent, or the ability to compel others, by coercion or persuasion, to do that which they would not have done otherwise. In this sense, the labour bureaucrat may be said to have power over others, though it may be a limited and relatively weak power.

The sources of the labour leader's power usually differ from those of the politician or boss. Most often it does not stem from the barrel of a gun, though on occasion it has. Nor does it result from the ownership of property and control of wealth. Typically it comes from two closely connected sources, authority and the control of information. Authority may be defined as the followers' recognition of the right of the leader to command or issue instructions that are to be obeyed. This authority, the so-called right to rule, may itself come from a number of sources. It may be granted freely and actively by the membership at large who have come together democratically to limit their individual freedom in order to protect the freedom of the collectivity. Such a stewardship of rights and freedoms, however, is rarely granted consciously and freely in a benevolent social contract. Often workers join unions because doing so is a condition of employment, and the union leader's authority is seen to rest on coercion and collaboration with the employer. Members may be faced with a *fait accompli*, in that union structures and officials are in place with entrenched powers before they join the union. The union leadership may be seen as having a relative autonomy from the membership, or may be viewed as a clique that represents a faction in a union. The leader's authority may be based on tradition and habit; it may be a recognition of past service and sacrifice; it may be the result of personal charisma, if someone appears to embody the spirit, will, and dreams of the membership. Authority may result from apathy if workers believe the leaders are handling affairs in such a way that it is not worth the trouble to try to replace them; it may be based on procedures and positions enshrined in a constitution created by unionists long dead. Authority may also be derived from expertise, for workers may decide to give power to those believed best qualified to handle union affairs. Regardless of the ways in which it is obtained, it is authority – the recognition of their right to rule – that supplies part of the power of the labour bureaucrats.

We may ask if this authority, however granted or grasped, is in fact legitimate. Max Weber held that authority was legitimate by definition, for people would obey only those whose right to rule they recognized and would not obey those whom they believed did not have such a right. The test for such recognition was coercion: if it had to be used to enforce decisions then clearly people did not recognize the authority of the ruler. This definition bolsters Zeitlin's argument, for it implies that people consent to be ruled. It also implies that some benefit is derived from surrendering one's autonomy to the leader, and that this benefit confers some legitimacy. Even if there is some truth in these claims, they obscure more vital considerations. First, we may dispense with the notion that derived benefits in fact represent either consent or legitimacy. Slaves may be said to derive some benefit from being slaves: they are supplied with food, shelter, and clothing, and are freed from the burden of having to secure these items. No one, however, would claim that this legitimizes the power of the slave owner. Similarly, the receipt of social benefits, a wage, or a collective agreement does not legitimize the power of the state, capital, or the union leader. Nor does it imply consent, for in none of these situations does the individual enter the relationship as an equal with other realistic options.

Next, we may ask how much and what kind of dissent are required before authority is declared illegitimate. Do the actions of a minority opposing the leadership serve to remove its right to rule? A simple majority? An overwhelming majority? What sorts of opposition count as registering a lack of consent? Petitions? Absenteeism? Motions from the floor? Storming of the union office? We may also want to consider what coercion consists of. Must it always be physical force? Surely any unpleasant externally applied consequences, or the threat of such consequences, ranging from abuse or ridicule at a union meeting to expulsion from the union, may be considered coercion. Similarly, how are we to decide what counts as consent? The mere absence of revolt is not precise enough, for it is well-nigh impossible to determine if the lack of opposition is the result of coercion or not. The lack of revolt or dissent may in fact be acquiescence to power, not the acknowledgment of a right to rule. Not all of us are able to be an Emma Goldman or a Joe Hill, always ready to hurl defiance at our oppressors. However, a lack of bravery, a sense of discretion, a pragmatic weighing of costs and benefits, or a sense of futility are not the same as consent. Whenever there exist any unpleasant consequences or the threat of such consequences, whether these be overt or implied, material or psychological, it is impossible to distinguish between consent and coercion. Union leaders customarily have some formal means of coercion at their disposal, ranging from fines to banning rebels from meetings to purging them from the union. They also have informal means, such as refined debating techniques that embarrass the less-skilled rank-and-file member or the ability to determine which grievances and demands will be acted upon by the union. Indeed, such forms of coercion are often deemed necessary by the union, as Hyman points out, in order to enforce the discipline that is believed to be a vital part of collective action. The labour leader may be able to dispense favours and rewards, such as personal service, praise, expedited handling of a grievance, even a staff job. These rewards are simply the other side of the coin of coercion, and are part of the bureaucrat's power. Insofar as union leaders have any means to coerce members, it is impossible to determine where consent begins and ends. If consent cannot be delineated, we must stand Weber on his head and argue that all authority is illegitimate. Such a conclusion was reached by Michael Bakunin, when he wrote the following:

We accept all natural authorities and all influences of fact, but none of *right*; for every authority or every influence of right, officially imposed as such, becoming directly an oppression and a falsehood, would inevitably impose upon us ... slavery and absurdity.

In a word, we reject all legislation, all authority, and all privileged, licensed, official, and legal influence, even though arising from universal suffrage, convinced that it can turn only to the advantage of a dominant minority of exploiter against the immense majority in subjection to them ...

The principle of authority ... becomes a monstrosity, a flagrant denial of humanity, a source of slavery and intellectual and moral depravity ... The only grand and omnipotent authority, at once natural and rational, the only one which we may respect, will be that of the collective and public spirit of a society founded on equality and solidarity and the mutual human respect of all its members.[54]

We must also consider how consent, or what passes for it, is achieved. Consent may be manipulated in any number of ways. Leaders may say one thing and then do another. Appeals to cherished, abstract ideals may be persuasive, and yet not accurately reflect the real policies and aims of the union bureaucrat. Such posturing may be more than hypocrisy or deception. The reformer and organizer Saul Alinsky pointed out it may be necessary to overstate grievances and aspirations to mobilize people. As Alinsky suggests, if the Declaration of Independence had presented a balanced view of the benefits and liabilities of being a British colony, 'the result might well have been a document attesting to the fact that justice weighted down the scale at least 60 per cent on our side, and only 40 per cent on their side; and that because of that 20 per cent difference we were going to have a revolution. To expect a man to leave his wife, his children, and his home, to leave his crops standing in the field, and pick up a gun and join the Revolutionary Army for a 20 per cent difference in the balance of human justice was to defy common sense.' This manipulation is especially obvious in contract negotiations, where no matter what the rhetoric, at the end of the day, the negotiators must compromise and sign an agreement with the same boss who was painted as the devil incarnate. This is a structural constraint forced upon all union leaders in the absence of a revolutionary situation.[55] In any case, it suggests that leaders may exaggerate their politics in order to achieve specific goals that all may support and then surprise those followers who believed them to be completely sincere. Nor is it possible for all people to investigate all the claims of those in office. To question and dissent, people must have the tools of reason, security, time, and information, and all of these may be disrupted by those in power. Since one function of the bureaucracy is to hold special knowledge, it is easy for bureaucrats to control the dissemination of information. This control both props up their authority and confers power in itself. Again, Bakunin warned that knowledge forms a kind of capital that can be used to exploit others:

Is it not evident that out of two persons endowed with a nearly equal natural intelligence, the one who knows more, whose mind has been broadened to a greater extent by science and who, having a better understanding of the interlinking system of natural and social facts ... will grasp more readily and in a broader light the character of the environment in which he finds himself? And is it not evident also that that person will feel more free, and that in practice he will prove the cleverer and stronger of the two? It stands to reason that the one who knows more will dominate the one who knows less, and if there were, to begin with, only this difference in upbringing and education between two classes, it would in itself produce in a comparatively short time all the other differences and human society would relapse into its present state; that is, it would split up again into a mass of slaves and a small number of masters, the first working for the latter as they do now in existing society.[56]

The kinds of knowledge and information used by labour officials to do their jobs vary considerably, but they represent a source of power that is not generally and easily available to the rest of the membership. Even the shop stewards are privy to a wide variety of information. They must quickly learn the contents of the collective agreement, the structure and constitution of the union, and the channels of authority in the company. The stewards learn to file grievances, to interpret the contract, and to determine which demands of the membership should be acted upon and how. They must develop a talent for 'reading' the boss and the union business agent; they have to be able to assess the shop workers as individuals and as a collectivity. They must be adept at gauging the militancy and solidarity of those they represent as well as the intransigence of those they fight. Their knowledge of union members is used by stewards in their own work, and is passed up to union officials who must coordinate the activities of other shops and locals. Stewards also receive information from employers and union executives and interpret and pass it on to the membership. To become better at their job, conscientious stewards seek out more information. They take courses in collective bargaining, labour law, and labour history; they read up on public speaking, leadership, contract interpretation, unemployment insurance, safety, and workers' compensation. At the very least they will listen to other union officials and try to learn from their experience. By virtue of their knowledge and their willingness to take on a job that requires some dedication and work, stewards, in some sense, are removed from the culture of their co-workers. If all workers are equal, shop stewards are a little more equal. They make decisions, and they interpret and administer the decisions of others. Workers go to the shop stewards to ask for advice and representation. If there is a problem on the shop floor, employers and workers alike turn to the stewards. They are no longer ordinary workers speaking for themselves; now they must speak for the collectivity. This imposes on them an outlook different from that of the rank and file. They must consider not only the good of the individual or the shop, but also the good of the union as a whole. They must examine the long-term conse-quences of the actions of the local membership, and must try to balance the demands from the shop floor with the strictures of the contract, the strength of the employer, and the strategy of the rest of the union. Stewards are required to think critically, to judge ideas, facts, complaints, opinions, and the like with criteria different from those of the members who put them forward. They must assume a kind of 'objectivity,' that is, they must remove them-selves from the individual, subjective, relatively short-sighted point of view of the rank-and-file member and consider a host of other factors when they decide when, if, and how to proceed with a grievance.[57]

The information and culture of the stewards, who are caught between the demands of the membership and those of the union hierarchy, may be valuable, even necessary, if they are to be effective. The price, however, is the relative isolation or separation of the stewards from the rank and file. They become authorities; they are seen not as superior, perhaps, but as special or different. Their role may open up opportunities that do not exist for other members. Companies often look to shop stewards when they need new lead hands or supervisors, for they have proven that they can work with and control other workers, that they can interpret the collective agreement, and that they have an ability to look beyond the immediacies of the shop floor. Jobs and privileges within the union may also become available. Of course, most shop stewards do not go on to become supervisors or union executives. Even those who do not, however, receive a certain status, some small privilege, some easing of the daily workplace toil. They alone among the shop workers may meet with company and union executives as equals. Often they take time off from work to do union business, to present grievances, to negotiate contracts. The work of shop stewards can be more interesting than that on the shop floor, for it requires creative thinking and analysis of a different sort. It allows stewards to work on problems of strategy and tactics, and it may infuse them with senses of responsibility and of doing the right thing for themselves and others. All of this has two sides, though. On the one hand, it advances the cause of working people; on the other, it encourages stewards to think of themselves as different from rank-and-file workers. It tends to reinforce the dependence of the workers on a special agent who is assumed to be above personal interest of any sort, yet like all of us, cannot be.

Thus, the shop stewards may be understood as part of the union bureaucracy. Their interests and concerns may be very different from those of higher union officials, but they are also somewhat different from those of the workers they are chosen to represent. If this is true of this first level of the labour bureaucracy, how much truer it is of the other levels that are almost completely removed from the day-to-day contact with the workplace.[58]

Hyman, therefore, like Michels before him, is quite correct to assert that bureaucracy is a 'relationship which permeates the whole practice of trade unionism.'[59] Now, the bureaucracy of the 1890s was very different from that of the 1990s. Most union executive positions were not comfortable sinecures, and the possibility of physical danger was a grim reality. Nonetheless, bureaucracy was not a crafty invention of the CIO or the TLC and CCL in the 1940s. It has always been a tendency in the labour movement, sometimes the result of pure self-interest, but often the result of what seemed at the time to be good, practical, legitimate concerns. When the state uses lawyers to draft labour laws it is negligent for unions not to hire and train their own experts to cope. Obviously, it is good for shop stewards to know more, not less, about a wide variety of matters. When under attack, or pressing home an advantage, it is useful to have experienced, practical, and tested leaders at the helm. If members, or potential members, are apathetic or cowed, the union's survival may depend on a cadre of class-conscious, highly motivated officials who have been removed from the day-to-day shop-floor struggle and can devote their time, energy, and knowledge to the cause.

It must always be kept in mind, however, that in creating a split between members and leaders a bureaucratic elite is formed. Bureaucracy stems from many sources, some more legitimate than others: a genuine need for efficiency; a need to delegate tasks; the personal motives of those who seek power, wealth, prestige, or pleasant work; the desire of individuals to put their ideas into practice; the belief that it is appropriate for one to speak and interpret for others. It may be that bureaucracy is not an aberration but a common, though hardly inevitable, outcome of organization, partly because it allows some to abandon responsibility or to be reluctant to get involved. Whenever bureaucracy is not recognized as a possible danger and is not attacked by an active, conscious, and alert opposition, it is likely to flourish. As Bakunin suggested, 'The absence of opposition and control and of continuous vigilance inevitably becomes a source of depravity for all individuals vested with social power.'[60] Insofar as this is not recognized and acted upon by the rank and file, unions become more bureaucratized over time. Leaders tend to hold on to their positions, and policy that encourages hierarchy and rule by experts becomes the norm.

To understand the labour bureaucracy of today it is necessary to understand the bureaucracy of the beginning of the labour movement. We look for those things that tended to separate union leaders from the rank and file. We may examine privileges granted by the union, such as dues refunds, salaries, offices, and the like. We may look for the development of expertise and calls for officials to be selected on the basis of such expertise. The control of information, elevated status, authority over members, and control of union policy and structures – all of which tend to remove union leaders from the shop floor and the workers they represent – offer clues to the development of union bureaucracy. We must also examine the people who actually filled union positions to look for factors that helped propel or maintain them in power and explain their particular ideology. Education, income, gender, and ethnicity all contribute to a world-view. This study will ask the following questions in particular: Is bureaucracy in itself a sufficient answer to the question of the ideology of labour leaders? Are there bureaucratic principles that are common to left and to right unionists? Is political ideology a guarantee of rank-and-file control? How and why are bureaucratic structures created? Does becoming a labour bureaucrat take a worker out of the working class? How are political ideologies reconciled with the concerns of bureaucrats? Are there pressures that tend to push leaders to the right? These questions, applied to the case study of the Vancouver Trades and Labour Council, may help explore the nature of the labour movement and bureaucracy in general.

2

The Vancouver Trades and Labour Council: Early Structure and the Beginning of Bureaucracy

As Bakunin wrote about the state, 'abstractions do not exist in themselves or for themselves, since they have neither feet with which to walk, hands to create, nor stomachs to digest.' Therefore, studying bureaucracy means studying the structures that were created, the people who created them, and the context in which they arose.[1] Starting with a handful of dedicated unionists in 1889, the Vancouver Trades and Labour Council soon developed the trappings of bureaucracy. From its ad hoc beginnings, over time, centralization, the exclusion of the rank and file, red tape, and regulation came to characterize the council.

Few of these measures were brought in to create a labour bureaucracy; most were adopted under the guise of necessity, for good reasons that would strengthen the labour movement. Many of the measures and policies were debated, and, for the sake of unity, council delegates moved cautiously. But by 1900 the VTLC was largely autonomous from the labour movement and the rank and file. It had its own life, controlled by a small clique of activists.

The unionists who formed the VTLC reflected the larger city and the economy they worked in. The nature of the city dictated the kinds of workers who would come to it, and by extension, the unions they would form. Vancouver was from its very beginning shaped and dominated by the interests of monopoly capitalism and government. The city owed its existence to the desire of the Canadian Pacific Railway (CPR) for a deep-water port that could service the expected traffic of its 'All-Red Route.' This was a vision of a grand transportation network that would use steamships and trains under the British flag to carry silk and tea from the Orient to Montreal and thence to Europe, and would carry mail in both directions. The original mainland terminus of the transcontinental railway had been fixed by federal statute, and was to be Port Moody, at the head of Burrard Inlet. Although the company did nothing to discourage the boosterism and land speculation in the town, it had decided by 1882 to extend the mainline twelve miles west to the townsite of Granville, or Gastown. Port Moody was deemed to have insufficient land available for the expansion of the railway yards and facilities, and the waterway through the Second Narrows posed hazards to shipping that would be eliminated if the docks were moved to Coal Harbour and the adjoining waterfront. Although it planned to make the move to Granville for its own motives, the railway played hard to get and convinced local and provincial politicians that it would not abandon Port Moody without lucrative incentives. A reasonable offer, the company suggested, would be a grant of 11,000 acres from a provincial land reserve. The province, headed by Premier William Smithe, was quick to give land to aid development, but agreed to surrender only 6,458 acres – a little more than ten square miles that included all the waterfront from First to Second Narrows and virtually all the land that is now downtown Vancouver and Shaughnessy. Local developers, keenly aware that the railway would greatly increase the value of their land, agreed to donate a third of their holdings to entice the company to extend the tracks. In 1886 the CPR signed an agreement with the province to take possession of the land and push the railway through to what would soon become the chartered city of Vancouver. In a move typical of the era, the company had in essence been granted land at the public expense to do what it had planned to do in any case.

The company sent out L.A. Hamilton to survey its lands, and the road system that defines the city to this day was planned and named by the CPR. The selection of docks, rail facilities, residential and business sections, even the dividing line of east and west that still separates the working class and the middle class, were the creation of the railway. By choosing Vancouver as its Pacific port, the CPR also helped determine the fate of Victoria, New Westminster, and Port Moody, for, without the railway, none of these cities could hope to become the dominant regional capital.

Politics and business were completely interwoven in the new community. The city's first mayor, M.A. MacLean, was a realtor; the CPR's surveyor, Hamilton, was an alderman on the first city council; the Oppenheimers were each aldermen, and David went on to become mayor and a partner in the first streetcar company in Vancouver. During the first fourteen years of the city, eight CPR officials acted as aldermen. In this, the city resembled the province, for in both arenas the line separating the state from business was blurred; indeed, often both roles were taken up by the same person.[2] The very notion of conflict of interest no doubt seemed strange to the men who moved into politics to enhance their investments and used their wealth to grease their way to political office. This combination of political and economic power meant that the government, supposedly neutral in a liberal society, was in fact an instrument of the business elite. Such an arrangement seemed logical, even moral, to the people involved, for it would be ungracious to have political power and not use it for the benefit of one's friends.[3]

Standing over the smaller speculators, merchants, industrialists, and politicians, like a king watching over squabbling barons, stood the CPR. The largest landowner and largest employer in Vancouver, the railway continued to influence development directly and indirectly. By refusing to sell off its lands quickly, the railway set the pace for business. Contrary to staples theories and the metropolis–hinterland thesis, the railway did not lead immediately to a rapid development of the regional resource economy. This meant that for a number of years, Victoria was still the regional centre for coastal transportation, distribution, and finance, especially for the dominant industries of salmon canning, coalmining, and lumber production. Business in Vancouver tended to look to the city itself, rather than the regional economy, for investment and profit. If the CPR brought a vision of industrialization and progress to Vancouver, old-fashioned real estate speculation, boosterism, and mercantile activity continued to fuel and shape employment patterns and economics. As a result, unionists tended to be clustered in the building trades and printing industries servicing the local economy and in the machine shops, stations, and roundhouses of the CPR. Later, unionism was expanded to take in service workers, such as retail clerks and streetcar railwaymen. Because of this particular economy, only a minority of workers and unionists resembled an industrial proletariat forced to work in 'dark, Satanic mills.'[4]

By 1892 Vancouver had a labour force of approximately 5,000. The CPR was the largest single employer, with between 500 and 600 workers in various jobs, ranging from the running trades to labourers. Other businesses were much smaller: the typical dairy, bakery, or hotel had fewer than six employees, and only a few of the foundries and machine shops had as many as twenty-five workers. Taken together, about 900 people worked in retail and wholesale firms; 800 were employed in bakeries, confectioneries, or machine shops; 700 were in the building trades; 500 worked as waitresses, cooks, or janitors; 300 were employed in transportation, with the streetcar company or drayage firms. About 150 were in real estate and finance, while the city had about 70 professionals. About 70 per cent of the workforce was employed in businesses that serviced the local population and manufacturing employed about 25 per cent. Only 5 per cent were engaged in primary industry such as mining, logging, fishing, and farming. Because of its development in the latter part of the nineteenth century, Vancouver did not undergo the same transition from a precapitalist, pre-industrial stage that eastern cities did; rather, it 'had sprung to life with all the trappings of the industrial–capitalist system.'[5]

Vancouver was incorporated in April 1886, and workers created unions soon after. The Knights of Labor organized two locals, Shaftesbury Assembly 5506 and Local Assembly 8608. These were 'mixed' locals, that is, made up of workers from a variety of trades and occupations. Both assemblies became active in two areas that would continue to challenge the city's unionists for some time: municipal politics and Chinese exclusion. Though the Knights' commitment to civic affairs and their anti-immigration policy were largely shared by Vancouver union members, the Knights of Labor as an industrial organization was already being eclipsed by craft unions. Both local and international trade unions were being formed in the city. The printers were the first workers to organize as a craft in Vancouver, and the International Typographical Union (ITU) issued a charter to local printers in 1888. Stevedores first joined the Knights, then like the longshoremen, formed a local union that later affiliated to the AFL. In the building trades, plasterers, bricklayers, and masons created their own organizations, and they later were granted charters by the internationals. Carpenters first signed up with the British Amalgamated Society of Carpenters and Joiners, but in May 1890 a number of them split off to create Local 617 of the American United Brotherhood of Carpenters and Joiners.[6]

Class conflict was also quick to appear in Vancouver. In 1887 a building boom fueled by the fire that had levelled the city the year before saw most construction workers putting in an eleven-hour day. Although the last hour was considered overtime, a pay scale of only 17 to 20 cents an hour made it clear that workers were not going to profit from the frenzied construction. As the rapidly expanding city tapped into the Capilano Canyon watershed across the First Narrows, struggles between labour and capital were literally spread via the water pipelines. In May 1888 Italian muckers on the pipelines demanded a pay increase. When their request was turned down by the contractors, the fifty men refused to dig the trenches for the pipes. After two days the men returned to work at the same rate, but were determined to reduce their daily output so it would more closely reflect the pay rate. Instead of slowing down or working to rule, each of the men cut off a portion of his shovel blade so that less earth was moved each day.[7]

To improve their conditions, carpenters in 1889 organized into two unions and started a campaign for a legislated nine-hour day. To this end they called upon other unions to confederate into a trades council that would advance the general interests of unionized labour by taking an active role in organizing and in municipal affairs. On 21 November 1889 delegates from the carpenters' unions, the plasterers, painters, the typographers, and the Knights of Labor met at Sullivan's Hall on Cordova Street to lay the groundwork for the Vancouver Trades and Labour Council. The delegates discussed fielding labour candidates in the upcoming civic election, but finally shied away from direct political action. Citing the rapidly increasing population as a constituency too difficult to influence by election day, the delegates refused to run their own candidates or to endorse others. Instead, a more cautious resolution moved by George Bartley of the typographers was carried unanimously. The resolution outlined labour's concern with working conditions and reforms, calling for the nine-hour day and better organization of the city's workers. In addition, the resolution scheduled another meeting to create a city-wide labour council.[8]

On 5 December delegates met again at Sullivan's Hall and voted to constitute themselves as the Vancouver Trades and Labour Council (VTLC). The labour movement in Vancouver was dominated by the construction and printers' unions, and the delegates and especially the first executive reflected this. Joseph Dixon of the United Brotherhood of Carpenters was elected president and George Irvine of the plasterers was made vice-president. David Jamieson, already secretary of the typographers, was made secretary of the council. Duncan Macrae of the carpenters was elected treasurer, and J.H. Clarke of the painters was made doorkeeper. A financial committee to oversee funds and expenditures was appointed, and George Bartley and two carpenters, F. Prosser and F.W. Adamswaithe, served on it. The domination of these trades would continue for two decades. Together with the machinists' union, these founding organizations provided three-quarters of the VTLC's presidents.[9]

Vancouver was surprisingly homogeneous for a port, and the labour council reflected the city's ethnic make-up as well as its employment patterns. In 1892 approximately 60 per cent of the population was Canadian born; about 20 per cent was immigrants from the United Kingdom and Ireland. Americans made up about 6 per cent of the city, Europeans about 3 per cent, and Asians, predominantly Chinese and Japanese, about 8 per cent. At least 85 per cent of the inhabitants spoke English, and most were Protestants: over 25 per cent of the population was Anglican; another 25 per cent was Presbyterian; 16 per cent was Methodist. The Catholic population was small: at just over 11 per cent, its adherents were out numbered by those who either had no religious affiliation or belonged to religious groups outside of the mainstream.[10]

Though much has been made of the alleged influence of British trade unionists and socialists in the British Columbia labour movement, and they were overrepresented in the council, their role in the VTLC was no more prominent, political, or radical than that of the Canadians.[11] Of the twenty-two people who served as president of the council between 1889 and 1910 eight were English, Scottish, or Irish; seven were Canadian, and one was American. The nationality of the other six could not be reliably determined. Presidents often held office for more than one term, and out of the forty terms between 1889 and 1909, fifteen were held by Canadians and fourteen by Britons. British and Canadian unionists shared other council duties as well. The first secretary of the VTLC, David Jameson of the ITU, had learned his trade in Ontario. Duncan McRae, first treasurer of the council, and a founding member of the United Brotherhood of Carpenters and Joiners local, had come to Vancouver from Nova Scotia, as had the painters' delegate F.P. Bishop, who served as vice-president in 1890, then as secretary for five terms between 1892 and 1895.

Two of the most important council members, George Bartley and Harry Cowan, were also Canadians. Bartley, who would fill many executive positions on the council and would edit its newspaper from 1900 to 1904, was born in Mount Brydges, Ontario. Working as a migrant printer, he set type for papers in Buffalo, Pittsburgh, Youngstown, New Orleans, Seattle, and Bellingham, before settling in Vancouver in time to help found the labour council at the age of twenty-two. Here Bartley worked closely with fellow Ontarian Harry Cowan, another member of the International Typographical Union. The two would become close friends. Cowan was born in Ottawa and had come to Vancouver by 1889, when he and Bartley first show up on the rolls of the ITU local. By 1891 Cowan was also active in the VTLC, serving as an ITU delegate and serving on its organizing and municipal committees. In 1892 Bartley became the president of the council and Cowan its statistician, and the two worked together on the Labour Day celebrations for that year. Bartley remained in the city, but by 1897, Cowan was in Winnipeg, where he helped to found the *Voice*, perhaps the most influential labour paper of the period. When the paper fell into financial trouble a year later, Cowan returned to Vancouver, where Bartley was president of the VTLC. Their collaboration on the council continued, as Cowan became VTLC president in 1899 and Bartley headed the parliamentary committee. In 1900 the two set up and ran the VTLC's newspaper, the *Independent*. Bartley edited the paper, and Cowan assumed the duties of business manager. The two shared more than business responsibilities and trade union politics: Cowan roomed in Bartley's home, and the two were staunch members of the city's lacrosse club. Two years later, they would become related, as Cowan married Bartley's sister, Connie. Bartley dropped out of the VTLC after his work on the *Inde-*

pendent, but Cowan stayed on for a time, serving as secretary in 1908 and 1909, before starting his own printing business. Together, these two Canadians played a formative role in the first twenty years of the labour council, as officials, politicians, and journalists.[12]

If historians have tended to minimize the contribution of Canadians to the local labour movement, they may also have overestimated the British contribution. Certainly the British trade unionists helped to shape the VTLC, but it is difficult to know how influential they were. In some cases it may be difficult even to assess how 'British' their culture and traditions were. Joseph Dixon, together with Bartley and Cowan among the most prominent of early council members, was born in Cumberland County, England, to a farming family. Sent to school and then apprenticed to the carpentry trade, he left England in 1880, at the age of twenty, and moved to Winnipeg. After three years in the prairie city, he moved first to Victoria, then finally to Vancouver in 1886. Employed steadily in the aftermath of the fire that levelled the city, Dixon was active in the local carpenters' union, and served as its president in the 1889 fight for the nine-hour day. Working with Duncan McRae, he helped sign the local unionists up with the United Brotherhood of Carpenters and Joiners the following year. Surprisingly, his English upbringing did not lead him to join the British carpenters union, the Amalgamated Society of Carpenters and Joiners, even though a branch of that union was chartered in Vancouver in the same year.

Dixon did well in the city. In 1890 he began to work not just as a carpenter but also as a contractor, presumably with men working under him. This was not seen as reason to bar him from the union or the VTLC, and he continued to sit as president of the council through the first half of 1890 and again in the first half of 1892. He married in 1892 and was less prominent in the affairs of the council until 1899, when he took up the vice-presidency. In 1900 he became president, and along with Francis Williams, ran as an Independent Labor candidate in the provincial election. Although Dixon was a successful unionist and businessman, it is not clear how his early years in England shaped his politics and commitment to the labour movement. Indeed, by 1890, when he became prominent in the city's union circles, he had been in Canada for ten years, gaining most of his craft experience in the new world, not the old. If he is considered a Canadian rather than a Briton, the total number of presidential terms held by Canadians rises to twenty, and those held by Britons drops to nine. In any case, Dixon's career in the labour movement and his politics differed little from those of Bartley or Cowan. The three men worked together and supported the same causes for years. When the decision to create a newspaper for the VTLC was made during Dixon's tenure as president, he supported the resolution to appoint Bartley and Cowan to head the paper, and in turn, the two journalists used the paper to support Dixon's candidacy in the provincial election of 1900.[13]

Other Britons rose in the council alongside Canadians, but their ethnicity had no calculable effect on their politics. In the case of Joseph Henry Watson, ambition and political expediency soon took precedence over any socialism he might have learned in the British union movement. Watson was born in England in 1854, and was a boilermaker by trade. He was a Vancouver pioneer, moving there in 1887 to take up his trade in the machine shops of the CPR. After working in the city for a time, Watson was transferred first to Kamloops and then to Revelstoke, the railway's mountain divisional centre. There he took an active role in union work, joining Eugene Debs's American Railway Union and becoming president of the local in 1894. Started in Chicago in 1893, the ARU was an industrial union that organized skilled and unskilled railway workers alike. It sought to break with the craft divisions of the past and especially the labour elite of the running trades, who often refused to make common cause with other workers. Despite this radical slant, however, the ARU delegates to the VTLC were not pitted against the more conservative members. Men such as Watson represented skilled trades, not navvies or sectionmen, and they reinterpreted and softened Debs's left-wing message. In 1895 Watson returned to Vancouver and was seated as an ARU delegate to the labour council. Fellow ARU delegate Charles Boardman was elected president of the council in the second half of 1895, and both men worked for the short-lived single-tax, reformist Nationalist party as VTLC representatives.[14]

Watson's political views were in flux in this period. A member of the left-leaning ARU, he nonetheless strengthened his ties to the more-conservative Nationalist party. In April 1896 he urged the council to work more closely with the party and its federal candidate, the Liberal-Labour politician George R. Maxwell. A month later, he pushed the council to invite Eugene Debs to speak in the city. With the decline of the ARU after the Pullman strike of 1894, Watson moved increasingly to the right. He strengthened his ties to the Liberal party and became its strongest advocate in Vancouver's trade union movement. With the collapse of the ARU in 1898, Watson helped found a boilermakers' local in Vancouver, serving as its first secretary and as its delegate to the VTLC. Like Dixon, he chose to join the American, not the British, union with jurisdiction over his trade. He started his climb in the labour council, becoming its doorkeeper in 1896, head of its organizing committee in 1898, and finally its president in July 1898. Watson also became a volunteer organizer for both the Dominion Trades and Labour Congress

(DTLC) and the AFL. In 1899, having relinquished the presidency of the council, he called upon the VTLC to create a new position, that of financial secretary, and in January 1899, became the first to hold the post.[15]

Watson's connection to the Liberal party was to provide him with both his chief rewards and later, his downfall as a labour activist. In 1899, in return for his support for the Liberal party, Watson was given a patronage job in the customs department. His party loyalties soon caused the only major rift in the labour council's first twenty years, in the dispute over Deadman's Island, as Watson sided with MP George R. Maxwell and against the bulk of the council on the issue of logging the island. Although he managed to weather the storm, even becoming VTLC vice-president in 1900, Watson's patronage job continued to make it difficult for him to serve two masters. No longer working as a boilermaker, he still served as the union's delegate to the council, and as the council's chief organizer. His work as organizer was strong: he organized twenty-seven different unions throughout the province, chartering some to internationals and some directly to the Dominion Trades and Labour Congress. His forthright activity may be explained in part by the way in which he was remunerated by the AFL and DTLC. Instead of a salary, Watson was paid a piece rate for every new charter he sent in. In 1901, however, his balancing act started to wobble. In April of that year, he asked Samuel Gompers for a job as a salaried AFL organizer. Gompers, while acknowledging Watson's work in British Columbia, replied that he could not 'see my way clear' to putting him on the payroll. A little later, Watson asked again, and this time was turned down by Gompers's secretary. Rebuffed by the American organization, Watson started to side with nationalists in the Canadian labour movement and against the AFL. In a letter to the *Independent*, he wrote of the need for one 'central body' and 'one supreme head' that could coordinate labour's political program. Defending his practice of chartering locals directly to the DTLC rather than to the international union that had jurisdiction over the craft, Watson's letter was almost identical to one sent by the labour congress's secretary, P.M. Draper, who was himself increasingly concerned with Canadian autonomy. At the same time, Liberal MP and DTLC president, Ralph Smith, whom Watson supported, launched his own campaign for Canadian independence, most likely at the behest of the Laurier government. Watson supported Smith, but events soon outpaced them both. The Nanaimo miners who had originally sent Smith to Ottawa now denounced his pandering to the federal Liberals, while Vancouver labourists were convinced that their future lay in independent political action.[16]

Watson, however, continued to back the Liberal party. In 1903 the conflict came to a head. The VTLC voted 41 to 20 to support the Independent Liberal Chris Foley in a federal by-election, while Watson plumped for the machine candidate, Robert Macpherson. Despite the council's decision, Watson remained true to his political masters. At meetings and in letters to the editor he railed against the council for its decision, insisting that the endorsement of Foley had been 'railroaded through,' and that Foley was no more than a 'liberal-tory.' If the labour council wanted politics, Watson maintained, it 'must have a machine, too,' and he continued to fight for Macpherson. Exasperated at his dogged loyalty to the shopworn Liberals, the VTLC moved to purge Watson.[17]

By the middle of 1903 Watson was no longer part of the labour council. Vancouver's socialist paper correctly noted that the cause of his downfall was the attempt to keep on 'riding two horses,' that is, the Liberal party machine and the labour movement. But Watson's career of nearly ten years as the Liberal party's chief advocate in the labour bureaucracy had paid him some rewards. He continued in his patronage job in the customs service, becoming the head of its post office parcel branch. When he died of a stroke at the age of fifty-four on 22 May 1908, the city newspapers gave his death and funeral service considerable coverage, referring to him as a 'wheel-horse' in the Liberal party and as 'an illustration, in his official capacity, of what a Civil Servant should be.' His tumultuous career in the labour movement was perhaps most important as an example of overriding ambition, as his politics reflected the expressed needs not of the labour council but of the Liberal party. Determined to hold on to his politically appointed job, Watson tried to bend the labour movement to the shape his benefactors required, until even his supporters could take no more. His example demonstrates that ethnicity was no particular guarantee of militancy or radicalism, and the influence of British labour activists could be a mixed blessing.[18]

The ethnic mix in the council continued throughout its first twenty years, and no easy distinctions of ethnicity and ideology can be made for any period. The VTLC of 1902 to 1903, often portrayed by British Columbia labour historians as a left-leaning council, was headed by W.J. Lamrick, an Ontario who had lived in the United States for some time before moving to Vancouver in 1896. Lamrick was a member of the Retail Clerks International Protective Association, and he served as its delegate to the labour council, becoming vice-president in 1901, then holding the presidency for four consecutive terms. The treasurer in 1903 was an American, A.N. Harrington, vice-president of the Waitresses and Waiters Union, local 28. From 1906 to 1909 the council was dominated by Canadians. Socialists such as James McVety and Parmeter Pettipiece were Canadians, as were the more-conservative Harry Cowan and A.R. Burns. These four served as secretary, president, financial secretary, statistician, vice-president, and trustee between them, often rotating among themselves. While Britons were undoubtedly important members of the labour council, their politics and trade union activity were virtually indistinguishable from those of the Canadians. Socialists and labourists were not divided by ethnicity, and Canadians were active participants in the creation of the council's ideology, culture, and structure.

The VTLC was created to be a 'fighting organization,' as Michels wrote of unions in general, and was organized along traditional, hierarchical lines with a president, vice-president, secretary, treasurer, and the like. Special committees were struck to deal with municipal affairs, political action, the 'Chinese question,' and the council's structure and constitution. Few of the council delegates were rank-and-file unionists. More often they were officers of the trade unions they represented. In many cases serving as a council delegate was one of the responsibilities of the union president. In other instances VTLC delegates were elected directly to the council by their unions, but even then they tended to be officers and former officers of the individual unions.[19]

Surprisingly for an organization created for the interests of labour, no efforts were made to limit membership in the VTLC on the basis of occupation or class. When asked if a contractor could sit on the council, President George Bartley replied that 'there was nothing in the Constitution to prevent him doing so providing that the Union to which he belonged thought fit to send him to the council.' Though one delegate opined that 'it was not right to allow contractors a seat in the Council as they might divulge the secrets to the Bosses' Association,' no action was taken to restrict the council to wage workers. This reflects both the nature of the building trades, where today's employee might well be tomorrow's employer, and the ability of artisans to move into the petit bourgeoisie without losing contact with the working class.[20]

When the issue of class did arise, it was often a cover for a factional debate within the council rather than a principle of solidarity or class consciousness. Less than a year after he had ruled that contractors could sit in the council, Bartley reversed his opinion and objected to the seating of G.F. Leaper on the grounds that he was an employer. In fact, Bartley's objection was based on a craft unionist's dislike of dual unionism, that is, rival unions in the same trade. Although Leaper was a compositor like Bartley, he was a representative of a mixed assembly of the Knights of Labor, not the ITU. In February 1893 he began to edit the short-lived *People's Journal*, a progressive labour paper. Bartley cited a clause in the constitution that forbade employers to sit on the council, but other delegates objected and gave notice of their intention to move to strike the clause. A committee consisting of Bartley, Pollay of the

Knights, and Gagen of the Brotherhood of Carpenters was empowered to find a way out of the problem. The committee finally recommended the replacement of the words 'but no person who is an employer of labor shall be admitted as a delegate' with 'but no person shall be admitted as a delegate to represent a mixed assembly or labor organization if a union or assembly of his particular trade or calling is in existence and working order.'

The wording of this new clause had nothing to do with keeping out employers. It was aimed instead at Leaper and other Knights who were competing with AFL-chartered craft unions. Fights over jurisdiction and the right to represent workers were nothing new to both organizations, and the ITU and the Knights had already clashed in eastern Canada. Furthermore, in this period mixed assemblies of Knights tended to operate not as trade unions but as political clubs, and this was often objected to by the craft unionists who preferred to deal with more immediate issues that arose from the shop floor. In any event, the resolution of the council indicates that class was not as important as union affiliation when choosing delegates.[21]

Bartley himself was soon forced to stave off a similar attempt to bar him from the council. In September 1894 the VTLC voted to ask the typographical union to withdraw George Bartley as a delegate on the grounds that he had become a government official. Bartley's defenders failed to have the motion quashed, but they did manage to amend it so that he was summoned to the council to explain himself before further action was taken. He defended his position adequately, for the request to have him replaced was withdrawn, and he was allowed to remain as a delegate.[22] The council continued to allow employers to be seated. In 1896 Delegate Hawson of the American Railway Union announced that he had become an employer 'in a small extent' and asked if there would be any objection to his continuing as a representative of the ARU. Bartley, now serving as the VTLC's statistician, voiced no objection to the seating of an employer; other delegates remained silent, and Hawson remained a delegate. This further suggests that Bartley's opposition to Leaper was politically motivated; more important, perhaps, it shows that the council was not prepared to see class as the most important line to be drawn.[23]

The debates over who should sit as a delegate also illustrate the federal nature of the labour council. Although the call for a central labour body implies a high degree of centralization, this was not the case in Vancouver. The unions were called upon to fight together for specific ends, such as the nine-hour day, but there was little attempt to combine the unions or to put them under a single, united leadership. In this the VTLC resembled the AFL and the Dominion Trades and Labour Congress. In each of these organizations, affiliated unions maintained their own leaders and independence when they joined. This included allowing each union to decide for itself whether its delegate was a fit representative, rather than insisting on uniform qualifications. The craft unions were careful to avoid treading on each other's toes and preferred to forge a relatively narrow alliance based solely on trade union matters and political issues that stemmed directly from trade union concerns. They tried to avoid larger issues on which reasonable minds could differ, for the difference could turn the unions against one another. This carefully limited solidarity reflected the delegates' fear of centralization and stemmed in large part from their experience as craft unionists. To protect the jobs of their own members, trade unions had to guard their craft jurisdictions jealously. No carpenter, for example, could idly watch a plumber turn his hand to framing on a job site, for that would take work away from another carpenter. Each union had evolved its own traditions, code of ethics, and work rules, and council delegates could hardly surrender any of these to the council in the interests of a greater solidarity. Ceding any authority to the council could only weaken the individual unions, and delegates firmly rejected attempts to have the VTLC assert autonomy. Thus, while numerous writers have suggested that centralization of the union structure was a project of conservative union bureaucrats, in Vancouver these leaders rejected centralization.[24]

Paradoxically, this federal principle was an attempt to build a greater unity than that achieved by the Knights of Labor with its all-embracing policy of organizing all workers in one union. In theory the Knights' structure united all workers, but in practice the union was troubled by the competition of sectional interests. Knights in Toronto were irked by the high dues they were forced to pay to help their union brothers who struck the city's streetcar system. Hamilton shoemakers organized in the Knights complained of the levies exacted upon them to aid Montreal shoemakers, even though they realized that the Quebec struggle was part of their own battle with employers. The Knights' aim of organizing all workers papered over another division in the working class, that between the so-called skilled and unskilled. The Knights held that the interests of the working class were ultimately the same regardless of job or skill level and organized workers by industry, not trade. While in theory this provided great solidarity, in practice it was a source of friction. The craft unions made this friction into a principle, as they based their strategy on competition between workers and on excluding people from the trades to limit the supply of labour. If this was an effective way to keep up the salaries of the unionized workers in some sectors, it meant abandoning the bulk of the working class to the predations of the boss. Since organizing the unskilled and the factory workers was difficult, diverting money and people from the day-to-day affairs of the unions was hard to justify. Furthermore, immigrants from outside the Anglo-Saxon countries tended to work in the unskilled jobs, and the terms 'unskilled' and 'foreigner' became practically synonymous. Union leaders often expressed their demands as rights that they were entitled to by virtue of their status as Canadians or British subjects and as whites, as well as their skill, and sought to forge links with the larger society based on a common ethnicity. Unskilled workers threatened this strategy by attacking the belief that skill and ethnicity should be rewarded. Thus Vancouver bricklayers squabbled with the hod carriers, or helpers, in 1891 even though, or more accurately, because, they were in the same union. The fight broke out when the hod carriers demanded $2.50 a day, a sum thought by the bricklayers to be too high. When the hod carriers stuck to their demand and were supported by the VTLC, the bricklayers resigned from the labour council. Their action was based on the belief that the wages demanded could not be gained without a strike, and the bricklayers did not want to jeopardize their strike fund to support the hod carriers. In order to minimize these inter- and intra-union disputes the VTLC asked for a more limited kind of solidarity and referred most calls for united action back to the individual unions. Decentralization and local autonomy were concerns of the right, not the left, in this period.[25]

This cautious solidarity extended to political issues as well as straightforward union matters. Again, the experience of the Knights illustrated that combining political action with bread-and-butter unionism could lead to disputes and factionalism, for workers in local assemblies often balked when their dues were diverted from local struggles to aid political campaigns. The Home Club affair of 1886 highlighted the differences between Knights who insisted on concentrating on unionism and those who favoured political action. The Home Club was a faction of Knights who followed the platform and ideas of the German socialist Ferdinand Lassalle. Chief among his ideas was the 'iron law of wages,' which held that no matter how workers fought or were organized the average wage could not rise much above the subsistence level, partly because employers could simply raise their prices to maintain profit levels and partly because workers would, in Malthusian fashion, take the opportunity of higher wages to produce more children. If the theory were correct, it meant that the struggles of the union movement could never achieve much. This in turn implied that other forms of action, such as co-operatives and involvement in politics, were more important. From this it followed that the actions of the workers were less important than those of the Knights who were politicians and that the middle-class intelligentsia was the proper group to head the organization. A seemingly abstract debate over a point of economics camouflaged a fight over who should lead the Knights and in what direction. The matter was further complicated when Home Club Knights in New York organized the Progressive Cigar-Makers Union and undercut the wage schedule of the AFL's Cigar-Makers International Union. The incident spilled over into Canada, although with little apparent justification, and the episode tended to exaggerate the differences between political reformers and unionists, and between the Knights and the AFL.[26]

To George Bartley, the history of the Knights indicated clearly that trade union autonomy and non-interference from the central bodies were important for the labour movement as a whole. Craft unions, he believed, could fight against the boss more effectively, while principled political battles were divisive and tended to replace traditional working-class leaders with political reformers. Bartley, who knew and worked with Vancouver Knights, wrote that by 1889 and the founding of the VTLC, 'the days of the noble Knights were numbered and the old movement of industrial unions, namely that all workers belong to one body, was being broken up by the American Federation of Labor.' Since the 'once noble order' now believed that labour could only achieve its rights 'through political action,' Bartley wrote, the Knights insisted 'that all public bodies must be controlled by "true" Knights.' Ultimately, he argued, this 'gave rise to factions in the local assembly,' and the result was the disintegration of the Knights of Labor. To Vancouver's trade union leaders, it appeared that far from guaranteeing solidarity, centralization could actually undermine it. At the same time, craft unionism remained the most effective way to maintain and improve the wages and conditions of the skilled worker. Although direct evidence is lacking, it may also be that union leaders, while receiving little in the way of salary, enjoyed a degree of prestige that would end if their positions as heads of unions were subsumed in one overarching organization.[27]

Craft autonomy within the shell of the VTLC was protected in several other ways. First, executive positions were generally spread out among the different unions, regardless of their size, to deny dominance to any single union. Second, appeals for solidarity were referred back to the individual unions rather than granted from the council's own funds. In this way aid to fellow workers could be given without compulsion and without alienating union members who might not be filled with empathy for other workers. In May 1890, for example, the VTLC called a general meeting of delegates and unionists to consider aiding strikers in Portland, Oregon, rather than enforcing a levy *en masse*. In November of the same year, the question of supporting Vancouver Island miners was sent back to each union to decide, while a request from the beleaguered steelworkers at Homestead in 1892 was 'referred to the different unions for their consideration.' The strikes of British machinists in 1897 and New York printers in 1899 brought forth a number of appeals for aid, and again, the council's response was to refer them to the affiliated unions. Although the request of funds from individual unions was sometimes successful, it held no guarantees: while the Portland meeting raised $165.50, two weeks of soliciting funds turned up only a single dollar for the Homestead strikers.[28]

This did not mean that the council was opposed to solidarity. It did mean that its first priority was maintaining the structural integrity of the Vancouver labour movement by avoiding both controversy and a top-down enforcement of political morality that could alienate unions. If the Knights taught men and women to dream of what might be, the VTLC preferred to take them as they were and refused to push them much further, hoping that in diminishing its expectations it might be more successful. The council did support other workers, but in ways that would create little stir. Although the Wellington miners received little direct aid, the Labour Day celebration of 1890 included a tug of war with a prize of ten dollars. The longshoremen won the event and were awarded the money 'with the understanding that they should forward to the Wellington Miners Association.' On the whole, however, the council acted on the belief that solidarity and charity began at home, and if its policy prevented sectarian squabbling it did little for the larger cause of labour.[29]

Political issues were handled in a similar fashion. Parliamentary committees were struck to draw up platforms, and those selected to serve on them represented a wide variety of unions. The final platforms were then presented to the council as a whole, debated and amended, then sent back to the individual unions for their approval. If such a procedure was complicated and time-consuming – it was undoubtedly a factor in the failure of the council to take effective political action in its early years – it minimized political squabbling and dissension.[30] The tactic was an effective one. In the first twenty years of the council, political debates took place, but rarely did they result in overt fractures in the council itself. Socialists and labourists feuded in the papers, at conventions, and at the polls, but the council itself avoided serious infighting. Indeed, the only issue that did split the council in this period was the fight over Deadman's Island, an early environmental battle that split political parties and businessmen as well as the labour movement.

Deadman's Island, today the site of the HMCS *Discovery* Naval Reserve Training Section, is a small islet in Coal Harbour, a few hundred feet off Stanley Park. The island had been used in the 1860s as a rendering station for whalers; before that, coastal Indians had used it as a burial ground. The island

and the 1,000 acres that were to become Stanley Park were originally part of a British naval land reserve and came under Canadian jurisdiction when British Columbia joined the Dominion in 1871. Since the land was under federal jurisdiction, it was held out of the speculation boom of the 1880s and 1890s. One real estate broker, A.W. Ross, believed that the undeveloped land could still help him turn a profit, if only indirectly. Reasoning that a large park would attract tourists and settlers, and thus drive up the price of his own nearby lots, Ross lobbied the civic council to ask the federal government to transfer the land to the city. In 1887 the Privy Council agreed to the city's request, and Stanley Park was created. Deadman's Island was used as a quarantine centre for suspected cases of smallpox.[31]

The island was commonly believed to have been included in the Stanley Park grant, but the Canadian government did not agree. In 1899 the issue was put to the test when the federal government, headed by Wilfrid Laurier and the Liberal party, leased Deadman's Island to an American businessman, Theodore Ludgate, who soon announced plans to build a sawmill and log the island. The population of the city quickly became aroused, and different factions sprang up to argue the respective merits of park space and industrialization. City council split on the contest, and the Conservative mayor, James Garden, used the police and the Riot Act to halt logging. The business community also divided. Leaders such as Henry Bell-Irving opposed the logging scheme, while others, such as Charles Woodward, supported it. Politicians fought among themselves and with their party members; even in the inchoate, non-party politics that typified British Columbia in this period division was acute and hostile. Ludgate's lease was fought in every level of court and was eventually decided in his favour by the British Privy Council in 1911. By then most of the trees had already been felled, and the decision was moot.[32]

The VTLC had long been active in securing park and recreational space for working people, and Deadman's Island touched a nerve. President Harry Cowan informed the council that Ludgate had received permission to log the island and run a sawmill for the nominal sum of $500 a year. The VTLC then voted unanimously to condemn the leasing of Deadman's Island for commercial purposes. Angry delegates decided to send Cowan to Ottawa as part of a deputation of business and community leaders opposed to the industrialization of the island.[33] This united front, however, soon proved illusory. At the next meeting, with Cowan on his way to the nation's capital, J.H. Watson, recording secretary of the Boilermakers and Iron Ship Builders Union, read a long letter praising industry and the leasing of the island to Ludgate. Delegates Harrison and Tyson then moved to reconsider the council's decision to oppose the sawmill scheme. Bartley, John Pearey, and Francis Williams worked to get the matter referred back to the constituent unions for discussion. This parliamentary procedure would have delayed any vote indefinitely, for it would practically amount to having the matter tabled and would let the original resolution stand. Although the council agreed, Watson and W.R. Lawson outmaneouvered Bartley and the others. Watson simply moved that the VTLC, 'after more mature consideration, does heartily approve the leasing of Deadman's Island or any other foreshore around the city, for manufacturing and commercial purposes, as being in the best interests of the working classes.' Ironically, Watson earlier had been in the vanguard of the labour council's park movement. In 1895 he had joined with Bartley to have the council petition the city to improve swimming facilities at English Bay. Watson had led the opposition to the selling of the city's foreshore rights and had clamoured for the clearing of land for a public park at English Bay. But this time he abandoned his earlier position and took the side favoured by the Liberal party. In what the newspapers called 'one of the most animated' meetings on record, the council voted 12 to 9 in favour of the motion and was then officially in favour of logging the small island. Cowan was notified of the abrupt about-face and returned to Vancouver.[34]

The matter did not die there. Those opposed to logging did not take Watson's actions lightly. President Cowan, Secretary J.H. Browne, Treasurer Joseph Dixon, and Parliamentary Committee Secretary and Auditor George Bartley turned in their resignations when Cowan returned. Together they denounced Watson's 'attempt to turn the Trades and Labor council into a political machine.' Charging that 'a number of members of the council have received government positions,' they deplored the fact that those members were 'amenable to government influence.' This was clearly aimed at Watson, a Liberal supporter since at least 1897 and a close associate of the Liberal-Labour politicians Ralph Smith and George Maxwell, both of whom supported the logging of the island.[35]

It is important to realize that this dissension was not a battle between those who favoured labour's engaging in politics and those who favoured Samuel Gompers's voluntarist policy of rewarding labour's friends and hurting its enemies, regardless of party. Bartley denounced Watson's partisanship, while he was himself on a ward committee for Conservative Mayor Garden and was later elected to the parks board as part of Garden's slate. The labour council as a whole was preparing to enter politics: in February 1900 it voted to take 'independent political action in municipal, provincial, and Dominion elections,' while in May it would nominate VTLC president Joseph Dixon and treasurer Francis Williams as independent labour candidates in the provincial election.[36]

What the wrangling over Deadman's Island does illustrate is the difficulty that faced the craft unions when they moved away from the 'pure and simple' issues of wages and conditions and towards the political field. The different trades could be expected to have different positions on issues, such as parks, depending on how each would profit or lose: boilermakers, stonecutters, and iron moulders supported the logging of the island, for it would create employment among their members, while those unlikely to prosper, such as printers, fought for the preservation of park space. Party politics, each union's perception of the interests of its members, and individual agendas made agreement extremely difficult, and the consequences of raising such issues could be bitter division. It should not be surprising then that putting forward an extensive political platform and forming a united political party to represent labour was such a difficult task. To succeed, the council and its politics had to be restricted to the most basic issues on which all unions could agree.

The council worked hard to repair the rift caused by Deadman's Island. What appears to have been a compromise resolution was hammered out in late April as the VTLC called for a city board to obtain the rights and control of the foreshore and False Creek area. This board, which was to include members of the VTLC, would be 'managed and controlled ... for public purposes, the promotion of industry, and the elevation of labour.' In September 1899 elections for the council executive returned members of both sides of the split. In January 1900 Dixon became president and Watson was made vice-president. Bartley gave up his council duties to become editor of the labour council's new paper, and he was unanimously voted to be the labour candidate for parks board. By 1902 no trace of the old animosity was evident, as Bartley and Watson served as delegates to the Provincial Progressive party founding in Kamloops. Nonetheless, the acrimony served as a warning to keep politics out of the labour council.[37]

To minimize such feuding, most controversial proposals were settled by sending them back to the individual unions for discussion. This reinforced the autonomy of the affiliated unions and made unity, albeit a tepid kind, more likely. When the building trades set up an arbitration committee in the VTLC, for example, delegates debated how the panel should be selected. Some wanted the council to appoint the committee, but after 'considerable discussion,' it was agreed to let the unions select their own representatives. When the Amalgamated Society of Carpenters and the Knights' Stevedores Union spoke on the desirability of a cooperative store for union members, many delegates were in agreement. When a plan for such a co-op was put directly to the council, however, it was decided that the VTLC itself 'could not take an active part in the formation of a co-operative association but that members individually would be willing to take shares in same.' When the council first conceived of publishing a labour paper, a committee was struck to see how much support could be garnered. The council, in now-typical fashion, moved to start the paper as soon as possible, pending the decisions of the affiliated unions and their success in raising the needed number of subscriptions. Given the limited resources of the council such a policy was wise, but the effect was again to reaffirm the independence of the unions that made up the central labour body.[38]

Unions asserted their reluctance to assimilate under one leadership in other ways. Fear of centralization was on occasion a strong enough reason for a union to be chary about joining in the first place. When the American Railway Union considered affiliating to the VTLC, it expressed great reluctance because of a clause in the council's constitution that placed the control of strikes 'solely in the power of the [council's] strike committee.' The council responded by changing the clause so it would 'apply only to strikes which are confined to the city of Vancouver and shall not affect Labour Unions or Brotherhoods who are controlled and in the case of a strike by officers living in other cities.' Apathy was an informal yet efficient technique used to prevent intrusion, and complaints over poor attendance of the delegates were common. 'Brother Cosgrove' was one of many who 'referred in strong terms to the laxity of some delegates sent by the various unions of the city to represent them in attending the meetings of the council.' Throughout its history the council found it necessary to pass resolutions to enforce attendance. Even this resolution illustrated the weakness of the central council, for it did not fine delinquent delegates or dismiss them. Instead, it returned the matter to the individual unions by stating that 'any delegate missing more than 2 consecutive meetings will have his union asked to appoint another in his stead.'[39]

More effective as a way to maintain a union's autonomy was the withholding of information and money from the VTLC. Concerned with wages and conditions of work, the labour council needed to garner statistics and figures on rates of pay, unemployment, union membership, and the like. One of its first tasks, therefore, was to elect Thomas Hallam of the Knights of Labor to the post of statistician. Hallam was energetic and drew up report sheets for the affiliates to fill out. Judging from the slow response of the unions to his repeated requests for information, however, the needs of the new bureaucracy were not treated with a great deal of sympathy. Despite previous resolutions to the same effect, delegates resolved in March 1892 to have 'the various unions bring in a monthly report of the state of trade, number of men employed, rate of wages, and as near as possible the number of Union and Non-union men in the city.' The reluctance to provide statistics may have had its root in economics as well as in a desire to control information, for union membership was used to calculate each union's contribution to the council. Unions were often in arrears, and the per capita levy could be a significant factor in a union's decision to remain with the council. In 1893 the Amalgamated Society of Carpenters tendered their resignation from the council, giving 'the chief reason for doing so' as 'their inability to collect the 10 cents per capita tax from their members.' After some pleading from other delegates, the society resolved to stick with the council, but a year later the Building Laborers Union and the Mainland Shipmens' Association announced that they had to withdraw because of financial difficulties. This time the VTLC asked them to continue to seat their delegates 'with the understanding that they be exempt from per capita tax until such time that they may be able to contribute to the funds of the council.'[40]

Despite the difficulty of raising funds and the opposition to anything more than a limited degree of centralization, the VTLC did begin to assert itself as a distinct organization. Attendance at the meetings was open to all trade unionists until May 1891. Then the council closed its sessions to the rank and file, deeming it 'advisable that only such members as were delegated to attend to the business of the council should be present and participate in its meetings.' A subsequent motion to allow former delegates to attend and speak, but not vote, was tabled, and several months later, the council voted to hold 'special meetings or secret meetings ... to discuss all private business.' These efforts to separate the membership from the council were mitigated somewhat when, after 'considerable discussion' the VTLC agreed that delegates would no longer be appointed to the organization, but would be elected by the unions on the basis of one for each twenty members. The general tendency of the council was away from control and influence by the rank and file it represented.[41]

On some issues the council was inclined to hold general meetings, but these relatively few occasions were still restricted. The selection of a delegate to the Dominion Trades and Labour Congress of 1890 was one such affair. A mass meeting was called to elect the delegate, but discussion was limited to five speakers, two of whom were the candidates. Voting was technically open, but 'everybody in the hall would have the privilege of voting, on condition that all who voted should contribute to the expenses' of the delegate, despite a prior council decision to fund the trip with a per capita levy. After his successful election, George Bartley made it clear that he held to a parliamentary, not a participatory, notion of democracy as he asked for 'resolutions and suggestions' that would 'guide' him but not 'bind' him at the conference.[42]

In addition to limiting attendance at its meetings, the labour council worked to restrict the flow of information regarding its business. Allowing newspapers, and thus employers and politicians, to be privy to the debates, divisions, decisions, and politics of the council could be harmful, especially in a period when trade unions and unionists had little legal protection or security. Therefore, early in 1892 the delegates discussed 'the advisability of allowing reporters into this council' and decided to ban the press and to furnish it with edited accounts of their doings. In May the Amalgamated Carpenters urged the VTLC to be 'more conservative with regard to publication of business transacted,' and delegates resolved to endorse this suggestion fully. In July the carpenters went further and called for an outright ban on the publication of the council's activities. The motion was tabled, but subsequently one was passed to make the secretary 'the only authorized person to report minutes of proceedings to newspapers.' Such a policy made sure that the press would not betray the council to employers, but it also prevented dissenting delegates from airing grievances. The restriction of information, together with the banning of the rank and file from meetings, also meant that workers could be made aware of the council's activity only through the official, edited channels of the press and the reports of delegates. Certainly opening the meetings to reporters would not guarantee the dissemination of accurate information, but by keeping close control over their meetings, even with the best of motives, labour leaders separated themselves from the membership they were to represent and aid.[43]

The council was unwilling to unilaterally levy assessments to aid workers, but it soon proved ready to assess the affiliated unions for its own purposes. When it decided to send a delegate to the Nanaimo Labor Congress in 1890, the council did not hesitate to charge each union member ten cents to cover the cost. Other taxes to fund the council were assessed without the deliberation of the individual unions. In September 1890 each delegate was required to pay the council five dollars for his seat. January 1891 saw a special assessment of ten cents per affiliated union member; the quarterly per capita charge was doubled to ten cents in March; a one-time levy of twenty-five cents per member was passed to provide money for May Day celebrations in 1892. Despite these fees and the regular per capita tax, the council was still operating at a loss, and it instructed the financial committee to calculate a new per capita assessment to eliminate the debt. The committee recommended a levy of thirty cents per head to put the council on a healthy footing.[44]

The need for funds and the difficulty in extracting money from the individual unions prompted the VTLC to adopt stricter accounting procedures and eventually to hire its first paid staff member. In 1890 delegates were told that 'as no books had been kept by previous secretaries, it was a difficult matter to find out the standing of the unions.' Delegates of delinquent unions were then asked to forward their arrears per capita tax, presumably on an honour system. To make accurate record keeping possible, the council secretary had special forms printed, and with the decision to keep better records came a motion to pay the secretary. An earlier attempt to give him a salary had failed, but in January 1891 it was resolved to pay him fifty cents a meeting. Six months later the rate was increased to five dollars per month and 'extra pay for extra work.' Part of his duties now included entering receipts and expenditures in the minutes of each meeting. Thus, the need for proper accounting, a must if the council were to survive, led to the first steps towards red tape and professionalization, or in Weber's terms, management based on written documents, a system of general rules for office management, fixed and official jurisdictional areas, and administration as a vocation.[45]

The 1895 Labour Day celebrations were considered a success for the council and the labour movement in general, but an incident that followed demonstrated to all the desirability of strict accounting and accountability in financial matters. The secretary, F.P. Bishop of the painters, resigned from the council, as he was moving to Seattle. However, he failed to turn over the books, the union hall keys, and cash receipts of about $19 before he left town. Without the books the financial committee was unable to report on the finances and could not settle accounts or figure out the costs and receipts of the Labour Day festivities. J.H. Watson was sent around to Bishop's house to collect the council's books and property, but discovered that the former secretary had already left for Washington. His wife was able to hand over the books, but the keys and the money had travelled with Bishop. A cursory examination of the accounts revealed some financial impropriety, and at a meeting of the council, 'several members condemned the conduct of our late secretary.' The Stevedores and the Steamshipmen's Union, a local of the National Seamen's Union of America, hinted darkly that they would take action as soon as the books were thoroughly audited, while ARU delegates promised to write to the Western Central Labor Union to inform it of Bishop's actions. It is possible that Bishop did not deliberately abscond with the funds, for he had been a member of the VTLC since its founding and had turned over a much larger sum to the council before heading to Seattle. The theft of union funds was quite common in this period, however, and it is probable that Bishop was leaving Vancouver to improve his lot. In this context theft may be the most likely explanation. Ultimately, the episode cost the council nothing, for the city band, to whom the money was owed, made their services a gift. The significance of the matter lies in the council's perception that tighter procedures were needed for its own protection, and in its resolution 'that in future the treasurer of the Labor Day celebration committee be placed under Bonds.' Necessity and prudence, then, were often a spur to bureaucracy.[46]

Political disputes within the council could also lead to the adoption of tighter control of finances. Eventually, even tighter measures were adopted. In addition to the financial committee and treasurer that had been part of the council's structure from the beginning, in 1899 a new bylaw was passed, creating a board of trustees to oversee spending. The bylaw also required that council funds be kept in a bank account and that withdrawals be signed by a majority of the trustees and countersigned by the president, financial secretary, and treasurer. Furthermore, withdrawals had to be authorized by a majority of delegates at a regular council meeting. Trustees were elected to a twelve-month term, and they were required to give regular financial reports. These measures were introduced during the Deadman's Island dispute, and the cumbersome arrangements were probably intended to prevent either side from controlling the purse strings. The one-year term for trustees – double that of the other council executives – also made it less likely that they would be embroiled in political manoeuvring. It is illustrative that these precautions seem to be standard procedures that any group today would take as a matter of course. But in the very different world of 1899, such red tape had to be worked out step by step, in response to specific situations.[47]

If revenue and accurate records were necessary to ensure the continued existence of the labour council, so too were stability and consistency. The council adopted informal ways to make sure that it would not be captured by demagogues or political fads that could divide the delegates. The constitution called for the executive to be elected for six months at a time, however, it was common for officers to be re-elected for a second term, in effect doubling the length of their tenure. This practice was especially prevalent with the positions of secretary and treasurer, and even longer tenures were not unusual. Keeping the same people in these jobs ensured that finances and record keeping would not be affected by ideological swings or transiency and gave the council some continuity in these key areas. It also created a semipermanent, though accountable, cadre of leaders that was selected on the basis of their expertise and experience. In this way the council protected itself from challenges to the status quo as well as from the uncertainties of the society and the vagaries of its members. Thus, the position of secretary was held by John Fulton of the ITU for three consecutive terms in 1890–1; George Gagen of the carpenters, from 1892 to 1893; F.P. Bishop of the painters for one term in 1892 and four terms in 1894–5; Walter Hepburn of the carpenters for three terms in 1896–7; J.C. Marshall of the ITU, from 1900 to 1901; T.H. Cross of the postal employees from 1901 to 1902; Francis Williams of the tailors from 1904 to 1905; and Harry Cowan of the ITU from 1908 to 1909. Treasurers had similar extended tenures. Charles Kaine of the Amalgamated Society of Carpenters served five consecutive terms in 1894–6 and two additional terms in 1897–8; A.W. Harrington of the Cooks and Waiters and Waitresses Union held the job for three terms in 1903–4. When the position of financial secretary was created in 1899 the first office-holder, J.H. Watson, was caught up in the Deadman's Island dispute, but the second, Francis Williams, then held down the job for two terms, as did his successor, W.J. Beer of the machinists. In 1902 J.T. Lilley of the freighthandlers took up the task for five terms, until the end of 1904. When the office was combined with that of treasurer, creating the new position of secretary-treasurer late in 1905, it soon fell under the guidance of A.R. Burns of the ITU, who stayed in office from 1907 to 1909.

The executive was further limited by the tendency of the council to rotate officers through the executive positions. As a result the tenure of one official in one particular office might be limited, but by moving to different positions, the same few people continued to dominate the council. Joseph Dixon, for example, served as president in 1889 and 1891; as treasurer in 1898–9, when he resigned over the Deadman's Island dispute; as vice-president in 1899; and as president again in 1900–1, when he ran as the VTLC-endorsed provincial candidate. Similarly, George Bartley served as president in 1892, statistician for seven terms in 1893–7, president for three terms in 1897–8, and editor of the council's newspaper from 1900 to 1904. William Pleming served but a single term as treasurer, in 1891; however, his influence continued during his tenure as president for the second half of 1891 and as the statistician in 1892. Harry Cowan had a varied career, starting as the statistician in 1892, then playing a less-active role until 1899, when he was elected president. Resigning in protest over Deadman's Island, Cowan became the *Independent*'s business manager in 1900. The paper folded in 1904, but Cowan returned as general secretary for three terms in 1908–9. J.H. McVety of the machinists served five terms as president in 1906–9, and added one term as vice-president in 1905.

Further continuity may be found at the levels of delegate and trustee. Often people would end their terms as officers, but would continue to operate as delegates, even serving on the committees that were struck. Thus, J. Rumble of the stonecutters served as doorkeeper, or sergeant at arms (the two terms were used interchangeably), in 1894, but remained a delegate as late as

1905. John Crow of the cigarmakers served a term as president in 1901 and was still active as a delegate in 1904; similarly, G.F. Lenfesty of the streetcar railwaymen stood one term as doorkeeper in 1901, but was still on the roll-call as a delegate in 1908. Council stalwarts such as Dixon, Bartley, Watson, and others could often be found working on committees even if they were not then serving as officers. The three trustee positions, together with the doorkeeper, were the least powerful positions of the council's executive, but they served both as a financial watchdog and as a kind of staging area for officers. McVety, for example, served first as a trustee in 1902, before later ascending to the presidency. F.J. Russell of the freighthandlers did one stint as trustee in 1901, then became vice-president for two years in 1902. W. George of the civic employees, C.N. Lee of the laundry workers, A.R. Burns of the ITU, and W.W. Sayer of the bricklayers, each moved from a trusteeship to positions such as president, vice-president, or secretary-treasurer. In this way, new delegates could be tried out and groomed for more responsible positions. At the same time the informal system ensured that dissidents could either be frozen out of the executive or brought along slowly, promoted once they had learned to go along with the council as a whole. They would, in essence, learn to contain their enthusiasm through stints of committee work and apprenticeships at the lower levels. By the time they moved up to more powerful positions, most would have learned important, bureaucratic lessons about politics being the 'art of the possible.'

This unwritten policy, based upon the need for officers to win the approval of their fellow delegates to hold elected positions, also meant in practice that leadership tended to change slowly. Five years after the founding of the labour council, four of the six executive officers were men who had attended meetings in the council's first year. At virtually every period of the VTLC's history, new officers sat with others who had some experience, and committees were staffed with a mixture of newcomers and veterans. This arrangement meant that marked departures from previous policies were unlikely, for new slates could not dominate the council. Consensus was necessary to win elections, and it required compromise and diplomacy. As a result, the council rarely took extreme positions or voiced sentiments that were much more than progressive or reformist. Rarely was the dominant cadre replaced; more often, the officers simply changed positions, as presidents would become the head of the parliamentary committee, treasurers would become presidents, committee members would become executives. New delegates would start at the bottom as trustees or sergeants at arms and slowly work their way up to more influential positions. This meant that officers would have some experience before they would staff the important council seats, but it also meant that an effective clique dominated the VTLC for its first ten years, and it trained the clique that would take over for the next ten. This system also weeded out transient workers and ensured that the council would be headed by older, more-established unionists. The common solution for the unsuccessful worker was simply to move on to greener pastures, and the structure of the VTLC meant that delegates who were not relatively well off and able to stay in the city would not have much say in the labour movement. The structure, however, reinforced those unionists who were successful and who could hold out in times of depression and unemployment. Older, more-satisfied, and wealthier unionists then tended to carry the day in the labour movement. Those whose existence was more precarious and who thus might be more inclined to push harder for aggressive, radical action were not around long enough to attain the leadership positions that would let them change the council's direction. William MacClain, for example, had little chance to influence the council with his socialist ideology, for his tenure as statistician – one of the first rungs of the bureaucratic ladder – was cut short when he left town. The control of the old guard helped ensure that 'young Turks' would not carry much weight until they had become established in the council and in the community, and it ensured that the politics of the union movement had a great deal of continuity. In this period it meant that the VTLC would remain reformist and cautious.

Unity and moderation were also maintained by the practice of electing officers from different unions. The council's first executive brought together Dixon of the carpenters, Irvine of the plasterers, Jameson of the ITU, and Hallam of the Knights of Labor, and later executives were similarly balanced. Never in the twenty years between 1889 and 1910 were the presidency and vice-presidency held by delegates from the same union; rarely was the secretary from the same union as the president or vice-president. When George Bartley became the first ITU delegate to preside over the council in 1892, F.P. Bishop of the painters was elected secretary. This was the first time the post had gone to a delegate who was not a member of the typographical union. In 1903 W.J. Lamerick of the retail clerks held the presidency, George Dobbin of the carpenters sat in the vice-presidency, and F.J. Russell of the freighthandlers occupied the secretary position. When Dobbin was elected president in 1904, W. George of the civic employees took over the vice-presidency and C.T. Hilton of the Amalgamated Society of Carpenters filled the secretary slot. This pattern held throughout the council's first twenty years, and presumably it was one of design rather than chance. The result was that no union, regardless of the number of its delegates, could hope to control the council. Ideologues of any stripe could direct the council's politics only by winning support from a wide range of delegates, and thus *coups d'état* were made unlikely.[48]

From its earliest years the VTLC worked steadily to separate itself from the rank and file it represented. By controlling the selection of officers, rotating established leaders, tightening rules and regulations, and limiting the access of press and of members of the rank and file, the council slowly increased its autonomy. At the same time the need for unity tended to act as a brake on militancy and radicalism of any kind, and a policy of cautious progress and compromise began to evolve. With time, and with the need for more concerted action by the labour movement, the council would create institutions and call for measures that would take it even further away from the rank and file.

3

The Development of Institutions and Formal Bureaucracy

The Vancouver Trades and Labour Council soon found it necessary to create a variety of offices and institutions to help labour in its struggle against capital and government. These ranged from government offices such as that of fair wage commissioner and factory inspector to institutions such as a union hall and a newspaper. Although all these measures were meant to benefit labour and to make it easier to win and to protect its gains, many of them divided workers as much as they aided them. The call for compulsory testing for boiler operators, for example, hurt less-educated workers who had learned the trade on the job; the creation of a labour press also created paid editors and business managers who equated support for the labour movement with support for their newspaper. To the degree that the council operated without the direct instruction and supervision of the workers it represented, virtually every new institution could help unify labour at one level while dividing it at another.

The first of these institutions was the council's first paid union position, that of the walking delegate. Contrary to many assumptions about bureaucracy, this position was created to foster unionism and militancy, not impede it. In November 1890 the VTLC began a uniform working-card system to ensure that all construction workers were union members. The system was an intermediary step between the traditional, informal job control exercised by craft workers and the development of formal, negotiated contracts. Unions would announce the hours of work and the pay scale they believed just and would down tools if the schedules were not met. To prevent other workers from underbidding them, unionized workers would refuse to work with non-union employees, and the working card made it easy to determine who was in the union and who was not. It was an attempt to enforce a closed shop without recourse to contracts or the hiring hall. The system reflected both class collaboration and class conflict, for it traded some freedom of action for a measure of stability, and yet reminded workers and bosses that their interests were not identical. The council defended the working card by maintaining that the employer would benefit, for it would guarantee agreed-upon wages and work conditions for an extended period and would provide ample notice when changes were sought. This would permit the employer to submit tenders with some assurance that the quoted wage bill would not suddenly change. It would also provide the employer with 'the best and most reliable workmen.' Workers, however, would benefit, for competition with 'underpaid workmen' would be eliminated. In addition, they would be reminded that 'fellow employees must assist in securing the amelioration of the laboring classes, for which the union men of this city have risked and sacrificed a good deal in the past.'[1]

To enforce the working-card system, the VTLC hired a walking delegate to go to job sites to make sure that all workers had union cards and were receiving the set pay and working the agreed-upon hours. The walking delegates have been described by Michael Kazin as 'the human glue connecting individual workers and their locals with the hierarchy.' Although American east coast delegates were infamous for their corruption, and were often characterized as 'petty grafters and despots,' on the west coast they 'acted more like labor policemen, helping to create an ethic of unionism.'[2]

The first walking delegate hired by the VTLC was its own former president and vice-president George Irvine of the Plasterers Union. Moral suasion was his primary weapon, and he noted optimistically that 'in every case where men were shown that they were acting contrary to union principles, they immediately quit work.' However, the staff position was expensive and difficult to maintain. A special per capita fee of 30 cents was exacted upon the building trades to cover the costs, but the expenses incurred by Irvine were still the largest single outlay in the VTLC's budget. The quarterly statement for April 1891 revealed that from total receipts of $204.35, over three-quarters – $156 – had gone to the walking delegate, even though the months covered were traditionally a slow period in the construction industry, and presumably the job was not overly difficult or involved at that time. Probably as a result of this financial report, the usefulness of the business agent was questioned, and some delegates moved to abolish the position. The vote on the motion was to take place two weeks hence. Between the meetings, however, events proved the worth of the walking delegate. Stonecutters working on the new post office building announced their new schedule of pay and hours, but contractors ignored their demands and found workers willing to work at the old rate. The stonecutters put down their tools and refused to work with the non-union crews. Although it is not known how the dispute was resolved, the need for strong organization was made obvious, and the motion to be rid of the card system and Irvine was soundly defeated.[3]

His survival was temporary, for Irvine now had to face the greater challenge of the employers and the courts. In August he was charged by a contractor, George Mesher, with besetting the new Bank of British Columbia. The section of the Criminal Code under which Irvine was prosecuted made it a criminal offence to beset or watch a house or other place to compel someone 'to abstain from doing anything which he has a lawful right to do, or to do anything from which he has a lawful right to abstain.' The contractor alleged that Irvine's efforts to have everyone on the job join a union was little more than extortion backed by the threat to shut down the work site. Mesher paid the union fees for several of his men out of his own pocket, but refused to pay arrears owed to the union by his foreman. The legal action threatened the ability of the building trades to enforce the closed shop, and the VTLC undertook to pay for Irvine's defence. The legal fees came to $215, and sorely pressed the council's limited funds. Another per capita tax was assessed, and money already pledged to the upcoming Labour Day celebrations was tapped. Not surprisingly, the council looked for ways to reduce its legal expenses, and a committee was struck to investigate the pros and cons of keeping an attorney on retainer. Irvine himself moved that 'a regular counsel be appointed,' and together with George Bartley reported that his attorney in the dispute with Mesher 'would like to handle all the law business that this council or any of the unions might have to do at a much lower charge' than on a piecemeal basis. The council was also prompted to take steps to amend the legislation under which Irvine had been charged 'so that trade unions will have more liberty of motion.'[4] From its beginning the Vancouver labour movement was forced to deal with the state's legal machinery and to hire legal experts to protect itself.

The employer's attack worked well enough, for Irvine soon resigned from his position and the walking delegate system was not reinstated, though a slump in the economy may have been a more important reason for its abrupt end.[5] The episode shows how the structure and demands of craft unionism exerted a subtle pressure towards bureaucracy. To maintain their wage rates and conditions of work, trade unions had to enforce the closed shop. The simplest way to do this was to delegate authority to a professional business agent. Presumably the spontaneous efforts of the workers themselves were not sufficient, while the temptation to freeload on the militancy and efforts of others may have been as hard to resist then as now. They may have lacked motivation; likely the employers were able to intimidate them, using the threat of firing to squash dissidents. A walking delegate hired by the labour council was not vulnerable to this kind of pressure, and could confront the boss without fear of losing his job or income. Indeed, he was paid to confront employers, and this independence could foster a kind of militancy as the delegate upheld the rules and traditions of the labour movement without regard to circumstances and without waffling. Accountable not to the workers he organized but to the leadership of the VTLC, the business agent could push aside individual concerns and cavils in the greater interest of solidarity. But as an employee of the labour movement, the delegate was also one step removed from the workers on the job. He was parachuted into the job sites, and this could harden relations between the union and the less militant or the less committed. While the newspaper account of Irvine's actions is clearly one-sided and prejudiced, it does appear that he was primarily concerned with applying the strict letter of the union law without regard to the wishes of the workers or to building a stronger, voluntary, and reasoned solidarity. Irvine was content to go behind the workers and have the contractor pay their dues and sign their names, even though some had indicated that they preferred not to join the union. It did not matter to the walking delegate if the union appeared to have cut a deal with the contractor at the workers' expense, or that the union appeared to be operating independently of the people it purported to represent. What did matter was that each worker had a paid-up card. This could be enforced and regulated; feelings and sentiments could not. This incident appears to have done little to build a sense of unionism: some of the crew agreed to join up 'just for the time that this work was going on,' on the condition that 'it was not to cost them anything either for membership or subscriptions.'[6]

It is not necessary to argue that Irvine and the labour council could have or should have done otherwise. It is to be noted, however, that the principles of good trade unionism, as defined by the leadership, required the hiring of a professional staff member with no shop-floor ties to the rank and file. Good unionism required the use of outside experts in the form of an attorney, and political action to forestall judicial harassment. To enforce the rules of the crafts, it was also deemed necessary to make a deal with the employer and to go against the wishes of some of the workers. Bureaucracy, the power of union leaders to force workers to do what they otherwise would not, was an integral part of the organization of the early labour movement.

Other standard trade union practices and objectives impelled the labour council to take a variety of bureaucratic measures. The enumeration of voters, for example, was an important issue for Vancouver unionists, for control over who voted meant control over the outcome of the vote. This fit into the general labourist ideology that held that the system itself was not wrong but had been usurped by powerful minorities. Thus, it was logical and reasonable for delegates to move that the VTLC appoint a member to make sure that union members were on the voters' list and to pay that official a 'reasonable remuneration.'[7] The motion suggests that the union leaders saw no conflict between hiring officers and class consciousness. On the contrary, the creation of staff positions was seen as a way of flexing labour's political muscles and turning consciousness into action.

Control over the employers' hiring practices was another matter of deep concern, and council members moved that the VTLC 'warn working men against so-called Labor Bureaus and that steps be taken to establish a Bureau of Labor in connection with this council.' Several months later another resolution called for a VTLC-sponsored hiring bureau to replace other agencies. After the troubles with the walking delegate, the council hoped to be able to create its own labour bureau to make sure that union workers could find jobs without recourse to the local job sharks. Although the proposed office was not created, the discussion indicates that new, bureaucratic offices were deemed necessary to protect the interests of union members.[8]

To maintain a favorable balance of workers and employment, accurate statistics were essential. In 1893 the council began to gather statistics on wages, unionization rates, conditions of trade, and the like, in order to supply the information to workers in other cities. This was not a point of academic interest. The trade unions of the VTLC, like trade unions everywhere, tried to keep wages high by limiting the supply of workers, by creating an artificial shortage of workers. Accurate knowledge of conditions would help the council attract workers in boom times, and more importantly, warn them away in bad times.[9] When it became apparent that the unions themselves were not up to the task of collecting the necessary information, the council began to pressure the different levels of government to take up the chore. Often this meant lobbying the governments to enforce already existing legislation. The council noted that the province had indeed passed a bill calling for a bureau of labour statistics, but 'nothing had been done in the way of appointing commissioners or arbitrators.'[10] In Ottawa similar bills had been passed by the Macdonald government, but, again, enforcement then became the issue. Five years after Macdonald's death, the VTLC announced that it 'would urge that its local as well as the Federal Government create Bureaus of Labor Statistics. We would then be in a position to obtain a correct knowledge of the financial, educational, and moral condition of our working people.'[11]

The call for government bureaucracy was not made with unbridled enthusiasm, however. Labour leaders were aware that the interests of the government and the union movement were not identical. When the provincial government provided unions with special forms for the collection of information, officials preferred to leave some lines blank, for answering the questions 'would be detrimental to the interests of the labor organizations.'[12] To make sure that the labour bureau worked for the working class and not business or the state, the VTLC maintained that the members of the Bureau of Labor Statistics should be selected by the council itself.[13] When the government rejected this suggestion, the bureau was viewed with suspicion and wariness. When delegates were sent to meet with the new head of the provincial labour bureau, the staunch Tory, Colonel James Baker, they were instructed by the council to provide Baker with the requested information only 'if in their opinion it is advisable to do so.' Commenting later on the bureau, the VTLC observed that it 'never was popular, as it seemed to have been enacted entirely for the benefit of the employing class.'[14]

Though it was aware of the dangers of government bureaucracy, the council was not hesitant to pressure other agencies to help working people. In the rough-and-tumble, boom-and-bust economy of Vancouver, real-estate speculators, contractors, and factory owners could not be trusted to put safety ahead of profits. Independent union action was neither sanctioned by law nor sufficient to ensure that adequate safety standards were met. As a result the council pushed for legislation and the appointment of government experts to inspect workplaces. Government officials, it was believed, would have the power and training to maintain professional standards based on science rather than tradition and the profit margin; furthermore, they would have a measure of independence from the business community. In 1891 the council called for the appointment of a factory inspector, and a few years later it petitioned the city 'to appoint a duly qualified architect to examine the Market Hall as to its safety and stability.' This was followed by demands to 'appoint a practical mechanic as building inspector whose duty it shall be to see the buildings constructed to original plans,' an attempt to forestall contractors and builders from making changes that had not been examined and approved. By 1899 the council was calling for city inspectors to make sure all new buildings conformed with the bylaws and for the city to appoint building instructors to ensure that all would know how to build according to the established standards. Finally, the VTLC endorsed the idea of a technical school for the city.[15]

Just as catastrophes were often the spur for new forms of civic government and the use of experts, as in the famous case of the Galveston hurricane in 1900 and the Halifax explosion in 1917, so too were they the impetus for demands from Vancouver's union movement. In November 1897 a boiler exploded at the Royal City Planing Mills, killing two men. The tragedy prompted a heated discussion at the labour council that condemned 'the want of a Stationary Boiler inspector for the province.' To prevent further disasters, the council passed a resolution moved by the delegates of the machinists and the amalgamated engineers calling for legislation 'making it compulsory for any man in charge of steam power to have a certificate of efficiency.'[16] Such legislation was finally provided in 1901 with the passage of the Steam Boilers Inspection Act. What seemed to be little more than common sense – who could argue against licensing requirements when lives were at stake? – had another, less benevolent side. The act was an important step in the professionalizing of the engineers, for it made running steam equipment dependent on the operator being able to pass tests and receive a certificate. If this was desirable for those who had the schooling, it also threw out of work those who had received their training on the job. A letter from Hugh Dixon to socialist MLA James Hawthornthwaite, who had been partly responsible for the act, illustrates how professionalism could work against some workers, while it rewarded others. The original spelling has been preserved to highlight the contrast between the formally educated and the less educated who were displaced by the bill:

I came to the cost 7 years ago thinking that in my old age I would go back to engineering but that law the Engineers Association got you to pass blocked me thair ... Your d–m law has blocked me at all points, but I sopos you feel all right you done what the Engineering Association told you to do. You had not much opasation – it was one calss [sic] of workers against another and you took the wining side the association. Them and the boiler inspection has got it all their own way thanks to you and [Socialist MLA Parker] Williams. So I may sterve as far as you caire, or go to school and lern to figar. When the 4 Class Certificate comes I will through it [in the] fire as it is no good to me as I would have to go firing are helping a snot that don't know nothing. So I have you and Williams to thank for getting sterved to death, well, well.[17]

If the call for expertise hurt workers such as Hugh Dixon, it helped others break the old boys' network of political patronage and favouritism. British Columbia politics was rooted in these practices, and one needed only to read the newspapers to see how members of parliament, premiers, mayors, aldermen, and the like rewarded their supporters and were in turn rewarded for their aid to schemers and power-brokers. Informal hiring practices in the construction industry further illustrated how jobs could be awarded on the basis of connections rather than merit. In this atmosphere the fight for hiring procedures based on demonstrated competence and adherence to written, presumably objective standards was an assault on the powerful and a defence of the honest toiler. Bureaucracy helped some workers even as it hurt others as labour leaders went to great lengths to oppose patronage and shady dealings between government and business. When the Vancouver Post Office was reorganized, the VTLC worried that new appointments would be made by the MP for the constituency and thus would be patronage appointments rather than appointments made on the basis of competency and efficiency. Instead of the MP, the council requested that the post office inspector of the province make the appointments, for 'only he knows the requirements of the office and [the] ability of those to be appointed and that he will be able to do justice to all concerned.'[18]

The members of the VTLC believed strongly in the maintenance of the Canadian political and economic system, but they insisted that working people be given equal access to the wealth and to positions of influence. Thus, the appointment of labour leaders to white-collar positions in the government and cooperation with bosses and politicians was not regarded as a betrayal. Indeed, such appointments were viewed as proof that the leaders and the movement were finally realizing their proper place in the scheme of things. Although others would interpret it as a reward for faithful service to his political masters, the VTLC newspaper, the *Independent*, applauded the appointment of Daniel O'Donoghue to the position of federal wage commissioner in 1900. The paper believed that making the Ontario labour leader a 'special government official will be heartily approved by all Canadian workmen ... This marks an important event in labor's history in Canada, for it is the most radical step the Ottawa government has ever taken.'[19] Similarly, labour leaders were pleased to note that 'as time advances, trades unionism becomes an important factor in the administration of our law-making institutions.'[20] This was not regarded as co-optation or incorporation, but as a sign that labour was finally getting its deserved recognition.

This very stability and pragmatism, however, tended to blunt the edge of labour reform. A letter to the *Independent* from ITU delegate and former VTLC secretary J.H. Brown revealed how pragmatism and bureaucracy could be used to score points against radicals who would take labour into the treacherous waters of politics. Brown called upon the VTLC to establish a 'bureau of information' and to pay an officer to maintain a list of unemployed union workers in the city. Unionists who wanted work would register with the bureau, and affiliated unions and members would be assessed 5 per cent per month to pay for the bureau. 'Everything should be done to enhance the cause we are all fighting for,' Brown wrote, 'and the duty of the VTLC was to see that the betterment of its membership is first and foremost in the battle of life and not the boosting of politicians (be they of whatever party or clique).' He appended to his practical suggestion a warning about politics in the union, reminding his readers that ' "Politics be d---d" is an old saying and I might add for the benefit of some of the members of the most humane institution we have in Vancouver – the Trades and Labor council – "Politicians be d---d." Our representatives in the council should look to the advancement of the men whose cause they should espouse and not to political tricksters.'[21]

Thus, the labour bureau would restrain militancy by directing labour away from politics and towards the preoccupation with bread-and-butter unionism. The labour bureau was also seen as a way to bring science and predictability to the chaotic world of the trade union movement. The purpose of such a bureau would expand from the gathering of statistics and matching the supply of labour with the demand to 'study society and explain the laws that underlie and govern social movements. It assumes that these are subject to general laws, and therefore, when understood, a solution of all questions affecting the general welfare is possible by scientific processes.'[22] If the movement were to have science it would need scientists, and the *Independent* was not afraid to call for them:

The establishment of a college or institution for the purpose of educating and training the leaders of labor organization by equipping them with the knowledge of the history and principles of economics and government is a great step ... If this proposition shall be carried out and as proposed, lectures and instructions be given by the most competent specialists in the various departments, it will not be long before the trade union secretary and president and walking delegate will be selected on the merit system and will be quite as capable of scientifically discussing the economic questions involved in labor controversies as the most experienced corporation manager. The trades unions would gradually become the training clubs for economic and social discussion, and by the force of intelligent information they would become more intelligent and forceful in their claims and many more times more successful in their undertakings.[23]

Such a call for experts and the selection of union officials by their book learning rather than by their abilities to organize, to agitate, or even to administer efficiently was more than a wish to put labour on an equal intellectual plane with capital. It implied that the tension between the classes was not fundamental, that the application of knowledge would be enough to bring about important social change. Incorporating a naive but widespread view of the objectivity of science, the wish for leaders trained in the manner outlined in the *Independent* was a kind of structural-functionalism that saw class conflict as unnecessary and costly rather than as the essence of capitalist society.

The particular class consciousness of the first leaders of the VTLC meant that they saw no necessary division between employer and employee. This in turn suggested to them that class conflict, when not between the people and the trusts, was not inevitable. The problems between the boss and the workers, they believed, could usually be worked out. If agreement was not possible, this signified not a clash of fundamental interests but unreasonableness and the failure to properly understand long-term gain. No less than modern employers, these leaders believed that stability was important, and that trust and a spirit of compromise should mark relations between union and boss and workers. As a result, arbitration and mediation were looked upon as a way to chasten employers who refused to be reasonable. Far from being a betrayal of class-conscious principles, the call for compulsory arbitration was the pinnacle of labourism, especially as the first generation of labour leaders reached the end of their union activism.[24]

Although the council created an arbitration committee as early as 1890, it was not until the creation of the *Independent* in 1900 that arbitration was actively discussed as a tenet of the union movement. The dual nature of labourism, that is, its class consciousness and its belief in the capitalist system, were both argued for in one article that characterized unionism as 'the broadest Christianity and the essence of loving–kindness among the children of men.' Thanks to unions, 'the days of Neroism are over. So are those of capitalistic extortion ... for unionism has stept [*sic*] in and cried "Hands off."' But in the same breath, the writer declaimed that 'Capital has its undoubted rights, and Unionism respects them – there is no body that ever was originated more ready to make reasonable concessions and to meet those with whom it has disagreements half-way, and to even concede a point or two.'[25]

Commenting on a proposed federal bill for the prevention and settlement of trade disputes, the VTLC organ editorialized that such legislation was a move in the right direction that could not 'fail to be effective of much good if worked in the truest and best interests of labor as well as capital. There is opportunity here to harmonize dividing factions and to bring about peace with honor.'[26] Other writers similarly called for state intervention to settle disputes between workers and employers. Compulsory arbitration, one maintained, would end the 'friction and consequent unrest' that was caused by 'a jarring in the machinery' of industrial relations. Such legal measures would 'remove that article that has brought about the friction,' and would 'let the machinery ... again work in perfect harmony.'[27] Strikes and lockouts, then, were viewed not as the product of the capitalist system but as deviations that could easily be corrected.

The aversion to strikes was, to some degree, an inducement to political action. 'Labor's two weapons are the strike and the ballot,' the *Independent* observed. 'Of the two the ballot is the more forceable, and at the same time, the more peaceable.' Furthermore, the paper noted, 'where labor unions are the thickest there are the fewest strikes ... when labor is well organized it puts a premium on strikes.'[28] The aim of organization, according to the VTLC paper, was not to intensify class conflict but to eliminate it while maintaining the system. The regular columnist 'Southern Cross' went even further in 1901, denouncing strikes as 'one of the most deplorable sights to be seen in any country.' Too often, the writer insisted, men struck 'when they had no just ground for doing so.' The 'want of education' produced strikes, and if such actions hurt employers, they brought a 'far greater wrong' to the strikers and their families. To prevent such hardships 'Southern Cross' advocated 'arbitration in every instance before a strike is declared' and looked forward to the day when education would mean 'the need of "striking" will pass away.'[29]

At times the hope for industrial peace echoed the sentiments of business boosters. 'Were British Columbia today like New Zealand,' the paper suggested, 'a land where there are no strikes, we would not lack capital to develop the mining industry.'[30] But the call for arbitration was not naive or strictly collaborationist. A strike on the Canadian Pacific Railway in 1901 showed, at least to the labourist mind, the necessity of using the power of the state to rein in capital. Rallying to the causes of the CPR trackmen and arbitration, the *Independent* insisted that 'the general good of Canada, which is more than the general good of shareholders,' required that 'clashing interests' should be resolved by a tribunal 'appointed by the people.'[31] But arbitration at any cost was not labour's answer. The VTLC was well aware that governments friendly to business were unlikely to favour labour in any dispute. The council expressed its distrust in government that did not act as a disinterested arbiter, arguing that 'we believe in the principle of compulsory arbitration. One great drawback to carrying it out successfully in British Columbia is that the government is not in sympathy with the working class.' If a compulsory arbitration act were passed in the province, the council believed, 'it would be so worded as to allow loop holes for capitalists or employers to go scot free, whereas labor would be compelled to submit to the arbitrary rulings of a judge.'[32] When the province considered a conciliation and arbitration act in 1903, the council denounced it, for it would 'rob our labor unions of their potency to favorably adjust the rates of wages and hours of work to meet the ever-changing conditions of industrial life.' The legislation would have severely limited the right to strike, and provided for penalties and fines to be levied against those who struck. Equally dangerous was the proposed tribunal, which was to be composed of one labour representative, one business representative, and a third appointed by the first two. If the two could not agree on the third member, he would be appointed by a supreme court judge. This, the council pointed out, meant 'putting the interests of labor in the hands of one individual.' When the 'corrupting power of capital' was figured in, the act was 'too slim a foundation upon which to rest the rightful claims of a body of wage earners.'[33]

Nonetheless, the appointment of E.P. Bremner as a federal labour commissioner in 1901 was greeted with enthusiasm. According to the *Independent*, Bremner had 'certainly earned his salary and has accomplished a large amount of good, being instrumental in settling more than one dispute between employer and employee.' Bremner, working under the federal Conciliation Act of 1900, settled strikes among fishermen, longshoremen, and miners, to the delight of the VTLC. His dismissal in September 1901 shook the faith of the labourist council in Laurier's Liberal government, if not in the arbitration process itself, and helped turn the council away from Lib-Labism and towards independent political action.[34] The Bremner affair also illustrated clearly the dilemma caused by the VTLC's hope in the power of arbitration. On the one hand, strikes were harmful: they hurt workers, fractured solidarity, and were signs of misalignment and friction in the larger society. On the other hand, compulsory arbitration schemes created by a non-labour government steamrollered over the interests of workers. No easy way was found to reconcile the dream of labour peace with the reality of class conflict.

If government-sponsored institutions simultaneously created solidarity and fragmentation, so too did labour's own institutions. VTLC institutions, such as the labour hall and newspaper, demonstrated that formal union structures both aided and undercut solidarity. The union hall offered several practical benefits to the movement. It gave workers a place to meet at their convenience; it assured that unions could not be denied a venue by nervous owners or hostile authorities; and it put an end to the running sore of rent, replacing it with a tangible asset. The labour press made it possible for unionists to get news and ideas that the daily papers deemed of little interest to their mass audiences, and it provided a forum for workers to discuss politics, social events, and community affairs. The hall and the newspaper provided psychological benefits as well. Each gave the labour movement a physical presence in the city and demonstrated that the unions were stable, mature, and responsible. Both the hall and the paper became sources of real pride to the council and its members.

The labour temple and the *Independent* also had drawbacks for the city's unionists. In some instances they became sources not of solidarity but of fragmentation. If both institutions were formally owned by the VTLC and its affiliates, in practice they were controlled by the council executive and the small cadre of the hall committee, the newspaper editor, and the business manager. Simply keeping the hall and the paper going required a great deal of work. Stories had to be written and typeset and rooms rented; equipment had to be purchased, money raised, and maintenance carried out. These ancillary tasks often came to be regarded as the end and measure of the council's efforts, rather than as the means to other goals and objectives. To the perennial question 'What have you done for me lately?' the leadership could point to the hall and the paper and justify their re-election by the health of the institutions they had created and maintained. Furthermore, maintaining the hall, and more particularly the newspaper, required the hiring of staff. This allowed some unionists to make a living not from their trade but from the union movement itself, and created a caste system in labour's ranks. To the degree that these union employees had a vested interest in keeping their positions they had to avoid running afoul of the council leadership. No matter what loyalties they may have had to the rank and file, they now owed some allegiance to the union executive as well. More subtly, these employees spent a great deal of time justifying their positions and the structures that made them possible. Stability and centralization became important to them. Hall managers called for dues increases to maintain the property, while the newspaper supported orthodoxy and loyalty to the leadership. For all of these reasons, the creation of the labour temple and the newspaper also led to the creation of a cadre of unionists who were distinct from the rank and file and had significantly different interests.

The VTLC first considered securing its own union hall in 1890. A committee was struck to find a building that 'would be a comfortable place for members to meet and where newspapers could be perused without let or hindrance.'[35] Little progress was made until 1896, when the United Brotherhood of Carpenters and Joiners announced that it could no longer afford to keep its own hall. The union offered the building and its furniture to the council free of charge save for the right to hold its own meetings there without rental fees. The council quickly agreed to the offer, and in March 1896 became the owner of the lease and the accounts receivable.[36] The VTLC soon outgrew the building, and in 1899 it appointed a committee to 'consider the proper step to take for the erection of a suitable building.'[37] The committee recommended that the council build its own hall at a cost of $10,000. The money to purchase the lot would be raised by assessing all members of the affiliated unions one day's pay. The bulk of the money would then be borrowed at 6 per cent interest, and this would allow the council to construct a two-storey building made of brick.[38]

The plan, however, had to be scuttled when the affiliated unions and their members rejected the suggested assessment of a day's pay. This was the first sign that the labour hall was the dream of the council leadership rather than the union movement as a whole.[39] Forced by this opposition to scale down its plan, the VTLC negotiated to purchase the Methodist church on Homer Street. A voluntary share purchase scheme replaced the compulsory assessment, and unionists were now implored to buy two-dollar shares in the building.[40] By September 1899 the council had obtained a mortgage and moved into the former church. A management committee was appointed to run the hall, and the committee was made up of VTLC officers and longtime members. Financial secretary J.H. Watson, Secretary D.C. Harrison, Trustee and Statistician J.T. Bruce, Trustee W.R. Lawson, and former Vice-President Francis Williams, soon to be a labour candidate for the legislature, made up the first labour hall committee. These appointments ensured that the hall would be controlled by seasoned unionists who would reflect and represent the more conservative element in the council.[41]

Once the building had been purchased renovations became the next item, and the committee made extensive changes in the layout and structure, including 'splendid plumbing arrangements,' no small matter in these early years of the city. The improvements meant that the council had 'ample accommodation for many years to come and also for public meetings whenever necessary.' The *Independent* boasted that the VTLC 'has become possessed of a property which will be of immense utility to all the working men of the city and indeed of the province.'[42] Not all of the working men of the city seemed equally impressed, however. Sales of shares were not brisk, and the council was forced to campaign and plead constantly for financial support from the rank and file. Making the scheduled payments on the mortgage was a close-run thing, despite the small contributions that were sought from each unionist. One appeal outlined the apathy of the membership, as it plaintively suggested that a small outlay of 10 cents per union member per week would raise $650 a month on the debt of $5,000. 'Can't this be done?' the paper implored. 'Can't even half this sum be forthcoming?'[43] Civic and union pride were played upon as the *Independent* pointed out that 'there are some 75 cities in the United States planning the erection of labor buildings. Vancouver cannot be behind in owning their own hall.'[44]

Still the funds were not forthcoming. Building committee secretary Francis Williams went on at length to chivvy reluctant unionists, using economic arguments and shame equally to convince them to pitch in. 'That the new Union hall is of immense benefit to the labor element of the city cannot be disputed,' he began. The central union building provided better accommodations for the participating unions at a lower cost than renting or owning separate halls, and it produced a profit of $400 a year as a result of the 'good management' of the executive committee. Nonetheless, still it was 'almost impossible to enlist the practical sympathies of many of our members. In view of the issues involved, many of them have manifested an apathy which might with perfect justice be designated as abominable ... In considering these facts are we not justified in concluding that with union men, as with churchmen, two half dollar pieces (or less) held close to the eyes, will shut out the whole landscape; will quench out the light of the noonday sun. Brother men get out of such selfishness or like the cankerworm, it will spoil the best fruit in the orchard.' Warning of the need to raise $3,000 in the next three months, Williams noted that some members 'have done more than justice demanded of them.' Others, however, were letting the side down, and he deplored the 'ignoble and unmanly spirit which grasps all benefit within reach and is not willing to render good services in return. In speaking these things, we are not talking of abstract speculations; we are dealing out truths that cannot be disputed or even called in question. We all know them, though we do not all act up to them.'[45]

Despite the impassioned plea, the hall was still in financial difficulty six months later. Part of the problem lay in the difference between those who benefited directly from the hall and those who were asked to foot the bills. The council had decided that it was necessary to move out of the 'cramped ill-ventilated quarters we endured so long' with little consultation with the rank and file and in the face of its refusal to pledge a day's pay to the cause. Williams himself provided a clue to the general apathy when he remarked that owning the hall meant that labour had acquired 'a home for ourselves – or to change the figure, to establish a *headquarters for Labor's executive* from whence to carry on with more vigor and effectiveness the Campaign for the rights of the people.'[46] The executive had unilaterally decided that a new hall was a pressing need, and later it lambasted the rank and file for refusing to support a project that was foisted upon it. The VTLC had to make the first payment out of general revenue because the membership declined to contribute to the fund, and the subsequent renovations were paid for in the same manner. Less than half of the city's union members purchased the $2 shares, and of these, several cashed them in within a few months. Rather than conclude that it had been operating in a vacuum, the council started to insist that unionism and the union hall were one and the same. Good unionists were now those who supported the hall, and bad unionists were those who did not. Apathy was seen as a symptom not of dissatisfaction but of treason: 'There are many of our members who have not lifted a finger to aid this enterprise as yet, but they share the advantage equally with the rest. Is it manly or just to take all and give nothing? This is what every unionist is doing who has not bought at least one share. It is a disgrace to the cause of unionism that in such a progressive city as Vancouver that these things should have to be said ... A citizen who refuses to defend his country in time of peril is no patriot, and a unionist who refuses to help in a case of this kind is a mockery and a sham.'[47]

But the chiding had little effect. Despite the oft-repeated assertion that the central hall reduced the rent that individual unions paid, several began to complain about or to be tardy with their payments. By 1902 the painters were in arrears, the Amalgamated Society of Engineers protested that their rent was too high, and the Building Trades Council, a short-lived federation of construction unions, asked for a rent reduction. To compound the problem, the hall caretaker's salary was under review, and some delegates believed that it should be raised to $50 a month. Desperate for funds, the VTLC struck a special committee to induce the affiliated unions to purchase shares in the building. The committee had little success. Early in 1903 the stevedores gave notice that they would vacate the hall, while the railway carmen made it clear that they were not interested in purchasing any shares. Subsequent attempts to sell shares and raise the mortgage had similar disappointing results. When revenue could not be gleaned from the rank and file, the council looked for other ways to raise money and to cut costs. The caretaker's raise was turned down, and it was suggested that the council could build a small house beside the hall and give free room and board instead of a salary increase. Tight money made this scheme impossible, and rather than free lodgings, the council voted only to repair the caretaker's existing quarters in the building. By 1904 the VTLC tried to become a landlord by building a 'good boarding house at the rear of the hall to rent as a probable good investment.'[48]

These first years of the labour hall were marked with financial insecurity and apathy on the part of the general membership. Far from being a means to unite the leadership and the rank and file, the hall tended to separate the executive, who were determined to maintain a headquarters for themselves, from the individuals and unions who could not or would not contribute to maintain it. The point is not that the council should not have had such a hall, but rather that something as apparently straightforward as a union temple illustrated the different priorities and agendas of the leaders and the led. By deciding on its own that the hall was necessary the VTLC executive exercised a degree of independence that was not widely supported. Instead of recognizing this, the union leaders used the gap between its own objectives and those of the people they represented as a reason to attack the membership for its apathy. In making support for the hall tantamount to support for the cause of unionism, the labour bureaucrats first drove a wedge in the movement and then moved to consolidate their control by taking further expenditures and plans on their own initiative.

A similar process centred around the VTLC official newspaper, the *Independent*. The paper first appeared on 31 March 1900, with long-time ITU and VTLC officer George Bartley as editor. The business manager was Harry Cowan, former owner and manager of the Winnipeg *Voice*, and a past president of the VTLC. As with the hall, control of the paper would be vested in the hands of men with a long history of close connections to the labour council.

From the beginning, reasonably enough, the paper urged workers to subscribe and support the venture. It noted with approval the 'professional press' of the German labour movement and enviously eyed its annual subsidy of $15,000 paid from compulsory union dues.[49] With no possibility of such a subvention in Vancouver, the paper was forced to rely on moral imperatives, and it was quick to identify its own interests with those of the labour movement as a whole. One appeal read,

A union paper is a real necessity in a community composed of wage-earners such as this one is, but in order to keep one alive it must be fed. The union men are the people who undoubtedly should see that it is properly taken care of. It is for their interests that it should be healthy and prosperous and possessed of sufficient vigor to make a square fight when necessary. Not that we are looking for a new fight or expect one, but such a thing cannot long be foretold and the unexpected is often the thing that happens. Therefore it is well to be prepared with all the ordinances and paraphernalia of war, and be in such a position as not to be caught in ambush. Remember, union men, the Independent is working for you. Don't you think you ought to do a little work for it? Send in your names and your subscriptions and be placed on the honor roll. The editor and the devil [i.e., helper] can't stand the wind much longer.[50]

Editorials and articles reprinted from other labour journals sounded a similar theme. Several bemoaned the fate of the faithful labour editor who fought on alone, while those who criticised his selfless efforts 'never give a cent to support the paper.'[51] Again the line was drawn between those members who actively supported the paper without question and those who, through poverty, indifference, or protest, did not.

The exigencies of newspaper publishing gave the pleas for money and support some urgency. Without regular subscriptions the paper could not survive, and its life was constantly threatened. One effect of this was to push the editor and business manager to seek support from the merchant class of the city. The paper actively solicited advertising from local merchants. Along with ads, it printed regular reminders to its readers to patronize those establishments that placed ads and to make sure they mentioned they had seen the ads in the *Independent*. More significantly, the editor maintained that such businesses and labour had interests in common and that one of these interests was the labour paper itself. 'Men of business,' Bartley importuned, 'are beginning to realize the necessity there exists of cooperating with the labor class in helping their paper.' He welcomed the support of businessmen, for 'if labor papers were patronized as they ought to be by business communities and workmen, it would not be so very long before there would be hundreds of daily labor papers.'[52] Practical business considerations, then, helped to blur class lines in the minds of the proprietors of the labour press.

The paper was also a medium consciously used by the labour leadership and the editor to put forward the views and policies of the bureaucracy. From the first, the editor announced that the paper would espouse the cause of reformism, even if it meant 'being vilified and dubbed a traitor to the cause by pessimists and extremists.' The *Independent* – its very name chosen to demonstrate the refusal to be controlled by any political party – was meant to 'be a reflex of the sentiments expressed by the Trades and Labor Council.'[53] This control was rarely exercised through overt censorship, as the paper often printed dissenting arguments in its letters page and printed articles from every labour and left perspective, ranging from Tolstoyan anarchism to Gompersism to DeLeonite socialism. Despite this open policy, however, the relative conservatism of Bartley and the VTLC leadership shone through. Sometimes their point of view was put forward explicitly, in articles that praised the council or supported particular policies or candidates. At other times, the political message put out by Bartley and Cowan was less partisan, if no less overt. Warnings against radicalism, for example, were a regular feature of the *Independent*, often in the form of a 'better safe than sorry' parable. In one such warning, a former editor of a 'really radical paper' reportedly told the *Independent* how the journal increasingly alienated readers with its radicalism. Soon the readership 'dwindled down to the extremists.' But even this loyal cadre was driven off, some by the editor's reference to social democracy as 'feudal oppression,' and the rest when he attacked 'atheism on the score of its superstitious tendencies.' Finally, the editor himself stopped taking the paper, for he found its radicalism 'too unsettling.' The moral of the story was plain: politics and religion were a source of division in the labour movement, and those who opposed moderation endangered both the cause and the paper.[54] This message was repeated constantly in different forms as the *Independent* drove home its assault on dissenters and radicals. 'The man who breeds dissension in a union,' one article maintained, 'is the greatest foe union labor has to contend against. He usually employs the cowardly weapon of slander and falsehood against someone who has incurred his displeasure, because he did not go the way the discord-breeder wanted him to go, and because he dared to think different [sic] on certain subjects foreign to the malcontent's reasoning. Harmony is the greatest force necessary to make the labor movement a success, and the man who for selfish purposes and without good reason tries to make life a burden to other members should be promptly sat on and squelched.'[55] Other attacks were launched against those who are 'the first to criticize the officers, the first to demand the benefits of the union, and the first to kick and swear that the union is no good ... He breeds more discontent and creates more strikes in his sneaking way than would a thousand good members ... If he is in your branch, "fire" him out, but don't kill him, as he would lose his last breath calling for the funeral benefits.'[56]

The labour newspaper applauded the virtues of common sense and pragmatism as part of its campaign against dissidents and apathetic nay-sayers. Encouraging members to support the status quo, the *Independent* insisted that 'labour does not want "wild men" to represent it anywhere.' Instead, it wanted 'the representation of sensible, clear-headed men who can state a case without exaggeration or undue heat.'[57] However correct such an assessment may have been of the will of the membership or the best tactical approach to take – and this is hardly clear – such appeals to 'sensible' action were a warning to those who might want to challenge the leadership. Other articles made the message plain: 'Discipline is indispensable to success ... All other things being equal, the army that is best disciplined is the one that is surest of success. As with other organizations, so with institutions, so with organizations of wage workers. Where wise rules are adopted and readily enforced, and where discipline has been maintained, the greatest possible achievements are the natural results ... Trade unions, being voluntary organizations, are incapable of enforcing the rigid discipline that law and necessity enforces [sic] but a great deal of it is necessary.' The piece concluded by enjoining workers to 'remember their obligations,' to 'live up to their promises,' and to 'adhere to the laws' of the union.[58] Another article reminded readers that 'trade unions are practical organizations ... advocating the practical desires and wants of workingmen by practical methods.' Unlike the socialists, unions did not 'dash headlong into wild theories, and hence are slow moving, conservative organizations.' To those who might argue that this was a fair description of what needed to be changed, the paper maintained that in fact, 'this is where their [the unions'] strength lies. This is why they have not been destroyed long ago.' Radicals, the article went on, had their place, for 'they are pulling us out of the "rut," which, without them, we would be inclined to rest in,' but moderation was the proper road. The interplay between radicals and conservatives explained why the trade unions were 'slow, but at the same time progressive.' Ignoring the braking effect of the labour leaders themselves, the paper concluded that it was important that the radicals did not get too far ahead of the masses and that more education was needed before the entire movement was as progressive as the radical element.[59]

Neither overtures to the business community nor aiming at the widest common denominator provided the paper with a sufficient income. Popular support among the city's unionists was not forthcoming, as the constant requests for subscriptions and money made clear. Less than one-third of the 1,500 to 2,000 union members subscribed to the paper. Such lack of interest had been demonstrated several years before, when the VTLC first broached the subject of a labour newspaper. At that time, weeks of soliciting had brought in only 130 promises to subscribe. Eight years later, when the *Independent* was launched in 1900, the magic number of 500 still could not be reached, though the city's population had doubled.[60] By October 1903 the lack of financial support forced the paper to cut back its publication from once a week to once a month. Determined to keep the paper alive, the council formed a special committee to help maintain it as a weekly, and with the renewed effort, the *Independent* continued in that format until its demise early in 1904.[61] But the reluctance of the rank and file to support the newspaper suggests that it, no less than the hall, was the creation and icon not of the union movement but of its leaders and paid staff.

The paid positions on the newspaper were themselves a sore spot in the VTLC. In January 1903 Bartley and Cowan came under attack for being employers. Ironically, Bartley had tried to purge the Knights of Labor editor G.F. Leaper on the same grounds a decade before. The first move came when some delegates questioned Bartley and Cowan's eligibility to sit on the council. The matter was referred to the bylaw committee for a ruling, but before it could report, a motion was made to have the ITU replace the two as delegates. They were, the motion asserted, 'considered employers of labor,' by virtue of their positions on the council newspaper and thus prohibited by the constitution from sitting. The council voted overwhelmingly to quash the motion, and Bartley and Cowan remained on the paper and in the council.[62] Although political infighting rather than any principled objection to employers seems to be behind the affair, the paid posts and the need to hire workers did put the labour council in a difficult position.[63] Despite this success, the editor came under fire again nine months later. While the council had voted to 'view with suspicion any labor man who espouses the cause of either of the old political parties,' the *Independent* had plumped for a Conservative candidate in a by-election. Angry VTLC delegates moved to withdraw the council's endorsement of the paper as its official organ, but withdrew the motion when it was apparent that it would fail. A subsequent motion to have the issue resolved by a referendum of the affiliated unions was defeated in a fairly close vote of 16 to 12, but a compromise created a press committee to supervise 'all copy pertaining to political matters' that was considered for publication.[64] The issue, however, would soon become moot, as the general lack of interest in the paper meant that it had only a few more months to live.

The history of the union hall and the newspaper demonstrate the profound differences between the leadership of the VTLC and the rank and file in Vancouver even when such differences did not lead to open conflict. Priorities and objectives were set by the leaders, who then expected members to follow uncritically. When such support was not forthcoming, bureaucrats tended to blame the rank and file, rather than try to understand apathy as a sign that they were not addressing the concerns of those they represented. In the face of this apathy, the council tended to see itself in opposition to the membership, and often acted accordingly.

The separation of the council from the rest of the labour movement created a vicious circle. Believing that they spoke for the whole movement, leaders created policies and institutions that reflected their own needs and perceptions. When workers disagreed or remained indifferent to the efforts made on their behalf, the leadership reacted by attacking the rank and file. This in turn separated the leaders from the led even more, for it allowed the bureaucracy to think that, in the face of an apathetic and even traitorous rank and file, it had the right, indeed the obligation, to press on without popular support.

4

Labourism, Bureaucracy, and the Labour Aristocracy

Along with a structure of organization and control, the labour council developed its political ideology. Contrary to many assumptions about labour bureaucracies, the VTLC did not become more conservative over time. From its earliest days, the council had advocated a progressive reformism, and not until the early 1900s did it begin to consider the question of socialism. An examination of the council's ideology from 1889 to 1900 suggests that conservatism is not necessarily a function of bureaucracy, for the first years of the council were less bureaucratic, had fewer paid positions, and were staffed by active trade unionists and workers rather than experts or professional officials. Where ideology and bureaucracy did merge was in the bureaucrats' ability to create and impose their own political agenda on the rest of the labour movement.[1]

The political program of the VTLC has accurately been described as labourism. While never tightly defined by the council or labourists elsewhere, the ideology nevertheless had at its core a belief in reform. Typically, this centred around improved conditions and wages for skilled or unionized workers. It also included workers' compensation, factory inspection acts, expanded suffrage, better access to political office for workers, arbitration, minimum wage laws, and public ownership of municipal utilities. It was not a revolutionary doctrine, for labourists sought to win reforms through the parliamentary system and through their efforts against employers on the job site. Many labourists observed that the system was indeed stacked against workers and trade unionists, but they still believed that adjustments, not revolution, could alter the balance.[2]

Labourism was a class-conscious doctrine, based on a labour theory of value, but neither the conception of class nor the labour theory of value were constructed along strict socialist lines. Unlike Marxists, labourists did not divide classes according to the relationship to the means of production, that is, between those who owned land, factories, or workshops and those who sold their labour to the owners. Instead, class was more often defined by one's relation to what was considered to be real work or socially necessary production. Farmers, artisans, small manufacturers, small proprietors – those who performed useful work that benefited society – were on one side. On the other were those who did not actually produce but reaped huge rewards. These included the great monopolists who accumulated outlandish sums by destroying small competitors and restricting the market; financiers who made gains by juggling paper; speculators who bought low and sold high without improving the land with their own efforts; and those who lived by clipping the coupons from their bonds. These people, labourists asserted, did very little to justify their existence and yet they sucked up the labour of millions. Productivity, actually creating goods and services for the society, was the cornerstone of labourism. Thus the council's newspaper, the *Independent*, asked, 'What would happen if all who work should suddenly cease to work? It might occur to some that labor is as important as the class that absorbs its product. Presidents, judges, heads of departments, etc., occasionally take vacations and are not greatly missed. Suppose cooks, engineers, firemen, etc. should take vacations, would they be missed?' Work itself was valued as the most fitting and noble condition for humanity, for 'labor is the life of life. Ease is the way to disease. The highest life of an organ lies in the fullest discharge of its function.'[3]

In this picture of society divided into parasites and producers, capitalism was not necessarily viewed as bad. Unrestricted capitalism, monopoly, unfair practices, and the centralization of wealth and power were the chief evils. Workers were not necessarily robbed at the point of production, as Marx insisted. A fair day's wage and a fair return on capital was possible, labourists believed, as long as both sides avoided greed and acknowledged the other's right to share in the rewards. From this it followed that the appropriate goal of political action was not revolution. But the power of monopolies to fix prices at an artificially high level meant that workers were robbed when they purchased goods. Large capitalists, blinded by avarice, holding no regard for the rights of workers, could take advantage of labour and use their great power selfishly. To combat this, progressive reforms were needed to end the abuses of the system and restore its harmony. This meant fair wage laws, lien laws, and protection of the rights of unions. It also meant public ownership of the so-called natural monopolies such as transit, power, and water, where high start-up costs and the need to avoid duplication of service and resources made competition unlikely to develop. In particular, labourists set out to fight the trusts, the organized cartels that had tight control over prices. John D. Rockefeller and his Standard Oil Company were favourite targets of Vancouver's labourists. They deplored his annual income of $72 million dollars and noted with alarm that 'this gigantic fortune, and other great estates wrung from the American people by the extortion of monopoly, are growing rapidly. Are they not a menace to the welfare of the masses? Are they not a danger to our representative system of government? Shall they be permitted to grow still more gigantic through favor of law and protection of hardened politicians?'[4]

In May 1900 the *Independent* printed a short critique that neatly sums up the labourist attack on the trusts:

The farmer, miner, carpenter, laborer, sells his labor to the capitalist. The capitalist, through the trust, sells him back the product of his labor and for his trouble in buying and selling, keeps just one-half of the fruits of toil. The time is ripening when the artisan will sell his labor to no man, when he will harness the trust and use it, not to accumulate gold but to distribute the good things of this world. In order that the day will come and come quickly, we must make 'public ownership' our battle-cry. We must first own the railroads, telegraphs, telephones, electric lighting, etc. and in due time the great trusts. Then fellow-workers and not until then, will there be an equitable distribution of the products of labor.[5]

If the fair wage settled on between unionists and their employers were chipped away by unfair prices, the obvious solution was to replace private monopolies with public companies that would be controlled by consumers. Thus, in 1893 the VTLC called for the government ownership of telegraph lines, and in 1894 it unanimously adopted a resolution calling for the city to take over and run the Vancouver Electric and Tramway Company. In September of that year delegates moved that 'It is a principle of the Vancouver Trades and Labor Council that the city should own and operate all its public utilities.' Failure to take over these privately owned ventures would only 'perpetuate unprincipled monopoly and speculation.' Later, the council opposed the twenty-five-year lease given to the private streetcar company, countering 'the city should secure the right to purchase the Railway and equipment,' and put itself 'on record as favoring municipal control of water, light, and tramways.' By the end of 1895 the call was expanded to include municipal ownership of gas, electric, telephone, and water utilities as well as ferry and street railway lines.[6] The *Independent* used examples from around the world to buttress its claim that public ownership was possible and, more importantly, would lower the money paid out by working people for necessities. The paper pointed out to its readers that one could talk for a year over the 6,000 miles of long-distance telephone lines in Switzerland for $16, while it cost $10 for a few minutes' call between New York and Little Rock. Why? Because 'Switzerland owns and controls her own telephone lines, and private corporations operate the Atlantic lines.' Using the United States as an example, the paper observed that, on average, the cost of power was 30 per cent lower in states and cities where utilities were taken out of private hands and turned over to the public. Locally, the high cost of heating coal in the winter of 1895 was blamed on 'the monopoly held by coal dealers in Vancouver,' and the council wrote to MLA Ralph Smith to obtain the price of coal at the minehead so it could calculate the mark-up of the 'trust.' Big capital was the chief enemy of the people, and the government was to be used as a countervailing power to protect consumers and workers.[7]

In keeping with the belief that they were exploited as consumers, the labour leaders also advocated reducing the costs of government. Government expenditures were watched closely, and the council was quick to protest monies given to large corporations or wasted on extravagances of little import to working men. In 1891 it applauded the city's offer of a bonus to the company constructing a new dry dock if the work was completed quickly, though it may be noted that such a proviso could result in a speed-up for the workers on the job. Two years later the VTLC opposed the city's plan to guarantee a new issue of street railway bonds to the tune of $50,000 and condemned its proposal to exempt the new CPR depot from taxation. This reflected the council's belief that no corporation should be supported, either directly or indirectly, by the taxpayers. The mayor and aldermen were blasted for spending $1,000 on an ad in the World's Fair Guide, on the grounds that 'the City would derive little if any real advantage from such a scheme.' City works were carefully scrutinized, and on numerous occasions the council complained to the Works Department of 'bad material' being used by a sewer contractor, or work on a new hospital being performed in a 'very unsatisfactory way.' Such attention to the spending of the city suggests that the labour council delegates viewed themselves as consumers and citizens no less than as workers.[8]

Federal and provincial governments were also barked at by the VTLC watchdog. The council protested 'the reckless handling of the people's money with respect to "Indian affairs,"' damned the British Pacific Railway land grant and subsidy, and labelled the proposed new parliament buildings in Victoria a 'reckless and extravagant waste of the people's money.' Careful attention to the direct financial considerations helped the council work out its position on free trade in 1895. The VTLC concluded that since the tariff had 'developed monopolies, trusts, and other combinations,' had hindered agriculture (and thus cheap food), and had 'oppressed the masses to the enrichment of the few,' the council resolved that the tariff 'should be reduced to the needs of honest, economical, and efficient government.'[9]

The concern with efficient government was balanced with union principles. For example, the VTLC urged the city to end contract labour, that is, work awarded to contractors who had tendered the lowest bid and made their profit by lowering wages. The council insisted that the work should be done by day labour, or labour that was hired directly by the city and guaranteed a decent, standard wage. Accepting the lowest bid for public works could prove to be a false economy, and one that unfairly rewarded contractors at the expense of labour and taxpayers. The *Independent* pointed this out forcefully, asking, 'Do our city fathers imagine that contractors are in the business for the good of their health? If the contractor offers to do a job for $100, he figures that $20 of that goes into his own pocket. And to earn that $20 what does he do? Absolutely nothing. This $20 will always be paid – to make his money, the contractor would not hesitate to substitute inferior material and labour; the lowest contractor bid is still inflated by the $20 of profit.'[10]

It was better economy, the delegates maintained, to have the city hire day labour and thus eliminate the $20 profit paid to contractors. Day labour would elevate wages, reduce competition among working people, protect unions, exclude Asians, and ensure that the highest quality work was done.[11] The labour newspaper quoted with approval the mayor of Haverhill, Massachusetts, who advocated day labour, claiming that under it 'all the evils of the contract system have thus been eliminated. Labor has been well paid, and the amount of public work done under these improved conditions has been much larger, with the same appropriation, than in previous years.' In the view of the council, there was no conflict between good unionism and smart public expenditure. Union principles could be put forward as measures that would benefit the society as a whole.[12]

On the political front, the union leaders sought to expand the franchise so the producers could exert their proper and deserved influence over the state and through it the trusts. This political call was not designed so much to alter the system as to ensure that politicians became accountable to the people and not the 'interests.' The VTLC declared that workers had to unite, not to tear down the state but to send 'the fittest and the best men' to fight for 'such legislation as will mostly benefit the wage-earners of the Dominion.'[13] The resolution illustrates the faith that this generation of labour leaders had in the system. The problems of the working classes, they believed, were not structural, were not an inherent battle between labour and capital. They were personal and could be eliminated when good men were sent to Parliament by an aware working class to represent labour. Thus, the first political platform adopted by the council was in the main devoted to increasing the participation of working people – that is to say, white, Anglo-Saxon, skilled males – in the political process. The platform called for manhood suffrage in municipal elections, abolition of the property qualification for those seeking municipal office, a legal half-day holiday for voting, a stronger Sunday observance act, the provincial franchise for all males receiving an income over $300 per year, temperance legislation, and an elected governor-general. Save for temperance and Sunday legislation, each of these measures was aimed at giving working men better access to the political machinery.[14]

Such demands continued to be a major part of the labour council's political agenda. In 1892 its parliamentary committee recommended asking the city to petition the province to amend the civic charter so the property qualification for municipal voters could be reduced from $500 to $200. Later that year the committee called for the payment of salaries to aldermen, and the demand was eventually won. This became a perennial concern, and in 1894 the VTLC called for a raise in pay to $400 per year. When the city threatened to eliminate the salaries in 1896, George Bartley fiercely opposed the measure. He insisted that it was imperative to maintain 'the present system of remuneration in order that the position of alderman may be open for workingmen representatives.' In 1899 the battle was waged again. This time the VTLC invoked the labourist principle of a fair day's pay for a fair day's work to buttress its claim, insisting that 'in every station of life, whether public or private, the laborer is worthy of his hire, and ... if carried, this by-law would practically debar workingmen from sitting in the council as aldermen.' The council resolved that it was strongly opposed to the proposed change and suggested that 'not only should the city aldermen be paid but that the salary should be increased to the sum of $400 per year."[15]

Other measures were advocated to increase the participation of working men in the political life of the community. By 1895 these included the right of any voter to run for municipal office, direct legislation in the form of initiatives and referenda, the abolition of the ward system, and the annual publication of the assessor's list and the city budget. The council disapproved of a provincial bill that would 'take away the franchise of the people' by allowing the government to appoint its commissioners, and it formally requested two seats on the Citizens Relief Committee, an early civil defence organization. Together with the reforms in trade union law, trust-busting, and the belief in 'producerism,' this political program made up the essential elements of the VTLC's labourist ideology.[16]

The intellectual roots of labourism may be found in several places. Thomas Loosmore has suggested that the reform measures, as distinct from the pure and simple trade union issues, stemmed from French and American republicanism and were imported to British Columbia by the Knights of Labor. Craig Heron has instead stressed British parliamentary struggles and nineteenth-century Radicalism as a source, and both are agreed on the influence of American populism. Undoubtedly both are correct to look so far afield for some elements of the ideology. But Canadian conditions and experiences also played an important role in defining labourism. Certainly the Canadian Knights of Labor developed their own 'brain-workers' and ideologues who could speak to the politics and issues north of the forty-ninth parallel. The British Columbia labourists drew heavily upon the Knights though they rejected much of that group's 'eclectic radicalism,' for local Knights were involved in the VTLC's early parliamentary committees.[17]

The British Columbia leaders also adopted ideas from the Canadian populist movement in Ontario. Indeed, the populist Patrons of Industry, in a political platform of 1893, strongly resembled that of the Vancouver labour council. The Patrons called for rigid economy in every department of the public service, simplification of the laws and a reduction in the machinery of politics, a tariff for revenue only, free trade, an end to railway bonuses, antitrust legislation, and more equitable electoral measures.[18] Even the language of the two organizations was similar. Like the labourists in British Columbia, populists held up the importance of the producer. *The Farmers' Sun*, newspaper of the Patrons of Industry, argued that 'one of the greatest evils society has had to contend with has been a faulty and unequal system of distribution, by which the actual producer, whether of the city or country, has been despoiled to enrich the non-producing class – capitalists, traders, professional men, and middlemen.'[19] Farmers and labour together created all wealth, and the following could have appeared as easily in the *Independent* as in the *Farmers' Sun*: 'On every field that bears a tempting harvest on its breast, on every brick in every building that was ever reared, on every book of value that was ever written, on every thought that burns to light the world, in every workshop, mine, mill, and factory – wherever labour sweats – are written the credentials of nobility.'[20]

In many ways the early ideology of the VTLC had more in common with rural protest than it did with Marxist socialism. This should not be surprising, for the first generation of labour leaders was itself making the transition from the countryside to the developing urban industrial society, and it was natural for them to build their analysis of the new world on the heritage of rural, populist criticism. They borrowed from the farmer the producer ethic, the emphasis on controlling consumer prices, the idea of fair wages and prices, and the ideals of community and a community of interests. The easy acceptance of small employers as workers, a suspicion of immigrants, the belief in the family, the position of women in the home and work economy, and the refusal to see all capitalist relations as essentially exploitative, were also rooted in the rural experience.[21]

Behind both the populist and the labourist ideologies stood the ideal of the free yeoman. Independence was at the very heart of this ideal, and farmers and trade unionists alike strove for a life and a society that would allow them to control their own destinies, to bow to no master, and to stand equal to any man. Among farms, the myth of independence was a powerful one, and many preferred a smaller income to the chance of greater wealth if it meant sacrificing independence. Although the leaders of the VTLC were workers, they too were at pains to avoid becoming proletarians. For they were artisans, working alongside their employer in small shops, able to exert some control over the conditions of their work and the work process. They were not industrial or factory workers; they were not wage slaves who had to bow and scrape to their boss. Early labour leaders such as Joseph Dixon and George Bartley had not emigrated to Vancouver to flee the sweatshops and mills of England and Ontario. As farming increasingly gave way to industrialization and urbanization, both men left the family farm to take up a trade. Learning a trade was a way to avoid the worst abuses that faced the proletariat, for it allowed them to maintain and extend their control and independence in the new urban frontier.[22] In Canada and the United States, the migration from the farms was rarely a movement from the petit-bourgeois occupation of farmer to the wage slavery of the factory. Instead, the farm worker moved into a variety of occupations and professions, many of them middle class. These ranged from law, banking, and accounting to the skilled trades. Populism and labourism were better suited to the experience of these people than revolutionary socialism, for these ideologies reflected their relative success under the developing capitalism of the late nineteenth and early twentieth centuries. Immigrants from other countries were much more likely to be factory hands, and this reinforced the labourist belief that ethnicity, skill, and success were intimately connected.[23] In Canada the rise of industrialization did not destroy petit-bourgeois property owners and force them into factories. Like farmers, artisans in the 1860s and 1870s tended to own property; as a result, their protest was not the protest of the exploited factory hand or sweated machine tender. It was rather the protest of those who feared such a fate. As Gordon Darroch has indicated, 'The political voices of Ontario's artisans were so articulate in this era partly because proletarianization was a real and visible threat not only to the independence of their craft communities and sense of traditional rights, but also to their considerable opportunities to gain small property holdings, which materially underwrote that independence.' The resistance to industrialization and wage work did not always turn into socialist protest; instead, this resistance 'often took the form of redoubled efforts to gain or maintain the promised independence of smallholding, as well as more recognizable forms.' Darroch concludes that 'petty property and its associated life-ways were by no means simply swamped or absorbed by the familiar institutional forms of late twentieth-century capitalism.' Labourists in Vancouver adapted the populist critique to fit their own similar experience of capitalist development.[24]

In the east, the similarities between populism and labour led the two groups to work together for a time. In 1886 the Trades and Labor Congress (TLC) sought an alliance with the Grange, a precursor of the Patrons, while in the 1890s, the Patrons and the TLC created a joint committee to explore avenues of cooperation. The organizations sent delegates to each other's conventions, and the Patrons were, for a time, given reciprocal membership rights in the TLC. Although the alliance was short-lived, it suggests that the general outlines of the ideologies had much in common. In 1894 and 1895 the Vancouver Trades and Labour Council worked with farmers in the Nationalist Party, a short-lived pro-labour party that favoured the single tax and sent the Lib-Lab George R. Maxwell to the House of Commons. Part of the council's political platform in 1894 was aimed at helping farmers, as it called for low-interest, long-term loans to farmers, these being 'to the best interests of the province.' Although the attempt at forging an alliance was unsuccessful, it does suggest that the class analysis of the early Vancouver labour leaders was closer to populism than to Marxism or socialism.[25]

Labour and farmers even shared the same intellectuals, writers, and speakers who formally articulated their ideologies. In its early years, the only newspaper the council as a body subscribed to was *Canada Farmers' Sun*. George Wrigley first edited the Knights' paper, the *Canadian Labour Courier*, in Ontario, then in 1892 he founded the *Canada Farmers' Sun*. From the populist movement, Wrigley moved to the Canadian Socialist League and edited its paper, *Citizen and Country*. In 1902 he moved the paper to Vancouver, where he joined with Parmeter Pettipiece to create the paper that would soon become the *Western Clarion*, the voice of the Socialist Party of Canada. Pettipiece himself left the family farm in Ontario to become a journalist, and his first paper, the Lardeau *Eagle*, was better fitted under the populist than the socialist rubric. As late as 1900 it supported the Independent Labour–Liberal candidate Chris Foley rather than any socialist campaign. Phillips Thompson, perhaps the pre-eminent Knights' ideologue, moved through the Patrons before taking up the cause of socialism. These spokesmen found a ready audience among the labour leaders of Vancouver, and the labour movement continued to draw upon the populist movement for information and analysis.[26]

The important question of the bureaucrats' ideology, however, is not whence it came. Rather it is, why did these labour leaders adopt and continue to hold the ideology they did? It is one thing to demonstrate that an ideology exists and has intellectual precedents and quite another to try to explain why it was appropriate for the group that held it. Clearly some of the common explanations for the conservatism of the labour bureaucracy do not hold in this case. For example, labourism cannot be explained as an ideology of salaried union professionals who are more or less removed from the working class. Only one officer in the VTLC, the secretary, was paid in the early years. The secretary generally exerted little formal influence on decisions, and his position in this period was at best a part-time job that paid five dollars a month. Professionalism neither propelled these officials into the middle class nor changed their material status significantly in this early period.[27]

Neither can contract negotiations and settlement be an explanation for conservatism in this period. Few unions in the first years of the VTLC negotiated contracts. Instead, unions decided upon a reasonable wage and announced their decisions to employers who would then accept or fight the proposal. The theory of 'institutionalized bargaining' put forward by Stan Weir and others does not fit either. The dominant unions in the VTLC, such as the building and printing trades, did not work for monopoly capitalists or for firms that sought tripartite schemes in the way Weir has illustrated in the steel and auto industries of the 1940s. Nor did union bureaucrats act as 'policemen' to force employees back to work in this period. Yet the council was still, in relative terms, conservative.[28] It may be that the very process of determining a wage rate in the union forced workers to be 'reasonable.' But this is a different argument from that of the incorporation theorists who suggest that the process itself of offer and counter-offer with the employer fostered compromise and conservatism. Even when contracts were signed, it is unlikely that they alone created a consensus among workers on the virtues of class collaboration in that period. Finally, the independence of the VTLC and its loose affiliation to the TLC and the AFL suggests that pressure from the central labour bodies was not the determining factor. The VTLC leaders had few qualms about rejecting TLC policies, and in fact, the areas in which they worked seldom overlapped. While the Vancouver council was in broad agreement with the general policies of the TLC, it would simply ignore anything that it disagreed with or that seemed irrelevant.

If the early VTLC leaders were not forced into their political stance of labourism by virtue of ascendancy into white-collar, middle class jobs in the bureaucracy, by the negotiating process, or by pressure from central labour organizations, it must be conceded that their ideology, for good or ill, reflected their class interests as they perceived them. Craig Heron has concluded that labourism indeed reflected the needs and aspirations of the skilled, unionized workers such as those who made up the VTLC from 1889 to 1900. What, then, were these needs and aspirations, and the sense of possibilities and change, based on? What was the common ground that allowed for considerable agreement among VTLC delegates on political action and ideology? Robert McDonald has suggested that the city itself acted as a conservative influence. Unlike the company boom towns of the resource frontier, Vancouver offered relatively steady jobs, higher pay in organized industries such as construction and printing, the chance to own a home and establish a stable life, and perhaps the opportunity to become a small contractor or businessman. All of these influences worked to make urban unionists conservative. There is a great deal of truth in this argument, but the theory of urbanism does not help us understand the different ideologies within the city itself, or the clash between socialists and labourists that would later rock the VTLC. What does explain these elements is the theory of the labour aristocracy.[29]

The *locus classicus* for the debate on the labour aristocracy is the work of Karl Marx and Friedrich Engels. Marx, in his inaugural address to the International Workingmen's Association in 1864, pointed to the tendency of modern capitalism to split the working class into castes and to advance the wages of a minority of the working class, while the 'great masses of the working classes' saw wages stagnate and fall. Those industries that were unionized and did not face the competition of women, immigrant labour, or machinery formed 'an aristocracy of the working class' that could secure a comfortable existence. A minority of workers in trade unions, the very workers Engels referred to as 'the advanced guard of the working class,' were, as the result of their ability to fight and their particular, historical place in the economy, able to win concessions and higher wages for themselves. With the achievement of these improvements, however, they became less and less interested in radical change; indeed, many were never convinced of the necessity for it in the first place.[30]

More recently, the historian Eric Hobsbawm has refined the concept of the labour aristocracy. He set out six defining characteristics of the aristocracy. These included the level of wages, security of social position, conditions of work, relations with the social strata above and below, the general conditions of living, and the prospects of upward mobility for the workers and their children. Most important of these was the wage level, for the worker who earned a good regular wage could put enough by to avoid the Poor Law, to live outside the worst slum areas, to be treated with some respect and dignity by employers and to have some freedom of choice in his job, to give his children a chance of a better education, and so on. The relatively well-paid worker, that is, the unionized worker who was not threatened by mechanization or cheaper labour, was, according to Hobsbawm, often able to merge with the lower middle class. This class included small shopkeepers, independent masters, foremen, managers, and even some white-collar workers such as clerks. Better conditions and upward mobility separated the 'labour aristocrats' from other workers and insulated them against socialist thought. As Robert Michels put it when describing privileged German workers and labour leaders, 'What interest for them has now the dogma of the social revolution? Their own social revolution has already been effected.' E.P. Thompson has argued in less condemnatory language that with the failure of Chartists to overthrow capital, reform appeared to be the only course left open to workers. And unlike radical movements, reformism did seem able to deliver some immmediate improvements. But when workers turned to reform, they 'became more reluctant to engage in quixotic outbreaks which might jeopardize gains acumulated at such cost ... [O]nce a certain climactic moment is passed, the opportunity for a certain kind of revolutionary movement passes irrevocably – not so much because of " 'exhaustion' " but because more limited, reformist pressures, from secure organizational bases, bring evident returns.' Thus, the very success of reformism both put the labour aristocracy in the forefront of the labour movement and took the edge off the desire for revolution or socialism.[31]

Did a labour aristocracy exist in the VTLC and affect its politics between 1889 and 1900? Robert McDonald has shown that the skilled unionists that made up the labour council were indeed better paid than other workers. From the beginning of the council, the income and conditions of work of the skilled craft unionist outstripped those of the labourer and the unorganized. By 1890 union carpenters were fighting for the nine-hour day and a daily wage of $3. Plasterers such as George Irvine earned $5 for an eight-hour day, and lathers were paid $2.25 per 1,000 feet of lath. Printers earned at least $3.50 per day for job work such as business cards, stationery, and business forms. Newspaper typesetting was essentially piece-work, as compositors were paid by the amount they set, based on a rate of 45 to 50 cents per thousand ems. The em was a variable measurement based on the size of the capital letter 'M' in the font being set. This worked out on average to about 40 cents per hour, or $4.50 per nine-hour day. Even longshoremen were unionized early in the city's history, and were relatively well paid at the rate of 35 cents per hour, with a shift differential paid to those who worked afternoons or nights. In contrast to these workers, non-unionized labourers were paid $2 for a ten-hour day. Labourers working for the CPR fared even worse, receiving only $1.70 for ten hours' work, roughly half the wage of a carpenter or printer. This pattern continued throughout the history of the VTLC. By 1908 ITU printers worked a seven-hour day and earned about $100 per month. Carpenters could make about $75 per month, or 50 cents per hour. Streetcar railwaymen working on the British Columbia Electric Railway made less per hour – about 35 cents – but their steady employment meant that their yearly earnings were nearly the same as those of the average carpenter, who would spend some time each year unemployed. Other building trades did a little better: bricklayers, masons, and stonecutters averaged about $80 per month; plumbers and gas fitters received a rate somewhere between that of carpenters and bricklayers. Labourers, however, would do well to earn $55 per month. Other workers who could not easily form unions could expect to do worse, and this was especially true of Asians and women. They were effectively 'ghettoized' in relatively unskilled, non-union jobs in the service and consumer goods manufacturing sectors and could expect to earn about half the wage of their white male counterpart in any setting. Women in the garment-making industry, for example, earned about $11.50 per week in 1918, men nearly double at $18.50. Domestic service, where about 40 per cent of the working women of the province were employed, was paid at an average rate of $70 per month, although this figure lumps together men and women and probably includes a cash equivalent for room and board.[32]

Higher income meant more than better food or living in better neighbourhoods. It meant a certain independence from the employer and some protection from the vagaries of economic depression and unemployment. It could even enable the labour aristocrat to move up a notch and start his own business. The *Independent* proudly announced in 1900 that former VTLC president and walking delegate George Irvine was now self-employed, making outdoor vases in Portland cement, while Dan Stewart, a former delegate from the tailors' union, was the owner of his own shop. George Wilks of the iron moulders, another VTLC delegate, left the city in 1901 to move to Grand Forks and set up his own moulding business. The *Independent* sent him off with good wishes, and the 'hope his best expectations will be more than realized at his new location.' Other early VTLC leaders left the working class to become contractors and small businessmen. William Pleming, council president in 1891, established his construction business a few years later. Walter Hepburn, who served three terms as secretary in 1896 and 1897, became a building contractor by 1903. A native Quebecer, Hepburn was a prominent member of the Liberal party, and in later years he ran successfully as an alderman and was chief movie censor of the province. George Bartley and Harry Cowan left the composing rooms of the daily newspapers to publish the *Independent*; later, Bartley would publish other papers and Cowan would own his own printing shop. Joe Dixon started working as a contractor in the 1890s. He took the first step towards establishing what would become a successful furniture business when he opened a carpentry-joiner shop in 1902. The *Independent* took the occasion to wish the VTLC founder 'every success in his new enterprise.' The union connections of contractors could even be used as advertising features. When former council secretary F.P. Bishop returned to Vancouver and set up his own painting company, the *Independent* put him on its list of fair contractors and told prospective clients that he and the others were 'reliable contractors of buildings employing union men only and who are on friendly terms with their employees. No danger of strikes or defective construction of buildings in charge of these contractors.' The promotion of workers to contractors, then, was seen as a way to reduce class conflict. Who better than a fellow worker and unionist to understand the needs of the employees?[33]

Even those unionists who were not tradesmen had some hope of becoming small businessmen. W.J. Orr, recording secretary of the Retail Clerks' Association, resigned his office in May 1901, having purchased a boot and shoe store. Described as an 'energetic man of business' by the *Independent*, the paper went on to wish him 'every prosperity in his new venture.' Another clerk, J.R. Jackson, also resigned from the union to start his own business, while council president W.J. Lamrick eventually ran a hardware store in the city. C.N. Lee of the laundry workers resigned the presidency of the council in 1904, and soon after he opened the Pier Tea and Refreshment Parlour.[34]

Business opportunities in the city allowed a significant number of labour aristocrats to move into the petit bourgeoisie with relative ease and gave these leaders a substantial stake in the existing society. The success of these artisans stood as examples of the myth of producerism and suggested that there was always the possibility of making it within the capitalist society. Such successes were applauded in the pages of their press by the labour bureaucracy, and far from being seen as exceptions to the rule, they suggested that the labourist values of hard, productive work and gradualism paid off. The craft skills and the mentality they engendered helped these workers leave the working class by working within the system, and the labour bureaucrats regarded this neither as treason nor as an aberration.

This description of the labour aristocracy strongly suggests that something other than bureaucracy explains the attraction of labourism to the early VTLC leaders. Income, occupation, ethnicity, gender, and status all contributed to shaping their world-view. Given the ability of the bureaucrats to control access to the council, such a world-view was a prerequisite, not a consequence, of holding an executive office in the VTLC.

Are income and social mobility sufficient to consider many of the VTLC leaders labour aristocrats? Some critics, notably Robert Gray, have attempted to define the labour aristocracy in terms of a 'cultural identity, a more or less self-conscious exclusiveness, by an upper stratum of skilled workers.' But this definition itself is predicated on the existence of an 'upper stratum,' that is, better-paid, workers. Furthermore, the cultural identity of this stratum pointed out by Gray was dependent on the higher incomes. Living in better housing and in better parts of town, refined leisure activities, the ownership of a piano, having a parlour: each of these is ultimately dependent on the wage. Instead of separating the labour aristocracy from its economic base, the cultural argument has reinforced it. Culture, attitudes, and lifestyles, control over one's own work, and the lack of direct supervision were certainly some of the factors that influenced the labour aristocrat. These were, however, the consequences, not the causes of, relative privilege. As Hobsbawm concluded, in his consideration of this culturalist argument, 'working-class culture, lifestyles and the nature of the actual work on the job, should not lead us to underestimate the actual level and predictability of the labour aristocrat's income, which was originally used as the main criterion of its membership.'[35]

Another criticism of the labour aristocracy argument has been the assumption that the theory implies that the labour aristocrats had to have been more conservative than other workers. Michael Kazin has insisted that 'the concept of a "labor aristocracy" is rather useless' when applied to San Francisco building trades, 'because it implies that "non-aristocrats" thought and acted in more class-conscious ways than the skilled minority.' It is a relatively simple matter for these critics to point to numerous examples when craft workers were more militant and radical than non-unionized and so-called unskilled workers to prove their contention. But the concept of the labour aristocracy does not hinge on the notion that the workers who made it up were more conservative than others and, in the words of Hobsbawm, does not imply that 'some other section of the working class was politically more advanced or revolutionary.' It is instead an attempt to understand the precise ideology and material position of the skilled, unionized worker. All the theory need prove is that the labour aristocrats were not revolutionary, and most work on the subject, including that of Kazin, has shown this to be true.[36]

It does need to be remembered that not all trade unionists in this period could be considered labour aristocrats. Only those trades that could defend their wages and job control could maintain their status. The membership of the labour aristocracy was never fixed, for it varied with changes in technology, the economy, and union strength. Vancouver tailors and cigarmakers were unionized from 1889 to 1910 and beyond, but were unable to cope with the employers' ability to introduce machinery. Their wages and conditions steadily worsened throughout this period. Other unions, such as metal workers and machinists, saw their income and status threatened, and they responded by abandoning labourism for more radical and militant doctrines. In the early years of the Vancouver Trades and Labour Council, though, the printing, building trades, and other unions that dominated the labour movement were largely able to defend their crafts and were not much interested in revolution. This conservative-leaning labour aristocracy intersected with the labour bureaucracy of the VTLC. Most of the leaders of the movement and most of the delegates and officers of the council came from this stratum of the working class. Regardless of whether these leaders held down more radical workers or represented their comrades accurately, they did not work to abolish capitalism or foment revolution. Because these men set the formal agenda for the labour movement, the political demands of organized labour reflected their position and their view of the world.[37]

5

Culture and Community

Despite the similarities in income and even their class position, strong differences remained between the labour aristocrats and the middle class. Unlike the middle class, the trade unionists of the VTLC often held to cultural and moral values that emphasized the working class and a limited class struggle. The labour aristocrat often maintained a strong sense of occupational and class identification, and it was the skilled trade unionist who set out the culture of union solidarity, labour ethics, and militancy. In Vancouver this code was first created in trade unions, but it was articulated chiefly in the newspapers and pronouncements of the labour council. In this way the aristocrats and bureaucrats were responsible for both labour's conservatism and its militancy.[1]

This culture was a mixture of class conflict and collaboration. It borrowed elements from the culture of the larger society, created some of its own, and sought to incorporate working-class traditions into day-to-day life. Much of this culture was the work of the leaders of the labour movement, rather than of the rank and file. Union officials and delegates to the VTLC set down rules for conduct, organized events, and planned the campaigns to instill in workers the proper attitude towards the union label, politics, and recreation. What they sought was not so much a spontaneous working-class culture but an official, controlled union culture that helped skilled workers come together as a class for specific ends on terms decided upon by the bureaucracy. Such a top-down relationship, however, could divide workers as well as unite them, and in this division it is possible to see the strengths and weaknesses of bureaucracy.

The most important cultural event in the union calendar was Labour Day. From the beginning, it was celebrated by Vancouver workers in September, not May Day, the day favoured by socialists and European workers.[2] The day was filled with activities, and the parade, games, eating, music, and dances brought together workers from all unions and trades. The first Labour Day, held in 1890, was a credit to the organizing abilities of the fledgling VTLC. The parade procession was three-quarters of a mile long and wound its way for two and a half miles from the city core at Cambie and Hastings to a ferry that took everyone to Brockton Point in Stanley Park. Banners proclaimed the unions that marched, bands played, and the parade was led by the VTLC president Joseph Dixon, who, 'on a gallant bay, assigned the various bodies to their proper place with great tact.' The planning of the parade, as well as the decorum and composure of its marchers, surprised many observers and reinforced the labour movement's insistence that its demands were fair, just, and non-threatening to the community. A reporter for the Vancouver *World* observed that 'those who pictured to themselves that labor organizations were composed chiefly of rash and irresponsible young men, were surprised at the thoughtful hearing, orderly conduct, and intelligent faces of the processionists. A large number of middle aged and elderly faces were noticed in the line.' The chief speaker at the festival spoke to applause when he put forward his labourist, gradualist position. 'Who was it,' he asked, who 'produced the wealth of the world? Why, the worker. Who enjoys the greater part of the blessings given by that wealth? Not the producer, but those who were enabled by the unjust laws to take advantage of him.' To remedy this, he continued, workers had to unite to change the laws. To the rhetorical question of who should be recognized as the best subject, he answered, 'He who produces the wealth.' The final goal of the labour movement, he concluded, was 'to bring about the time when each man shall enjoy the just rewards of his labor, when, as the Good Book says, if a man labors not, neither shall he eat.'[3]

Subsequent Labour Days followed a similar pattern. Athletic events proved popular, and in 1893 the games included bicycle races, running races, a sack race, a three-legged race, and a one-hundred yard fat man's race. Joseph Waldrop, a Populist from Portland, Oregon, spoke to the crowd, and local Indians were featured in the parade. The council arranged for cheap ferry rides to take people to the events and funded the celebration with a per capita levy of twenty-five cents, with the stipulation that unions would contribute further assessments if a deficit were incurred. Such precautions were unnecessary that year, for the council was left with a balance of nearly fifty dollars, but the willingness to risk a debt illustrates how important the ceremonies of Labour Day were to the fiscally conservative leadership.[4] The following year saw a downturn in the economy, and the reduced labour movement was forced to cancel the procession of the trades. Other celebrations continued to be held, however. The city band marched and then headed to North Vancouver to play during a picnic organized by the VTLC. Workers and their families played games and listened to speeches from MPs and MLAs who were friendly to labour. The afternoon was filled with dancing and a baby show, and the evening saw a 'grand concert' in the Market Hall. J.C. Brown, future finance minister in Joe Martin's provincial government of 1900, was brought in from New Westminster to give an address on 'the Labor question.'[5]

Over time, however, Labour Day did less and less to bring workers together and remind them of their common aspirations. The ceremonies and activities began to lose their labour trappings, and the day became hard to distinguish from other holidays. From the first, local politicians and businessmen, not all of whom could be considered genuine friends of labour, were invited to take part in the activities. Businessmen were also counted on to participate in the events. As early as 1894 the labour council noted that only 'through the liberality of the Businessmen in the city' was it 'able to present an attractive program.' Thus, in that year parade floats representing local factories and businesses rode beside those of carpenters and tailors. With the contributions of money came parade floats bearing the banners of local factories and businesses. By 1898 Labour Day had changed substantially. The games were there, as people played and watched lacrosse, tugs of war, and sack races; a successful smoker was held in the city hall. But the customary march through the streets was no longer called the 'procession of trades'; now it was the 'Industrial Parade.' Unions and workers contributed banners and marchers, but they were outnumbered by floats hawking the wares of the Royal City Planing Mill, local soap manufacturers, hardware merchants, an advertising agency, and the Sons of the British Empire. No longer was the parade led by a proud unionist on a prancing steed. Instead, it was headed by the militia band, followed by the police and the fire department. Fourth in line came the VTLC contingent. Many attended the concert and the smoker, but there were no speeches on 'the labour question' to remind workers why they had marched together. Instead of cheering the speeches of fiery orators, spectators cheered those who competed in athletic events for prizes put up by local businesses.[6]

The following year's Labour Day was another illustration of the VTLC's desire for some degree of class collaboration and the incorporation of labour into the larger society. The day was dominated by corporate sponsors, including the Conservative *Province* newspaper, the Imperial Bank, the fish-canning Bell–Irving Company, and the B.C. Electric Tramway Company. Business floats were by far the most prominent. Prizes were given to the best float in three categories: merchants, manufacturers, and unions. Significantly, the first two categories were awarded a prize of forty dollars each; the best union float on Labour Day had to content itself with a first prize of only twenty dollars. The traditional smoker featured songs, boxing matches, military drills, banjo and cornet solos, sketches, and dances, but no speakers were brought in to rally workers and make them aware of their own traditions and cause. If Labour Day had any political purpose, it was to reassure business and the state that the union movement was not a threat to them. In 1897 an editorial in the *World* noted that in Germany and France, and even in 'Conservative England,' Labour Day had some socialist colouring and evoked the traditions of rebellion in Anglo-Saxon cultures that were symbolized by myths of Robin Hood and the like. But 'even this,' the writer maintained, 'when examined carefully will not be found to be cause for alarm for the principle of true democracy.' To those who still feared the spectre of workers marching in the street, the *World* soothed that 'Labor Day in Canada has no meaning or significance if it fails to offer all classes of fellow-citizens a message of peace and good will.'[7]

Other manifestations of trade union culture sent out dual messages of conflict and collaboration. The labour council delegates made sure that the deaths of their fellow workers and supporters were properly mourned and that their services and sacrifices for the movement were known to all. When a founder of the VTLC died in 1894, the council gave a stirring tribute in language that echoed labourist values. Duncan McRae, it solemnly noted, had 'filled the office of Treasurer and served on committees with credit to himself and honor to the council.' He was 'always on watch to oppose any legislation that in his opinion was not in the best interests of the working men,' and his work on committees was 'exact and painstaking.' In private life, the notice continued, he was 'always of an optimistic disposition, reflecting in his conduct the qualities of Faith, Hope, and Charity, and was in every respect a good and desirable citizen.' In conclusion, the council resolved to express its sympathy to McRae's family, to forward a copy of the resolution to them, and to record the tribute in the official minutes. In similar fashion the council mourned the death of Catherine Maxwell, mother of Liberal–Labour MP George Maxwell, who was a 'favored son' of the VTLC. Thus, the labour bureaucracy looked after its own and buried its dead, extending the world of the union movement to take in not just politics and wages but life and death.[8]

Such cultural ties were not always removed from financial concerns, however. When United Brotherhood of Railway Employees organizer Frank Rogers was murdered by CPR police in 1903, the VTLC was quick to organize memorial services, pay for a wreath and a funeral band, and to call upon all union men to attend the funeral. This solidarity was somewhat marred, however, by the subsequent haggling over who would pay for the funeral itself. Nearly a year after Rogers's death, the council refused to pay the funeral director's bill of $97, arguing that 'it would be a dangerous precedent for the council to assume this or any other unpaid account of the UBRE as in that case we might be saddled with them all.'[9]

Mourning ceremonies were also used to reinforce labour's identification with other classes and the nation. A resolution of condolence was passed when John A. Macdonald died in 1891, and delegates spoke of his accomplishments. If the passing of the Old Chieftain was a momentous occasion that transcended class, surely such could not be said of the death of John Thompson in 1894. Despite his lacklustre tenure as prime minister for a little more than two years, the council was impelled to express 'its sorrow [over] the death of Canada's eminent statesman the Right Honorable Sir John S.W. [sic] Thompson.' It extended to 'Lady Thompson and family the council's earnest sympathy in their sad bereavement,' and ordered a letter containing these sentiments sent to the widow. Odder still was the eulogy for the Republican president William McKinley. McKinley had been assassinated by an anarchist and the *Independent* went to great lengths to dissociate the labour movement from the act. Even though McKinley had defeated the liberal, populist William Jennings Bryan and had taken the United States into the Spanish–American war, the *Independent* still gushed that 'no man ever held high office who provoked fewer enmities or had such a multitude of friends. His personal integrity and the purity of his political and private life made his political career one typical of the best of American public men.'[10] These eulogies indicate that the labour leaders did not always see themselves in opposition to capital and the government. Rather they sought to insert labour into a more prominent place in the workings of the nation. The death of a Tory politician or an imperialist president required the intervention of the labour council as much as the death of one of its own members, and in this way the labour leaders blended working class culture and ideology into the larger society.

At the same time the council did work to create and instill a culture of militancy in the union movement, and it laid down rules and an ethic for workers. The leadership taught that the cause of labour was more than enlightened self-interest, for in advancing their interests, unionists were advancing civilization. As one editorial in the council paper put it,

At this time the trades union movement is engaged in the noble effort to secure the eight-hour workday for the overburdened toilers, and create the opportunity for work for the unemployed; to rescue the children from the factory and the workshops, and to place them into the school-room and into the playground; to secure a better and higher life for every man, woman, and child; to mentally improve themselves and to educate the educated ignorants that self-interest is best advanced 'when each man sees in another's good, the establishment of man's brotherhood.' The sooner all are enrolled in the unions of labor, the earlier will come the day for improvement in home and life, and the dawn of the brighter day for which the whole world has struggled.[11]

In addition to this lofty vision, the labour council established a practical code of behaviour for the good trade unionist. From the beginning, the VTLC held that the ballot was crucial for working men, and it urged them to get on the voters' list and make use of the franchise. At one of its first meetings the council resolved that it was necessary to canvass workers and to show them 'that only by having their names on the several voters' lists can they ever hope to secure ... the elevation of the working classes, mentally, morally, and physically.' Careful, conscientious attention to the workers' business was another part of their moral code, and early in 1892 the council passed a resolution that would allow it to seek the removal of delegates who missed more than two consecutive meetings.[12]

If the council were to survive, it needed money, and the labour leaders set out to make the paying of dues another moral imperative. Francis Williams, a tailor, council officer, and VTLC provincial candidate in 1900, stressed the need for unionists to keep up their dues, even when they were unemployed. Dues equalled solidarity, and the failure to provide them constituted a moral lapse. Even worse were those short-sighted workers who dropped out of their union to get 'more work at a lower price.' Williams pilloried 'These men [who] have no proper respect for themselves. They do not care for their fellows. They injure their craft for the basest motive. They plunge into a depth of moral degradation themselves, and worse still they "carry others" with them.' Other groups had learned the value of solidarity, Williams continued, but 'when will working men learn to have the same eye to their present and future welfare as the physician, the lawyer, and the capitalist? To this last we might add the preacher. All these men know the value of union and cooperation. By this means they have obtained and retain special immunities and privileges. But the worker, who ultimately considered is the brain, nerve, and muscle of the nation, is, as far as organization is concerned, only a rope of sand.'[13] The article illustrates the attempt of the labour bureaucracy to appeal to a culture and moral code that would inspire workers to move beyond their selfish concerns and work for the common good. That these dues would be used, in part, to pay for the candidacy of Williams and others need not diminish the sentiment.

Good, effective trade unionism also meant rewarding labour's friends and depriving its foes of support. This could be done effectively, and at little cost to the unionists, with the boycott and the union label. These tactics were important symbols of union ethics and political awareness, and the *Independent* put the case firmly:

The wage-earner who will spend even a single cent over the counter of a merchant who he knows to be unfriendly to the welfare of the toilers is playing deliberately into the hands of his enemies ... There is no reason why the workers should invest or spend one cent to support their enemies. There are enough merchants friendly to the cause of labor to do all the trading of the laboring class, and what is more they are honestly entitled to the trade ... Even an idiot would laugh at the idea of the British soldiers putting rifles in the hands of the Boers to use against themselves, but it is not one whit more foolish than to put money into the pocket of the merchant who would like to down you ... [I]f you have an ounce of common sense in your make-up you should know enough to stand by your friends, and when you do so you will be making friends to stand by you.[14]

Printers made similar claims and won the support of the central labour council for a resolution condemning 'businessmen, storekeepers, and societies that had their printing done elsewhere,' as 'this is detrimental to the master printers, the entire printing business, and the city's best interests.' This was followed up by a call for the city council to have its bylaws printed locally. Since most of the large printshops of the city were unionized, this was in effect a call for the union label on these products.[15]

Other unions too made the union label one of the acid tests of labour culture. Support for it provided a simple way to determine allies and signify one's own support for the cause. Thus, in 1892 the VTLC voted to have its affiliates fine their members who patronized non-union shops. More often moral suasion was used to remind union workers of their duty. One editorial asked, 'Do you believe in trades unionism? Are you a union man? If so, see to it that you purchase, whenever possible, union-made articles. The cigars you smoke should bear a blue label, the clothes you wear should carry the label of the Tailors' Union, the bread you eat should carry the label of the Bakers' Union, and the stationery you use and the printing you order should both bear the impression of the Typographical union, and last, but not least, have your superfluous hirsute appendages removed by a member of the Barbers' union.' The virtues of the union shave were further lauded in verse:

They found him in the gutter
In a most appalling state;
His face was cut and bleeding,
His sufferings were great.
Said one: 'Some foul assassin
Tried to send him to his grave';
But between his groans he muttered,
' 'Twas a ten-cent shave.'
A crowd began to gather,
And then two policemen came;
They tried for many minutes
To ascertain his name.
An ambulance was sent for
He continued still to rave,
And the only words he uttered
Were 'A ten-cent shave.'
It proved, sad to relate,
To be his final ride;
For when he reached the hospital
'Twas found that he had died.
The coroner held an inquest
And the verdict that he gave
Was 'This man has been the victim
Of a ten-cent shave.'[16]

Because the union label was so important and so difficult to enforce, on occasion the campaign for it could reach almost ridiculous heights. In 1902 the VTLC passed a resolution that all delegates were to wear at least one article of clothing with the union label. A special committee was struck to inspect the delegates' clothes every three months. This quickly prompted the question, who shall guard the guards themselves? After 'some discussion' it was resolved that the president of the council would be responsible for examining the members of the label committee to see if they themselves had the requisite union label.[17]

The solidarity of the union label campaign was especially hard to enforce when it forced workers to choose between their dual roles of producers and consumers. Here the so-called free-rider problem created tensions between a leadership that tried to create and instill the principles of good unionism and a less-visionary membership. It was one thing to pay dues to remain in the union and receive higher wages as a result, but supporting other workers by paying more for union-made goods and services meant putting one's money where one's mouth was. The high cost of union-made products often put them out of the reach of local workers, while shopping only at unionized stores could be expensive and inconvenient. Many Vancouver unionists failed to meet the standard of ethics outlined by the VTLC. As a result the retail clerks union foundered, largely because other unionists failed to ask for the clerks' union card when shopping. The union of waiters and waitresses regularly complained that organizing was difficult because too many workers preferred to eat in non-union restaurants and hotels, while cigarmakers regularly deplored the stench of non-union cigars evident even at council meetings.[18]

Even at its best, however, the union label was divisive. As often as it was used to promote solidarity, it was used to discriminate against Asian workers. Even while it reminded its readers of the virtues of solidarity, the *Independent* was quick to point out that 'the presence of the blue label of the International Cigarmakers' Union on any box of cigars is a guarantee that it isn't made by Chinamen or in sweatshops. Remember the golden rule.' Vancouver workers were also warned that a Victoria brewer 'employed Chinamen to a large extent' and that they should buy their beer from a local branch that 'paid out $1200 per month in wages chiefly to white men.'[19]

The union label could also be used as a way to minimize class conflict. George Bartley, editor of the *Independent*, praised and reprinted an article written by an AFL organizer that maintained that the union label 'supersedes the strike, the lock-out, and the destructive boycott. It is the outward manifestation of harmony between employer and workmen, binding both parties to maintain their friendly relations and the continued approval and patronage of a discriminating public.' Thus, even a principle such as the union label could be used simultaneously to increase class awareness and reinforce racism and class collaboration. The point is not that the union label was bad. Rather it is that the the labour movement was sectional and divided along lines of race, income, and even occupation. Creating a culture and code of ethics was fraught with contradictions and competing interests. The labour bureaucracy of the VTLC had to tread carefully as it tried to reconcile the need for discipline and solidarity with the particular and even selfish demands of the workers it represented. It is not surprising perhaps that its policies therefore were cautious and limited, rather than sweeping and bold.[20]

Another important element of the official labour culture was politics. But entering the political arena also carried some consequences for the ideology of the labour leaders. Organized labour did not make up the majority of the city's population; indeed, unionists did not even make up a majority of the workforce. In 1891 the city's workforce totalled about 5,000, roughly 40 per cent of the population of 13,000. By 1911 the total workforce was a little over half of the city's 100,000 residents, but wage-earners numbered about 33,000. Unionized workers, almost exclusively white men, were a subset of this figure. Vancouver's unionized sector made up about 15 per cent of the workforce, a figure that corresponds roughly to the rate of unionization for the province and the nation.[21] This ratio was hardly unique to Vancouver or to North America, and it carried some implications for political action. Simple arithmetic demonstrated that organized workers could not expect to control the electoral process at the municipal, provincial, or federal levels. As a result, the labour bureaucracy set out to seek alliances with other classes. When the question of 'a working man's candidate or a platform suitable for working men' was first taken up by the VTLC in 1890, George Irvine noted that at best 'working men had the balance of power' rather than a clear majority, and president Joe Dixon argued that if the council were to take part in elections, 'the best way was to cooperate with the business men.' In 1894, when labour took part in the short-lived Nationalist party, it tried unsuccessfully to work in conjunction with the province's farmers.[22]

The provincial election of 1900 reinforced the need for cross-alliances, at least in the minds of the VTLC leadership. The council put forward two candidates, Joe Dixon and Francis Williams, but the two did poorly in the polls. In the aftermath of the election Williams argued that if labour wanted to triumph it would have to drop its appeal to class consciousness and reach out to other groups. It was necessary, he wrote, to win over those outside the labour movement. The craft unions had to approach 'unorganized labour,' 'for these are our brothers in heart and mind and the right hand of fellowship belongs to them.' But if this hinted at a greater class solidarity, Williams also insisted that it was necessary to woo those 'who do not belong to the "horny-handed sons of toil," yet who are workers in the true sense of the word. Merchants and office men, who realizing that a prosperous working class always means a prosperous mercantile class, were with us in word and act.' Williams evoked the rhetoric of populism to call for labour to help form a 'Reform league, or a People's league,' to elect a 'government by and for the people, instead of as heretofore by and for the classes.'[23]

This appeal across class lines was taken up again in 1901. The VTLC's parliamentary committee reported that if the true cause of reform 'is to make steady, substantial progress, it must be instituted and carried out on broad, liberal, lines, care being taken that all sections of those interested in reform be duly represented from its very inception.' Labour should go into politics to support its principles and friends, but the committee was 'opposed to a movement of this kind of any class claiming a monopoly to rule, not only over itself, but over all other classes.' Instead, labour should work to include 'all men engaged in productive industry, whether *employees or employers*, and whether members of trades-unions or not, so long as they are in sympathy with the cause.' Thus, political action tended to push labour leaders to consider expanding class solidarity to the unskilled and simultaneously push them to seek alliances with 'progressive' elements of the middle class.[24]

The labour council could also be used as a platform to bring union leaders into the elite circles of the city and to launch political careers. This tended to make them identify their interests with the community, rather than their class, as they had to appeal to a broad, interclass electorate. J.L. Franklin of the carpenters union served as a delegate to the VTLC in 1891, becoming a member of its Labour Day committee and treasurer of the council. In 1892 Franklin worked on the council's parliamentary committee and, from there, launched a successful aldermanic campaign, running with the endorsement of the VTLC. Bartley ran successfully for the parks board in 1900, again under the banner of the VTLC, while the following year saw John Morton, former council vice-president, and J.H. Watson make unsuccessful attempts to win election as alderman and school trustee, respectively. Morton was more successful in 1903, when he became an alderman for Ward 5 and held the job until 1906. Similarly, Francis Williams, VTLC financial secretary in 1900, then secretary from 1904 to 1905, sat as alderman for Ward 6 from 1904 to 1906. The labour bureaucrats actively sought positions as city licence commissioners, who were responsible for the granting of liquor licences. Robert Todd, ITU delegate and VTLC trustee, received the council's endorsement for the position in 1901, while Samuel Gothard, active in the ITU since 1895, and a perennial delegate to the labour council from 1900, ran as a labour candidate in 1902 and 1903. Some, such as Frank Russell, could move from being a delegate from the Freight Handlers' Union to the vice-presidency and secretaryship of the labour council, and from there to appointed government positions. When Russell was appointed by Premier McBride to help enforce the immigration act, this was widely regarded as a victory for labour; it also gave considerable power and status to Russell.[25]

In this way unpaid careers in the labour movement could be parlayed into political careers and thus help elevate the status of the labour bureaucrat. Though parks and licence commissioners served without salary, aldermen were paid, and the issue of their salaries was an important one for labour leaders. Arguing that their wages as workmen made it difficult to volunteer their services as aldermen, the council advocated aldermanic salaries of $400 a year in 1894, about half a year's wages for a skilled workman who could find steady employment. Although workers were hardly in a position to give up evenings and other time to carry out the city's business, the salaries did open up the possibility to improve both labour's position and the position of the successful labour politician. Political action gave labour a voice, while at the same time it integrated labour leaders into the larger community. The commitment to community that participation in municipal politics implied carried with it a commitment to compromise on the issue of class. This was necessary, first, to allow labour candidates to appeal to a wider audience and, second, to allow labour politicians to work with politicians from other classes.

Membership in the VTLC could also help leaders work with business in less-formal settings. The skills acquired by the labour leaders of the VTLC from organizing events such as Labour Day, for example, allowed them to forge personal relations and alliances with members of other classes. This usually worked to replace class consciousness with a community consciousness that sought to minimize class conflict. As early as 1890 George Bartley met with Vancouver politicians and businessmen to plan the celebration of Dominion Day. The twenty-three-year-old printer worked with such notables as R.G. Tatlow, real estate speculator and later, finance minister in Conservative Premier Richard McBride's first cabinet; Dr Bell-Irving of the fish cannery dynasty; *World* editor J.M. O'Brien; newspaper owner and maverick politician F. Carter-Cotton; Bank of Montreal manager C. Sweeney; city coroner Dr McGuigan; store owner Charles E. Tisdall, another Conservative who later would become mayor of the city and the anti-labour Premier Bowser's minister of public works in 1915; and Mayor David Oppenheimer, dry-goods merchant, real estate speculator, former mayor, and head of the Westminster and Vancouver Tramway Company. Bartley was made secretary of this committee in 1893, and continued as a member for several years. One of his duties as secretary was to write a thank-you letter on behalf of the committee to the CPR, the long-time foe of populists and labourists alike, expressing gratitude for the special round-trip fare the company laid on for the celebration. Paid fifty dollars – the better part of a month's pay – for his role, Bartley also issued appeals for money to the city's inhabitants. He was aware that such appeals had to go beyond class lines, and the wording suggests that to the degree that Bartley saw himself as a spokesman for the city, he placed less emphasis on class conflict. Community, not class, was the key element in his press release. Bartley requested money, not for any 'private or corporate object,' but rather for 'the purpose of celebrating the confederation of the Dominion, and keeping our national holiday in a manner becoming a progressive and up-to-date city like Vancouver. It is consequently a fund to which every citizen having Vancouver's best interests at heart should contribute.' His 1900 appeal to workers to support Dominion Day was even more placating. Bartley called upon unionists to put aside class differences for the good of the community. 'Whatever the politics of the individual may be,' he urged, 'we are learning more and more as the years roll by the lesson of toleration.' Similarly, S.J. Gothard, ITU delegate and secretary, and vice-secretary and editor in later years, moved freely between the labour camp and the civic offices, serving as the Grand Marshal of the Labour Day parade in 1900 and the Dominion Day secretary the following year.[26]

In 1897 Bartley helped plan the city's celebration of Queen Victoria's Diamond Jubilee. When he again became involved in the Labour Day committee in 1899, it no doubt seemed natural and correct to change the focus of the day from being a celebration of workers to a more general holiday open to all and with little political content. The decisions to make the 1898 Labour Day more of an exercise in class collaboration partly reflected the ability of its chief architect, J.H. Watson, to fit in with both the union movement and the political club of the Liberal party. It could be argued that such cooperative relations between labour leaders and the city's business and political leaders could give labour a stronger voice and perhaps a better hearing. It is equally arguable that the ability of these leaders to mingle with politicians and businessmen showed them that class lines were not fixed, that working men could work with and benefit from collaborating with elements of the bourgeoisie. This upward mobility was limited to a handful of privileged working-class leaders and depended on a labour leader playing down class conflict, at least while sitting on the committees. It could be rationalized away on the grounds that it was better to have labour represented at the highest levels than to remain outside the formal and informal corridors of power. Socialist critiques of their action could easily be dismissed as the jealous whining of those who were denied access to the inner circle. At the same time, however, it is likely that working with their erstwhile class opponents diminished the fire of class conflict in these labour leaders.[27]

Such unity with the civic officials and business leaders was not complete or without criticism of the middle class. When the Duke and Duchess of Cornwall and York (later George V and Queen Mary) visited Vancouver in 1901, the labour paper strenuously objected to the 'fuss and flummery' of the city elite. Proclaiming its loyalty to Britain and the monarchy, the newspaper maintained that 'the plain people are quite good enough to receive and entertain royalty in a plain and hospitable fashion.' It opposed the 'epidemic of snobbery' that had infected the city and denounced the 'so-called "upper set" of British Columbia.' One reader, signed 'Gander,' put the sentiment in a verse entitled 'The Duke':

> The Dook an' his old bloomin' family is comin'
> 'Ark to ther geese comin' over ther plains;
> Cacklin' an' squackin' an' scrapin'
> an' cacklin' and squackin' an' lowin' agen'.
> 'Ark to ther geese thet we 'ave in our city
> Each one apickin' the other one's down.
> Tryin' ter prove thet 'e isn't ther fittest
> Ter welcome ther bigger geese into ther town.
> Feathers an' frills an' some gold-painted plumage
> What are they all when you've added the sum?
> Back to yer work. Don't be standin' an' gapin'
> Keep to yer slavin' an' let ther geese come.
> Ye are the workers an' they are the shirkers.
> Ye feed an' clothe every goose in the flock.
> Ye live by work an' the geese live by lyin'.
> Don't yet be trying the geese fer to mock.[28]

Thus, the culture of this generation of labour leaders cannot simply be understood as 'embourgeoisement' or a simple absorption into middle-class mores. Though much of it did represent alliances and similarities with the middle class, the culture – the experience – of the union bureaucrats was filtered through their own lives as working people. Their responses to social events were not identical with those of the middle class; by the same token, they were not necessarily identical with those of the rank and file or of the factory hand.

Recreation was another cultural arena for the labour movement that demonstrated the contradictory pressures of class conflict and collaboration that worked on the VTLC leadership. When steel baron Andrew Carnegie offered the city of Vancouver an endowment to establish a new library, the *Independent* heatedly informed its readers that 'Mr Carnegie's money, morally speaking, belongs to the poor, down-trodden people who work for him in Pennsylvania.' Although it stopped short of calling for the city to refuse the money, the paper reminded workers that far from philanthropy, the $50,000 was 'an unwilling gift from the ironworkers of that state.'[29]

Unfair treatment by civic officials in allocating park space and time could easily be turned into a conflict of classes, as it was in 1900. When the elitist Vancouver Cricket Club monopolized the cricket grounds at Stanley Park, the labour paper lashed out at those who trod on the right of the workers to equal time. There was, the paper editorialized, now 'little chance for the man who works for a living ever getting a chance for a game.' This stood in marked contrast to England, 'the home of cricket,' where the sport was 'essentially democratic, all meeting on a common ground.' The Vancouver Cricket Club, however, barred non-members and showed little respect for the game. In the hands of bankers and the like, 'it takes on more of the aspect of an afternoon affair, and in reporting a game more space is given to the ladies' gowns and "dear Charlie's waistcoat, just too sweet for anything," than to the play. Let the people, though, take a greater interest in the park, and the remedy is in their own hands.'[30]

This fight over the use of parks was not an isolated one. The council's interest in recreation and green space dates from the Deadman's Island dispute and before. As early as 1891 the VTLC called for public beaches. In August 1895 the council requested the city to clear rocks from bathing beaches and to put out depth buoys and a lifeboat. Later in the month the council protested the 'monopoly' that the Brockton Point Athletic Association exercised over a section of Stanley Park. Labour delegates were especially incensed over a $10,000 loan the association had received from the city to clear and maintain its site. Since the association made non-members pay for the use of its section of the park, the VTLC charged that working people were effectively 'debarred from entering such grounds without being taxed practically twice.' To provide equal access to recreational grounds for all, the council resolved that a 'portion of [the] English Bay side of Stanley Park be cleared, levelled, and sowed with grass, the same to be known as the Vancouver Public Park.' The debate continued for over a year as the labour council fought to prevent the selling of foreshore rights and to create a public park. In 1898 the council passed a resolution calling for municipal voters to support a referendum that would enable the city to buy lots that would be turned into parks to provide 'breathing spaces' for the residents. Voters were urged to band together to stop 'some of the larger tax-payers in this city [who] intend to kill the [proposed] by-law.' Despite the activity of the VTLC, the city did not build parks for working people. Instead, local groups, 'usually dominated by those in business,' pressured the municipal government to create parks in the wealthier areas. The city council, then as now, listened more carefully to the rich and powerful. As a result, neighbourhoods such as Kitsilano and Grandview had parks early on; working-class districts had virtually no park space until well into the twentieth century.[31]

Recreation could cross class lines as well as delineate them. Sports and unionism could meet on one issue: the shorter work week. The *Independent* noted approvingly that 'the lacrosse boys are a fine lot of fellows, whose sympathies are with the Saturday half-holiday movement. They know that if their patrons can get off on Saturday afternoons they will be sure to take in the matches.' At the same time, sports could bring men together across lines of class and occupation, in the classless, male atmosphere of the locker room and the clubhouse. The *Independent*'s suggestion that patrons and employees would both gain if Saturday afternoons were given over to lacrosse is an example of the labourist belief that there was no essential contradiction between employers and employed and that class conflict could and should be forgotten once all were in their team uniforms. Such a description appears to fit George Bartley who, as president of the Vancouver Lacrosse Club, worked and played with men from different classes without hostility. Bartley served as toastmaster at a going-away party held at the Merchants' Exchange for one of the club's members, A.E. 'Bones' Suckling, who was about to leave the city to take up 'a lucrative position as traveller for Brenner Bros., the well-known tobacco and cigar manufacturers of London, Ontario.' Bartley led the club in toasts to the queen, the army, and the navy, and supported the speech of the secretary who suggested that the businessmen of the lacrosse club should hire the better players, so they could devote more time to the sport. This would 'foster ... healthy lacrosse,' while circumventing the taint of professionalism.[32]

Thus, culture and community could work for and work against class conflict in this period. Even as the labour bureaucracy buried and eulogized its dead, it praised Conservative politicians. Labour Day parades showed labour's might, then suggested that capital and labour could and should peacefully co-exist. Enforcing the union label was a way to impose discipline and solve the free-rider problem of the labour movement, but it also made it possible to discriminate against Asian and women workers. Visions of community could unite workers to fight for park space, but recreation and sport could blur class lines.

Even working class politics, as articulated by the leaders of the VTLC, sought to unite workers and to make overtures to capital at the same time. Their position as labour aristocrats and labour bureaucrats gave these leaders privileged access to politics, civic committees, and business leaders. This cooperation flowed naturally from the ideas of labourism and was believed necessary given labour's relative weakness, but it also worked against class conflict. To the degree that the VTLC leaders saw themselves as members of the community, rather than as members of a class, their culture, even their political culture, became more conservative and compromising. As the men most responsible for shaping formal working-class culture and politics, their own vision of labour politics put a conservative stamp on the whole union movement. This does not mean the labour bureaucrats were class traitors who should have been socialists; rather it suggests that it would have been nearly impossible for them to become socialists, for everything in their experience demonstrated that change and success were possible within the system. Because of their class experience and their experience as labour leaders, the working-class culture they sought to create was a peculiar blend of militancy and pacifism, conflict and collaboration.

6

Relations of Race and Gender

The ideology of the VTLC leaders went beyond political action and trade unionism. If class was one important element of their world-view, so too were race and gender. The bureaucratic control of the union structure, institutions, and policies by a handful of white, Anglo-Saxon males had important consequences for those who did not fall into the same categories. Women and other races were ignored, even attacked by the labour council throughout its first twenty years. Ironically, in calling for measures that most today would find abhorrent, the labour leaders were acting in accordance with the sentiments of those they repesented. Far from being the preserve of a more conservative bureaucracy, racism and sexism were in the mainstream of the labour movement, and the make-up and structure of the labour council ensured that changing these ideas would be a slow process.[1]

The nature of racism in the British Columbia working class has been the most debated issue in the province's labour historiography. Two competing explanations have been advanced. Historians such as W. Peter Ward have maintained that racism 'was a daily experience, a living reality in a way that class among whites seldom was.'[2] Other historians have pointed out that this view is in essence 'idealist,' for it is based on a notion that a prevailing 'social psychology' and preconceived ideas create racism. Insisting on a materialist explanation, that is, one that maintains that ideas arise from social conditions rather than innate characteristics, these writers have quite properly argued that racism cannot be understood outside of the 'explicitly racist captialist social relations.' When Chinese labourers were brought to British Columbia's coal mines by employers, for example, it was with the explicit intention of using them to drive down wages and to break trade unions. In this context, transferring labour conflict into racism was an easy, if deplorable, step.[3] It is not so clear, however, that these two conceptions of racism need be mutually exclusive.[4] American historians have been able to argue that social psychology and economic conditions blended together to form the particular racism of the labour movement. Alexander Saxton points out that white workers in California were 'both exploited and exploiters' as they were forced to compete with the cheaper labour of non-whites and benefited from the low wages paid to Chinese. Acknowledging that workers were structured into racism and that the labour market was indeed segmented by occupation and colour, Saxton insists that the 'cheap labour' argument is inadequate. White workers did not respond in the same way to the threat of cheap Irish and Slavic labour, and trades that had no fear of competition were often in the forefront of the anti-Asian agitation. Hostility towards the Chinese and Japanese was 'composed of a rational economic argument mingled with and disguising an older complex of ideas and emotions,' including a pioneer ethic, nativism, pride of craft, and xenophobia.[5]

In his study of the San Francisco building trades, Michael Kazin has similarly argued that the craft union movement was 'not merely a device to press the economic demands of its members but a bulwark against the incursion of a hostile race.' Kazin maintains that belief in class solidarity and racism 'did not pose an agonizing contradiction ... for white labor leaders.' On the contrary, both were vital for their self-defence as they defined it.[6] In Vancouver, as in San Francisco, racism was complex and enmeshed in labour ideology and politics. The economics and social relations of capitalism have strong explanatory power. However, they alone do not account for the depths of the hostility expressed by the delegates of the Vancouver Trades and Labour Council, and this explanation does not easily account for their strong sense of ethnicity.

Within the VTLC, a highly developed racial consciousness coexisted with class consciousness. Indeed, the two often seem to be completely intertwined, and sorting out the relationship is a complex task. It is hard to hold to a strict economic theory that sees racism as a response to competition for jobs and wages, for neither the bureaucrats of the VTLC nor the union members they represented were actually threatened by Asian labour. Asians were restricted to work in mining, the lumber industry, salmon canning, market-gardening, domestic service, laundering, tailoring, and fishing. Even in these sectors, whites and Asians were often separated by geography, as Chinese workers were often employed in and by the Chinese community itself and tended to settle in specific areas of the city and the province. None of the unions affiliated to the VTLC in its early days represented workers in these occupations, and none of the unions was interested in organizing in these areas. There was no competition for wages or jobs between whites and Asians in Vancouver, and no reasonable fear that Asian labour would in any way affect the economic interests of the union movement or its leaders. When whites did try to organize in industries in which other races were employed, such as fishing, they quickly learned that success meant organizing all races. The economic explanation for racism, then, must be more subtle than that put forward by most of its adherents. Although they are correct to observe that ideas do not form in a vacuum and that any system that gives power, wealth, and privilege to a few will create other divisions, the racism of the labour bureaucracy must be understood as a more complicated issue.

Racism or, more precisely, Asian exclusion, was an urgent matter for the VTLC from its start. One of the first committees drawn up by the council was a joint standing committee on lien laws and alien labour. Two issues – ensuring that workers were paid for their toil and barring Asians – were thus placed high on the council's agenda. The committee was a powerful one, made up of Joseph Dixon, president of the carpenters and of the council itself; Duncan McRae, treasurer of the VTLC; and George Bartley, perennial ITU executive, founding member of the trades and labour council, and future president.

At its fourth meeting, the council voted unanimously to support a recent deal worked out between the city and B.T. Rogers, an American businessman supported by the CPR. Rogers wanted concessions from the municipal government to set up a sugar refinery in Vancouver. The city council agreed to give Rogers and his B.C. Sugar Refining Company a $30,000 grant, a fifteen-year tax waiver, and free water for ten years. William Pleming, spokesman for the VTLC, informed the city that labour was in favour of progress and industry, but it would vigorously oppose the granting of concessions if Rogers were to employ Chinese workers. Once Rogers promised that he would not hire Chinese, the VTLC voted to support the deal. A year later, the full extent of the labour council's opposition to Asian labour was tested. A Glasgow firm that used Chinese workers began to import sugar to Vancouver and sell it for less than B.C. Sugar charged. Rogers, playing a neat double game, insisted that it was up to the labour council to take action against the cheap sugar, for it was the council that had kept him from using Asians and thus from providing sugar at the lowest possible price. Pleming and the VTLC quickly organized a boycott of grocers who sold the so-called Chinese sugar, and enlisted the support of the Victoria Trades and Labor Council. Although the VTLC leadership believed that it was important to keep out cheap labour, two observations suggest that racial hostility played an equally important role. First, the VTLC had neither unions nor members employed at B.C. Sugar. No economic hardship would result to organized labour from Chinese sugar workers in either Vancouver or Glasgow; indeed, the importation of cheap sugar would end Rogers's monopoly and reduce prices. Second, if cheap labour were the only concern of the VTLC, vigorous union organizing would seem to be the appropriate solution. William Pleming himself suggested that racism was the real cause of the council's actions. Commenting on the original concessions and the subsequent boycott, Pleming wrote, 'I do not know that another shipment [of "Chinese" sugar] ever came, but labour felt it had won the first round anyway ... This was a whiteman's country.'[7]

Other examples reinforce the argument that race hostility fueled the VTLC's reaction to Chinese immigration quite as much as economics did. In 1892, the council voted to endorse the lawsuit of the Laborers' Union against a Chinese worker who had fallen on and injured one of its members. Twenty-five years before British Columbia passed Workers' Compensation legislation, civil suits were the only form of redress for work injuries. Normally, however, they were directed at the employer and not other employees. Since a Chinese labourer would be unlikely to be able to pay substantial damages, the decisions to launch and to support the lawsuit appear to be inspired more by a desire to punish the Chinese than a desire to compensate an injured worker.[8]

In March 1893, the council struck another committee to investigate the 'Chinese problem.' Reporting for the committee a few weeks later, George Bartley stated that it had 'procured considerable evidence in the shape of cuttings from the Chinese press of the deplorable ignorance, superstition, and vice of the Chinese and their unfitness to associate or assimilate with the white population of this country.' Claims of this sort pictured the Chinese as less than human, or at best, several rungs below whites on the evolutionary ladder, and similar stories percolate through the minutes of the council. In September 1899, the VTLC heard a lurid tale of child molestation that struck at the very hearts of the delegates. One member told horrified unionists that white children were being 'lured to out-of-the-way places not only by white men but by Japs and Chinamen' in the alleys and corners near Powell and Alexander Streets. The *World* newspaper reported that the delegate had declared that 'one Chinaman had been seen with a child almost in his clutches, but on help arriving he fled, and unfortunately could not be caught. According to [his] statement, this was not by any means an isolated case but a common occurrence.' This spectre of evil but cowardly Chinese preying upon white children smacks more of urban legend than fact, and there is no evidence to suggest that the episode did take place. Nor is there evidence to believe that kidnapping or worse was a 'common occurrence.' That the tale was told and repeated does illustrate the fear and hatred the white trade unionists felt towards Asians, and it reinforced the belief that the Chinese were fundamentally different and impossible to assimilate. After hearing the story, the council suggested that 'if the facts were as stated, a little lynch law would not be out of place.' The mob violence that characterized labour's response to Asian labour a decade earlier, when Knights of Labor attacked a camp of Chinese workers, had been channelled into political action, but had not been entirely forgotten.[9] With the creation of the VTLC newspaper, the *Independent*, in 1900, anti-Asian propaganda became more pronounced. In its first issue, the paper announced that 'one person in four is a Mongol' in British Columbia. The author proved the contention by arguing that the population of the province was roughly 125,000, of whom 25,000 were Indians and could thus be discounted. Of the remainder, nearly one-half were women not in the work force. Subtracting children and 'persons decrepit or otherwise incapacitated' left a total of 40,000 workers. The number of Chinese in the province was approximately 10,000, and another 2,000 were Japanese. Thus, 25 per cent of the male work force was made up of 'Mongols.' Buttressing its nativist sentiments with an 'objective' economic argument, the author held that such a large proportion of Asians would discourage 'desirable immigrants' and 'would have the tendency to stop capital ... Capital will not invest ... without confidence and it is impossible to have confidence in a British colony peopled by Japanese and Chinese.' The 'solution to this vexed question' was the 'total exclusion of Oriental cheap labor.'[10]

Other stories took up a similar theme. The newspaper criticized a recent arbitration that disallowed the rule that required underground coalminers to be able to read in English. Though the rule was ostensibly in place to make sure all could read and understand safety regulations, the absence of the requirement meant that 'the mines of Vancouver Island will be more and more flooded by cheap Oriental labor to the exclusion of white workers.' Yet another article deplored the entry of Japanese workers who were 'rapidly ousting the white worker from many of our leading industries, fishing, lumbering, and coal mining and railroad construction work ... They accomplish this by selling their labor for a mere song.' A month later, the paper insisted that those who distinguished between Chinese and Japanese immigrants did so at their own risk. 'It may be argued,' one columnist wrote, 'that the Jap is a notch above the Chinaman. That may be so; he may be a mile above him in the social scale. But it is a fact, and one that is too apparent to be ignored, that absolutely no white man can work for the wages he does, for the very simple reason that the remuneration would be altogether inadequate to existence.' Again the alleged fundamental and unchangeable differences between whites and Asians were affirmed. The economic issue addressed in these pieces is clouded by the absence of a call to organize the Asians to end competition and the insistence that exclusion was the only answer.[11]

The labour council believed that the federal government's immigration policy was at worst collusion with the CPR and at best based on ignorance. The *Independent* noted with satisfaction that 'some of the British Columbian Chinese seem to be making East, in which movement many here will wish them good speed, as the sooner that Eastern Canada learns something practically about the Chinese problem the better.' The assumption was that once politicians and labour leaders met Chinese workers they too would quickly come to appreciate the need for Asian exclusion.[12]

Proving that it was not immune to other forms of racism, the *Independent* ran an account of 'a negro and a native of Alabama who entertains the public by giving exhibitions of forcing different articles inside his mouth which would seem to be an impossibility. One of his feats is to completely envelop a saucer six and a half inches in diameter ... It is not to be questioned that he may before his old age be able to eat a watermelon grape-fashion.' The stereotypes of the Irishman and the Jew were regular themes, often presented in the form of dialect jokes. One Irish joke managed to present its subjects as dirty, criminal, and favouring drink all at once: '"De water-cure is somet'ing dat's got to be stopped," exclaimed Meandering Mike. "It's too crool and unusual to be stood." "Do you know it is?" asked Plodding Pete. "Course. I've been froo it. I hadn't been in jail fifteen minutes before dey made me take a bath."' The miserly Jew was similarly treated. 'That plackguard's [sic] hookin' it with von of my coats on. Fire at hith trousers, Ikey,' one snippet went.[13] But if these stock characters were little more than a figure of fun, the 'Asian menace' was seldom joked about, for the Chinese and Japanese were viewed as a real and immediate threat. The murder of Police Chief A.D. Main in the neighbouring village of Steveston by 'Chinamen' was, to the VTLC, proof of this. The murder of 'one of our most highly respected citizens' was further evidence that federal legislation was needed to 'stop the enormous increase of the migration of Chinese and other Asiatics.'[14] The careful noting that a 'citizen' had been murdered by outsiders may be interpreted as another way in which the council members distinguished between themselves and the Asian workers. Their fear is indicated by the allegation that 'Chinamen' in the plural had killed the officer; in fact, only one was responsible, but the vivid suggestion of a mob attacking a lone upholder of the right was irresistible.

The spectre of disease added to the hysteria. A letter signed 'Physician' warned that Chinese grocers used urine to blanch celery stalks and put green bananas in their beds so 'the heat of his filthy body effectually ripens the fruit in a few nights and gives it that rich foreign flavor so much desired by those who prefer a filthy Chinaman to a clean Anglo-Saxon.'[15] A report on alleged health violations by keepers of boardinghouses that catered to Japanese harped on a similar theme. According to the story, the Vancouver city health inspector issued several summonses to the proprietors, who slept the men ten to a bed. The fault was not attributed to the owners who created and maintained the conditions, but to the Japanese themselves, who were presumed not to care. Disease and filth were assumed to be a necessary condition of Asian labour, rather than the result of poverty, unscrupulous hoteliers, or profit-maximizing shipping lines. The causes were not attacked, only the victims and 'carriers.' The concern for health and safety, natural enough in a port city, became tied to racial exclusion. Thus, the *Independent* wrote: 'There cannot be too much care exercised by our municipal health authorities in inspecting the hordes of Japanese immigrants now arriving. The scourge of smallpox now visiting Winnipeg came via Japan, Japanese coolies brought the plague to Hawaii, and it is known that the native steamships which bring the laborers to Victoria are in the steerage quarters, foul almost beyond conception ... The more legitimate restrictions are imposed on the hordes of Oriental laborers for whom there is no scope without ousting our own people from work, the better.'[16]

Like their counterparts in San Francisco, the VTLC leaders linked class-consciousness to racism. It even extended a hypocritical fraternal hand across the ocean. Commenting on the famine in India, one article pointed out that 'the prime curse of India is not caste but the exploitation of native labour and the vampires of usury.' The writer called for relief efforts, but noted that real relief could come only when the government 'and the class they represent cease to make financial profit' out of war, pestilence, and famine.[17]

The labour council's desire to prohibit Asians helped propel it towards political action. Anti-Chinese planks were an integral part of labour's political platform from its beginnings. In May 1892, the VTLC passed a motion of non-confidence in the provincial government, complaining that it had not passed legislation to aid workers, had endorsed a deep-sea fishing project that would create jobs for immigrants, and had failed to take effective action on the 'Chinese question.' The council then petitioned the federal government to end Chinese immigration and employment, and lobbied the national TLC to call for an increase on the entry tax and for an annual tax on Chinese residents. In the federal election of 1896, the VTLC threw its support behind the Reverend George Maxwell, an Independent who supported the Laurier Liberals and pledged to work for anti-Chinese legislation. The council constantly supported the provincial government's efforts to block Chinese immigration, and was outraged when the federal government regularly disallowed the restrictive legislation. When overt measures foundered on the rocks of federal disallowance or political manoeuvring, the council was quick to find other ways to press its attack. In addition to prompting local health authorities to harass Asians, the VTLC supported the city's amendment to its charter that disenfranchised Japanese and Indians in addition to Chinese. The VTLC then called for provincial laws to limit the granting of public contracts and public lands to British subjects. As the population of the city and the province grew, the labour council called for new measures to make sure the restrictions were not flouted. In 1899, its parliamentary committee resolved that the Alien Naturalization Act should be amended to compel aliens seeking citizenship to appear before a Supreme Court judge, in order that the official could verify that the naturalization requirements had indeed been met. These new, formalized, bureaucratic procedures were necessary, for 'in cities of large dimensions and thousands of inhabitants,' it was impossible for the community to know everyone and informally ensure that the appropriate steps had been taken, unlike the 'small villages where everybody is known.' In this instance, federal bureaucracy, in the form of red tape and rules on policy, were encouraged by the labour leaders as a defensive mechanism. If informal community control were no longer effective, institutionalized codes and official authority would take its place.[18]

Racism was a defensive response of craft unionists and their leaders. As skilled tradesmen, they prospered by controlling access to the labour market and through restrictions such as jurisdictions, hiring halls, apprenticeships, and walking card delegates. These unions were organized by trade and craft, and their ability to control the labour supply allowed them to win higher wages. It also allowed them to base their demands on the basis of skill, rather than simple need or a larger argument about the necessity of all labour. It was their ability to organize that defined their work as skilled, since there is no objective measure of skill that applies to most work. Printers could lay claim to the nobility of their trade and insist on a four-year apprenticeship, but this represented the strength of the union more than any one arcane skill or mysterious technique that could not be learned by anyone in much less time than the apprenticeship required. Seeking to restrict workers by race was thus a logical extension of their traditional practices. Refusing to organize the unorganized or the Chinese was not simply a measure of their conservatism or social psychology. It flowed naturally from their pragmatic approach to craft unionism.

Indeed, extensive organizing outside the trade could weaken the skilled workers' position, as it would dilute the craft. Trades that could easily restrict the flow of labour, notably those that worked in areas such as construction and printing, were more successful in protecting their members than trades such as tailoring and cigarmaking. These trades could be flooded with goods imported from other provinces and countries. If employers were to make money by reducing expenses, they could only cut costs by cutting wages. This in turn meant that employers continually sought to lower wages and to replace highly paid workers with cheaper ones. The nature of these businesses also played a role in the union's ability to organize and fight. Cigarmaking and tailoring required little capital investment; much of the work could be contracted out or done in a sweatshop with little machinery. These trades and their unions won few battles in this period. Despite efforts by the VTLC and the tailors and cigarmakers unions to enforce the union label and to boycott shops that employed Chinese or sold goods made by Chinese labour, these organizations were soon to lose their effectiveness in Vancouver.

Furthermore, both cigarmaking and tailoring produced for the consumer, and both produced luxury items. The building trades worked on business projects that could pass on the cost of labour to the consumer or on houses that were a necessary purchase. Printers worked on job printing, most of which was done for local businesses, or on newspapers that relied on advertising for revenue. The cigarmakers and tailors were caught in a bind, as many working people, including union members, preferred to buy less expensive items from non-union shops. Building and printing did not face the same problem. Thus, union label campaigns to promote organized cigar and tailor shops were constantly launched by the VTLC and constantly failed. The Waiters and Waitresses Union had similar problems. J.H. Perkins, secretary of the union, complained to the VTLC that 'there were many Union men patronizing Japanese and Chinese restaurants' and thus hurting those establishments that hired white union labour. If labour leaders reflected the racism of the times, they still had difficulty enforcing their boycotts and campaigns among the rank and file who put consumerism ahead of race.[19]

Racism was also a useful tool in the ideological battle with employers. Relying on the language and assumptions of a common British heritage, labour leaders could invoke images of an independent yeomanry, the nobility of toil, and the virtue of the producer to justify wages and access to politics. By stressing the lines of a shared ethnicity, these labour leaders sought to make an alliance with politicians and employers to prevent harsh treatment. The 'Chinese threat' was not a direct threat to their wages; it was a threat to the dream of a white society in which all could be equal. Devalued labour struck at their claims about the nobility of toil, which was in part a claim about political rights and control. If the Asians, described by most Anglo-Saxons as inferior, were considered part of the working class, the white workers of British Columbia could not make the same arguments about deserving high wages and a voice in politics. Such reasoning was used against so-called unskilled workers of all races and ethnicity in the labour council's struggle to keep out cheaper labour and to reject attempts to justify wage reductions on the grounds that the producing classes were not the moral and racial equals of the employers. Thus, the VTLC paper denounced 'the influx of Japs, Chinks, and the scum of Europe' in a single breath. All unskilled workers combined to form a 'terrible vampire, whose morbid appetite will never be appeased until ruin and desolation stalk through the land.'[20] The fact that Asians were highly visible and were placed near the bottom of Anglo racial hierarchies gave racism a particular virulence and fervour that supports, to some degree, Ward's position on a 'psychology of race.'

Attitudes on race would not change until circumstances changed the perceptions of the leaders, or more often, changed the leaders themselves. Such was the case with the fishermen's union. Started by VTLC organizer J.H. Watson, the union grew when two socialists, Frank Rogers and Will MacClain, began organizing for it. This industrial union broke from the mould of the craft unions and had to adapt to different conditions if it were to survive. Unable to restrict access to the fishery in the way printers could restrict entry to their trade, the fishermen's union had to organize all the workers for its success. Since so many fishermen were native or Japanese, the union could not be racist in the same fashion. The *Independent* commented on the 'necessity' of organizing 'Japs' into the union, and called upon whites to 'fall in line' with the Japanese organizing in Steveston. Such necessity did not affect Watson, however. In letters to the newspaper, he continued to insist that it was 'better to starve the Mongol out than to starve our white worker out of an occupation.' No economic or practical consideration could have much of an impact on his views on race. Until structural changes in the population and the economy affected other unions, racism continued to serve the VTLC's interests more effectively than inclusive appeals to class.[21] Hostility towards the Asians who were synonymous with unskilled, non-union labour reflected the specific class position of the labour leaders. If the delegates of the VTLC were something of an aristocracy of labour because of their ability to organize and fight, their positions as leaders and spokesmen gave them another kind of status and power. As successful workers and later, often contractors, publishers, and the like, these men had made it in the pioneer society of Vancouver. The system had given them a measure of success, and thus it seemed to be a system that worked. The labour leaders could meet with, and perhaps to a degree, identify with, Vancouver's political and business leaders. Asians, brought in by monopolies such as Dunsmuir and the CPR had little in common with these men. Not surprisingly, the VTLC supported those who seemed more like themselves – local politicians, shopkeepers, small businessmen, professionals – against the outsiders who appeared able to wrest control away. In this way, the 'Asian menace' was linked to the populist ideology of the day, for it appeared to be the final arm of the triad of state, monopoly, and foreigners that challenged the way of life and the day-to-day control these people exerted. Racism was the ugly side to the populist critique, but it was seen as essential and relevant to the members of the VTLC. Like the critique of big government and big business, it was a fight over who would control the politics, wealth, and culture of the city. To ally themselves with Chinese workers would mean that the frontier myth and the producer ideology were finished; it would mean that society was absolutely divided by class, that movement between classes was not easy and fluid, and that working people could not expect or proclaim any rights that flowed from their position as creators of wealth equal to businessmen and merchants and farmers.

Understanding the labour bureaucrats' position on what was labelled 'the woman question' is difficult, largely because discussions of women rarely figured in the council's activities between 1889 and 1910. This silence is in itself significant, but apart from illustrating that men largely ignored women's issues it offers little insight or room for analysis. Some evidence of their attitudes towards women is available. The core of the labour leaders' ideology in regard to women was the belief in the two separate spheres of women's work and men's work. Men worked in and produced for the market, while women worked in and produced for the home and family. Men were assumed to have certain skills that would be rewarded with wage labour, while women were assumed to be nurturers and care-givers who would use their very different skills to run and maintain the household and to raise children. They were also expected to provide support for the wage-earning male. Thus, one writer suggested in the *Independent* that 'The girl that polishes up the cook stove until it shines like "dad's dinner pail" will make a good wife for any man.'[22] Another reflected on the contemporary craze for bicycling to ask in verse,

> Where is the wheel she rode last year;
> Her bloomers, where are they?
> Why is she never seen upon

The bicycle paths today?
The lover whom she rode with then
Did not lay down his life
Upon the field of battle but
He took that maid to wife.
Her tyres now are all flattened out
Her bloomers hung away –
Beside a baby's crib she sings
Sweet lullabies all day.[23]

The corollary for women of putting away the things of youth was to marry and raise a family.

The labour leaders assumed that women were to act as the moral influence in the family, and the official paper was quick to reprimand women who stepped out of this role, usually by printing jokes and anecdotes to make the point. One story had a mother asking her young daughter where good girls went when they died. The child answered that they went to heaven. The mother then asked where bad girls went, and the daughter replied that they went to the train depot, 'to see the travelling men come in' – a not so subtle reference to the hoary jokes about travelling salesmen and prostitution.[24] In another, aimed at women's alleged vanity and artifice, Tommy, aged five, asked,

'What's a fictitious character, Aunt Em?'
Aunt Em – 'One that is made up.'
Tommy – 'Oh, then you're a fictitious character,
ain't you, Aunt Em?'[25]

There was little suggestion that the two spheres of work attributed to the sexes were separate but equal. For a time, the *Independent* ran a women's section that paid little attention to political or economic affairs. Instead of trade union information or discussions of women's rights, the paper carried recipes, grooming tips, and hints on stain removal, smart consumerism, and the like.[26] Women's responsibilities were often the subject of jokes based on the motif of exaggerating a characteristic believed to be part of women's different nature. For example, thrift was considered a valuable trait for working-class wives, but was often parodied as overwhelming consumerism. In one anecdote, several castaways were adrift in an open boat on the high sea. They were near death when a male sailor spotted a ship in the distance. 'A sail! A sail!' he shouted. A woman passenger, half dead from thirst, reached for her purse and shrieked, 'What, a bargain [on] salt?'[27] Women were often portrayed as cunning manipulators who would turn into tyrants once they had ensnared a man in marriage. One writer even compared women to 'the big trusts. The instant she acquires a controlling interest in you she becomes a regular ring master. She will make you jump through, lie down, roll over, walk lame, and play dead. And don't think for a moment that you won't do it, either.'[28]

Although men were often chided for not fulfilling their part of the marriage agreement, the jokes seem less pointed and more accepting of the follies of the male. In one short item in the paper's miscellany column it was dryly observed that 'many a man protests that he would lay down his life for a woman, who after marriage he won't lay down a carpet for.'[29] In another, a woman at a party freely admitted that women were vain, but that men were not afflicted with that particular vice. As the men nodded wisely in agreement, she added that 'by the way, the necktie of the handsomest man in the room is up under his ear.' Her real point was made when 'every man present put his hand up to his neck.'[30] Women might have wisdom, but power was denied them; men could be tricked into admitting their vanity, but could not be confronted with it. While it is easy to make too much of these anecdotes, they do suggest that relations between the sexes were fundamentally uneven. Marriage was a trap for men, a fulfillment for women. Women were fierce perhaps in their attempts to make men obedient, but ultimately could not prevail upon husbands even to lay a carpet.

The power of men in the household was, however, restrained by a moral code. The labour newspaper ran several articles that outlined the proper conduct for men. This meant more than just bringing home wages, and included a standard for behaviour in the family. In one item, for example, it was observed that 'the true measure of a man is ... at his own fireside ... If his children dread his home coming and his wife swallows her heart every time she asks him for anything, he is a fraud of the first water, even though he prays until he is black in the face and howls hallelujah until he shakes the hills.'[31] When the Vancouver *World* accused VTLC candidate Chris Foley of being 'henpecked,' the *Independent* lashed back, insisting that 'the man who would assume the role of dictator in his own home or interfere with his wife's affairs is a pretty low and contemptible being.'[32] A parable entitled 'The Two Men' was reprinted several times, and its message, that money was not the only contribution men were expected to make was clear: '"I would like to, but I haven't the time." The door of one of our most splendid mansions closed and a man hurried to his office ... A wife and family were his, but he no longer had time for family associations ... Elsewhere a man with a dinner pail kissed his little boy good-bye and the door of one of our smallest homes closed as the bread winner hurried away. All through the dust and grim [*sic*] and toil he thinks of his wife and boy and they think of him and at night the lad runs out to meet him. At night he holds the little youngster close to his heart and reads the paper on the door-step. He has time.'[33] But in spite of the sentimental imagery of the article, it was fairly clear that work in the day-to-day maintenance of the home was not the man's responsibility.

The concept of the two spheres was a reflection both of the larger society and of the particular class location of the labour bureaucrat. Able to command a relatively healthy wage, or at least able to see such a wage as his due, the successful labourist could avoid the necessity of having two wage-earners in the family. The belief that men should be the sole wage-earner in the family, however, often put women in a double-bind. Deprived of an independent income, yet responsible for maintaining themselves and the family, they had to request and receive money from the husband. The resulting tug-of-war, with women in the subordinate position, was a source of jests and jibes among the men of the labour elite. Women were pictured as avaricious and scheming, as one wife was portrayed in an anecdote: '*Wife* – I've mended the hole in your trousers pocket last night after you had gone to bed, John dear. Now, am I not a thoughtful wife? *Husband (dubiously)* – Well – er – y-e-s; you are thoughtful enough, my dear; but how the mischief did you discover that there was a hole in my pocket?'[34] If financial dependence required women to plan for a possible future in which they might be widows, this too could be interpreted as greed. The *Independent* complained that 'six men out of ten who leave behind liberal life insurance have no monument. In a majority of cases the widow uses the life insurance to attract another husband.'[35]

To preserve the integrity of the sexual division of labour, the VTLC leadership argued that their wages and jobs should be protected from the unfair competition of both immigrants and women. The idea of the 'family wage' was used to support their position, and many articles in the *Independent* argued for wage levels that would allow men to support wives and families on a single, male income. One such item set out the position strongly and ended up blaming working women for contributing to the prostitution of their sisters: 'the women who take the places of men in our stores, offices, and factories are largely girls who get part of their living elsewhere ... [that is they] live at home or have brothers or relatives who assist them, and they can afford to work for from $1 to $3 per week ... The husband's and father's ability to keep the woman in the home where she belongs is diminished by woman's taking his place in the shop at less wages, thereby cutting his wages and reducing his chance for a job, the women themselves making wages by

that means drive the weaker natures to sell their persons for a better existence and he who blames them is both cruel and unjust.'[36]

Similarly, the editor of the *Independent* commented with alarm on a magazine ad for a simplified system of accounting that was so straightforward
'that a girl at $4 a week can take care of records and accounts that, with
books, demand an expensive man.' This deskilling, lamented the editor,
explained why young men 'find it harder than their fathers did to find
employment at wages that will enable them to support a home decently.'[37]
Such a home was crucial to the labourist world-view. When the 'federal
bureau of labour' allegedly announced that nearly 90 per cent of workmen in
twenty-two Canadian cities were unmarried, the VTLC newspaper was
alarmed. 'These figures,' the writer complained, 'indicate that there is something radically wrong with the environment of the workers.'[38]

Good trade unionism meant, to these leaders, keeping the traditional structure of the family intact by organizing to defeat the inroads of capitalism. 'If
trade unionism prevailed,' one contributor wrote, 'every little girl and boy
would be running up and down school steps, women would be taken from the
factories where they sew and stitch their lives away, and every parent would
receive sufficient wages to provide for his care, so that he would not be
obliged to rob childhood of its sunshine and joy.'[39] The council took action
along these lines in 1904 when it formally called for legislation to appoint a
factory inspector and to limit the hours of work for women and children.
Though these measures were advocated to change conditions 'inimical to the
physical and moral well-being of females and young persons,' it is more accurate to see them both as progressive measures and as attempts to restore the
vision of separate spheres with women in the home.[40]

The concept of 'manliness' was an important part of the culture and world
view of the labour bureaucrats. The 'Recipe for a Union Man' called for

... an ounce of gumption
Just a grain of sand.
A little independence,
Some manly spirit, and
Mix them well together
With patience – if you can.
Add to it unselfishness –
And you have a union man.[41]

Unionists who did not do their part were accused of having an 'ignoble and
unmanly spirit.' When attacked by political opponents, J.H. Watson decried

the 'want of manhood' in his foes and enjoined them to 'be men above all things.' The 'trade union principle' itself was portrayed as a traditional, male figure, standing as the 'mighty protector against all forms of wrong and injustice.' The union instilled 'courage, manhood, independence, fraternity; the love for the good and the true; it lives in the hearts and minds of the toilers, and must live; it will not die.' In contrast, women were often portrayed as a wedge that forced men apart. For example, when the *Independent*'s business manager Harry Cowan married editor Bartley's sister Connie, the wedding notice appeared under the headline 'Cowan a Benedict.' If such jokes were meant only in fun, they still suggest that a solidarity based on the mythology of masculinity and 'manly virtue' left little room to include women.[42]

However, there were important exceptions to this general attitude. In 1900, 'J.H.B.,' probably J.H. Brown of the International Typographical Union, wrote to the Vancouver *World* to defend the pragmatic reformism of the AFL against the socialist movement. He argued that among the 'general objects' of unionism were shorter hours, better pay, and 'the equalization of the wages of both sexes for similar work.' A month later, the *Independent* pointed out that Seattle had already signed up 65 women into a waitresses union, and urged the regional AFL and VTLC organizer to 'move in this direction in Vancouver.' The newspaper called for a waitresses union to address the 'great need' for better wages and hours and was pleased to note that both men and women helped to found the Cooks' and Waitresses' Union in August. Most of the VTLC leadership applauded these efforts, and President Dixon, Financial Secretary Francis Williams, organizer Watson, and the *Independent*'s editor Bartley and business manager Harry Cowan all addressed the new union's members to give their support. The newspaper also noted with approval that the retail clerks' association had resolved unanimously to invite 'lady clerks' to join, and the association soon elected women as vice-president, assistant secretary, and 'guide.'[43]

Solidarity was also extended to women in other occupations. The *Independent* noted with sorrow and respect the death of a city hospital nurse, 'an administering angel in caring for the sick' who died from blood poisoning 'during the discharge of her duties.' Joseph Watson deplored the conditions that women in domestic service faced, and he called for reduced hours, a six-day work-week, and a systematic training, schooling, and certification process. This would raise the benefits and status of domestic work and make it more attractive as a career for young women. When telephone operators, virtually all of whom were women, struck in 1902, the VTLC was quick to vote its support and to organize rallies, fundraisers, and boycotts.[44] From these examples it may be concluded that the opposition of the VTLC leaders to women in the workplace and the union movement was not absolute. But their support was limited to women who worked in areas that were an extension of women's work in the home, that capitalized on traditional ideas of women as care-givers, or were already dominated by women.

While the labour bureaucrats stamped the labour movement with their own ideas of women's roles, it is not clear that their positions as bureaucrats were the key determinant of these ideas. In language similar to that of the early incorporation and corporate liberalism theories, Marie Campbell has argued that male trade unionists joined with government and industry to end 'the threat women posed to men's jobs, as well as providing a pool of cheap labour to aid capitalist growth.' Employers were deskilling the work process and hiring women to replace high-paid artisans in some industries. Yet the labour leaders who opposed women working were in those trades least affected by the hiring of women. Women were not becoming bricklayers or painters or printers; they were teachers, clerks, and garment workers. Men in the craft unions were in fact more likely to encourage women to unionize, though they were rarely responsive to the real needs of women. This suggests that more than a straightforward economic calculation based on the exploitation of working women was at the bottom of their analysis. Instead, women working outside the home threatened them in a less direct, though equally powerful, fashion. The 'spectre' of women in the work force challenged the traditional way of life these men sought, and it challenged their picture of a stable world in which men and women had clearly defined roles. Working-class women also attacked the producer ideology, for it had always seen the production of value for the market as a part of men's work. This view stemmed from a sexist society that was not the creation of labour bureaucrats. Furthermore, for the first generation of Vancouver labour leaders, both industrial capitalism and women working outside the home were a new and relatively rare experience. Just as most of the labour leaders did not work in factories, most did not encounter women in the workplace. Two years after the VTLC was founded, women made up little more than 4 per cent of the British Columbia work-force; during the *Independent*'s run from 1901 to 1904, women were barely 6 per cent of the labour force. Indeed, in the province as a whole, women comprised only a quarter and a third of the entire population from 1891 to 1901.[45] The difficulties that labour leaders had in understanding and developing strategies for working women were caused in part by the very newness of the situation.

In addition to their small numbers, women tended to work in areas that were low paid or under attack in this period. This work also tended to be very difficult to organize. Domestic service, teaching, clerking, and tailoring provided the vast majority of jobs for women: in 1891, 68 per cent of working women were employed in domestic service and the professions, primarily teaching. By 1911, when women made up nearly 14 per cent of the labour force, over 40 per cent were employed as domestics; about 8 per cent were saleswomen; 9 per cent were stenographers or typists; close to 6 per cent were teachers. Most women, then, worked in sectors that were unproductive, that is, in which the employees did not actually produce surplus value for the employer. As a result, winning concessions or even union recognition was usually very difficult. In occupations where employers made money directly from the work of their employees, such as construction, wages represented profit. The wages of a domestic, a clerk, or a public schoolteacher, however, no matter how important or necessary the work was, represented a direct cost to the employer. This tended to heighten employers' intransigence in the face of wage demands. Sectors of productive labour, such as tailoring, were faced with other difficulties, as the British Columbia industry was in competition with eastern Canada and the United States, where factory production, technology, and economies of scale provided significant advantages. Men and women both faced enormous difficulties when they tried to organize in these industries. The tailors' union vanished during the depression of 1893–5; when it was resurrected in 1898, it had little success in protecting wage and piece rates. The retail clerks fared little better: despite electing its president and international organizer to the head of the VTLC in 1902, their union was forced to disband in 1904.[46]

None of this, of course, excuses the labour bureaucrats for their inability to understand and press for women's issues and to include Asians in the labour movement. It does suggest that it was not primarily their position as bureaucrats that shaped their sexist and racist ideology. Rather, it was their status and income as unionized artisans, as men in a sexist society, and as progressives who were adapting to the spasms of industrialization by building on their own experience and their utopian notion of the artisan and yeoman. But it was their position as bureaucrats, with control over the political agenda, the money, and the press, that ensured that their voices, and not those of women and Asians, would be heard.

7

The Clash with Socialism:
Intellectuals versus Artisans

By 1900 the ideology of producerism and labourism was no longer the most radical position in the Vancouver labour movement. It still had many adherents among trade unionists and especially among the leaders such as Dixon, Bartley, and others who had established links in the economic, political, and social circles of the city. But the evolution over ten years of a system of officials, experts, and leaders had taken place under the guise of expediency and ad hoc responses to immediate conditions. The labour council and labourism appeared to some as a structure and ideology of entrenched bureaucrats. Increasingly, the leadership of the VTLC was challenged by a new faction bearing the banner of socialism, and the two ideologies clashed in the press and at the polls. Both sides argued that they were the logical representatives of the city's working class and denounced the other as being out of touch with the real needs of the rank and file. In fact, neither labourists nor socialists were much interested in bringing the rank and file into the labour council. These fights were not over hierarchy and democracy, but over ideology, and over who would lead the labour movement. Moreover, the positions of each side reflected their class position more than objective principles of right and wrong.

The early socialist movement of the city was an odd agglomeration of Marxism, Christian socialism, and reformism. The strongest Marxist line was taken by the local chapter of Daniel DeLeon's Socialist Labor Party (SLP) and its 'economic arm,' the Socialist Trades and Labor Alliance (STLA). Both groups upheld DeLeon's assertion that trade unions were largely futile and their leaders reactionary. During the 1900 provincial election, for example, the STLA's Vancouver local, the Pioneer Mixed Alliance, openly attacked the Lib-Lab Ralph Smith and the labour council's candidates Joe Dixon and Francis Williams. The STLA denounced Smith as a 'traitor to the working class' and condemned Dixon and Williams for their 'weak-kneed attitude towards the capitalist parties.' The labour council's reform platform was labelled a 'compromise with cockroach business interests,' and the STLA called upon unionists to 'repudiate their fakir leaders, convicted as they are of incapacity and unfaithfulness to the interests of our class.' Instead, the paper urged, workers should 'rally to the standard of the Socialist Labor Party ... avoiding middle class socialism and the would-be labor champions who pose at election time as "friends of labor."' Not surprisingly, the STLA request to affiliate with the labour council was rejected out of hand.[1]

The mutual rejection of the DeLeonists and the VTLC posed a problem for those socialists who wanted to work within the labour movement. Men such as William MacClain, Frank Rogers, and Allan Boag tried to adopt a middle course of advocating socialism without needlessly alienating the labourists. In 1900 they and others broke away from the SLP to form the United Socialist Labor Party (USLP) and ran MacClain as a socialist candidate loosely backed by the VTLC. The SLP attacked the new party in print, calling MacClain a 'so-called socialist candidate' and a 'fakir' and denying that Rogers had ever been a representative of the SLP.[2] The new party fared little better than the DeLeonists, but it did point the way towards a less rhetorical, more pragmatic and conciliatory socialism. The moderate socialism of MacClain and the USLP called for direct legislation and government ownership of key sectors of the economy, demands that were not far removed from the labourist platform of the VTLC.

At the same time, the influence of Christian socialism was spreading. The Canadian Socialist League (CSL) was founded in eastern Canada in 1899 and was led by George Weston Wrigley. Wrigley maintained that Christ had been the first socialist and that socialism was a movement for reform, not revolution. Seeing the way of the future in government ownership of the post office, the Intercolonial Railway, schools, and libraries, Wrigley was a kind of Fabian. He combined many of the populist planks, such as the initiative and the referendum, with the call for public ownership and direct democracy to cobble together a moderate left-leaning program.[3] A blend of Methodist reform and middle-class socialism, the CSL was a pink alternative to the SLP. With its emphasis on education and popular reform, the CSL was more akin to the USLP, and in 1900 the two groups met in convention to join together in a provincial federation. Although the new organization had little success, it provided the direction and the base for a revived party in 1901, the Socialist Party of British Columbia (SPBC). Headed by Ernest Burns, the SPBC combined the platform of the Socialist Party of America, the national demands of the CSL, and a list of reforms of particular importance to British Columbia.[4]

The new party quickly became the centre of socialist activity in the prov-ince and the city of Vancouver. Its dominance was assured in 1902, when the former DeLeonist, E.T. Kingsley, brought the Revolutionary Socialist Party of Canada into the fold. Kingsley represented, in the words of A.R. McCor-mack, the socialism of the 'pre-1900 Socialist Labor Party.'[5] He and his sup-porters, based in the coalmining district of Nanaimo on Vancouver Island, rejected trade unionism and political reformism. Instead, Kingsley called for class warfare, his chosen battleground the provincial legislature, and the exclusive reliance on the ballot box. Thus, his group and the CSL both shared a distaste for unionists, although from different perspectives. Kingsley viewed the union movement as reactionary, for it strove only to ameliorate the conditions of workers without trying to remove the causes of exploita-tion. The Christian socialists, however, had no great interest in the working class; their program represented a concern with improving the position of a stratum of the middle class. Both of these socialist tendencies had platforms and ideas that they shared with the labourists, but neither represented the world and the world-view of the artisans and master craftsmen who domi-nated the VTLC. While uneasy alliances could, and would, be forged, the different factions eyed each other suspiciously as each sought to lead the working class for its own particular ends.

The old guard of labourists did not give in easily. It fought to preserve its control over the labour movement by moving, grudgingly, to the left, and by launching frontal assaults on the upstarts. As early as 1898, George Bartley fired a warning shot. Speaking on the occasion of his re-election as president of the VTLC, Bartley observed that despite 'many ups and downs in the industrial barometer,' the labour council had survived. One of the most important keys to this survival 'had always been neutral[ity] in party poli-tics' and Bartley maintained that the unions were not ready to change their stand on the issue. The economy was on the upswing, he noted, and this bode well for labour. If the union leaders wanted to 'be up-to-date,' they had to continue to oppose party politics. Partisan politics led to 'restriction, narrow-ness, and monopoly, which have so much retarded the progress of the labor movement.' Furthermore, he continued, organized labour had to 'keep at arms' length self-opinionated, hot-headed, and would-be czars, the source of disruption in nearly every organization. Whenever they could not deal with these worthies in reason, more forcible and effective methods must of neces-sity be resorted to.'[6]

J.H. Watson took a slightly different tack, posing first as a socialist sup-porter whose disagreement was over tactics, not ends. As a member of the boilermakers and the IAM, Watson faced some competition from others in the unions representing CPR workers. Chief among these were William MacClain and Frank Rogers. MacClain was, like Watson, an emigrant from England and employed in the CPR's machine shops. Unlike Watson he was a newcomer to Vancouver, having jumped ship in Seattle shortly before coming to the city in 1899. Also unlike Watson, MacClain was an ardent socialist. At first a member of the Socialist Labor Party, he soon became disenchanted with its doctrinaire and sectarian politics, especially its attacks on the labour movement. When the VTLC refused to accept STLA representatives as delegates in 1900, MacClain, now president of the IAM local, delegate, and statistician of the VTLC, was forced to choose between the party and the union movement. He broke with the STLA, and helped form the United Socialist Labor Party. This allowed him to continue to agitate as a socialist and to work within the main house of labour. MacClain ran as a socialist candidate in the 1900 provincial election, and though not part of the VTLC's Independent Labor slate of Dixon and Williams, received some support from the council. MacClain then joined with fellow socialist Frank Rogers and with Watson to organize the fishermen of the Fraser River. Fired from the CPR because of his militancy, he devoted all his considerable energy to the fishermen's union and was responsible for much of its success.[7]

That MacClain and Watson were both active in the machinists' union and with organizing the fishermen did not mean that the old Liberal supporter had embraced socialism. The IAM itself was split on the issue of left-wing politics, and events in Vancouver were an echo of the battle taking place at the national level in Canada and the United States. In part a fight between industrial and craft unionists, it was also a conflict between socialists and those who supported the National Civic Federation and its policy of conciliation and collaboration. In general, conservatives favoured craft unionism, while socialists fought for industrial unionism. The NCF supporters could count Samuel Gompers as an ally, and Watson, with his ties to the craft unions and to the Lib-Lab Ralph Smith, was decidedly on the side of the conservatives.[8]

The struggle between the factions was evident in the fishermen's union, as Watson concentrated on organizing whites in New Westminster, and the socialists organized Asians and whites together in other areas. While New Westminster fishermen and Watson debated admitting the Japanese, Vancouver, 'with a spirit of freedom and liberality, and, fully realizing the necessity of such a course, opened its doors freely to Japs and Indians and to those of every other nationality.'[9] Although Watson was also pushed by necessity finally to endorse signing up Asians, he continued to press for Oriental exclusion and restriction, and complained bitterly over the large number of

'Japs and Chinamen' working as bartenders' assistants in Vancouver. Allowing Asians to work alongside whites allowed the 'Japs' to 'watch every move you make' and soon become skilled enough to replace the better-paid white worker, just as they had, he warned, 'busted nearly all the white cooks and bartenders in the city.'[10]

Watson was similarly pressured to make gestures towards the left, and similarly he snapped back to his original position later. In a series of articles for the labour paper, he outlined a labour theory of value, challenging the notion that the capitalist paid the workman. Instead, he showed, 'It is not the capitalist who gives bread to the workingman, but the working man who gives himself a dry crust and sumptuously stocks the table of the capitalist.'[11] In the next issue, Watson went on at great length on this theme, even suggesting that workers should 'call things by their proper names and tell the capitalist that he steals from the men who earned the money he received, and is therefore a robber.' In words that echoed his socialist foes, Watson concluded that 'between the working class and the capitalist class there is an irrepressible conflict, a class conflict for life. It crops up in all sorts of ways and manner of ways. It is a struggle that will not down and must be ended only by either the total subjugation of the working class or the abolition of the capitalist class.'[12]

Watson's conversion to class conflict, however, was only temporary. Nor did his strong statement imply a commitment to socialism. Watson soon returned to the labourist themes of craft unionism, avoidance of 'politics' in the union, and moderation. If these had a progressive ring to them in 1890, by 1900 they were the last refuge of the labour bureaucrat trying to stave off the socialists. Because his writing summed up the position of the labourist union leaders so aptly, it is worth quoting at some length. Cloaking himself with the mantle of science to appear to be in the vanguard of modern thinking, Watson penned a passionate defence of craft unionism. 'Specialization of functions is one of the most universal of all the laws governing the evolution of the social organism,' he wrote. In primitive societies, each member had to do everything. But as society became more complex, 'not only are the trades and professions differentiated, but these divisions themselves are subdivided, so that a craftsman will make possibly the hundredth part of a shoe, the lawyer deal entirely with one class of cases, the physician becomes a specialist of one class of disease, and so on.' Trade unions, with their insistence on craft jurisdictions, were simply following this 'law of specialization.' Industrial unions, favoured by socialists in this period, were therefore a violation of natural law and progress.

Having established the historical necessity of the trade union, Watson went on to deplore politics in the union hall, holding that 'a man's religion is his own business, his politics is his own business, his personal relations outside of his sphere as a craftsman are his own business.' Carefully avoiding any reference to his own close ties to the Liberals, Watson denounced the socialists who 'would divert the trade union from its proper work; who would apply political tests to trade union members ... and who rail at trade unionists as being content in seeking to achieve what they superciliously denominate as palliatives and makeshifts.' Craft unions, he argued, had won the evolutionary battle to represent the working class, and the proof lay in their 'record of achievement.' While socialists wrapped themselves in 'the folds of the red flag' and proclaimed themselves 'apostle[s] of a new and grander dispensation,' they bore 'the dagger of the assassin that they strive to plunge into the vitals of trade unions.' 'Hands off!' Watson warned, to 'those who would attempt to tamper with the economic integrity of the craft unions.'[13]

His attack on the socialists was followed up with an analysis of class consciousness that accurately reflected the labourist position. 'There is,' he wrote, 'possibly no phrase in the English tongue which has been worked overtime so much as "Class conscious."' It was true, he acknowledged, that the trade union movement could not exist if workers did not realize that 'they have certain distinctively class interests.' But it was the trade union that was best situated to understand these class interests and to shape workers' 'awakened desires and aspirations into cohesive and rational endeavours.' Nor was it necessary to set the craft worker 'on the one side as a social Ishmaelite' or to 'wage war in every institution of the existing social order.'

From this suggestion that workers might indeed have some common interest with the employer, Watson moved on to defend the 'pragmatic' unionism he had championed in the city. 'All great movements,' he contended, 'in a degree compromise between the cold, hard facts of environment and the ever unsatisfied longing of humanity for the ideal.' And his left-wing critics were indebted to the reformers such as himself, for the 'shortening of the hours of labor [gave] them an opportunity to study the science of socialism.' The conservative battles for better conditions gave 'men an opportunity to read and think.' Trade unions also created 'a greater spirit of independence against the exactions of the shop tyrant,' and infused workers with a 'spirit of solidity,' [sic], thus bringing out 'the better side of human nature and thereby building up the better citizen and the better man.' No matter how the left might rail, these accomplishments put the labourists firmly on the side of progress. They differed from the socialists chiefly because they refused to speculate on what the ideal society should be. That, he maintained, would be left 'to those who make up the membership of the pool of infallibles.' Believing that 'when

the minute hand goes round, the hour hand must progress also,' Watson concluded that unlike the radicals, 'The trade union does not disdain the day of
small things, knowing right well that all of civilization, nay, of life itself, is
but the aggregate of minute details. The trade union represents the principle
of opportunism in social reform. It does not refuse the small gain, but neither
does it waste its ammunition in shooting arrows at the sun. It recognizes the
limitation of human nature, but it helps to modify those qualities of human
nature which have kept men dependent and in bondage.'[14]

Other labour stalwarts took up a similar theme. Dividing the reform
movement up into spheres of influence, one writer asked, 'Why should there
be a dissenting rivalry between trades unionism and socialism? Neither, in
truth, should trespass on the rights of the other.' Trade unions had for their
mission 'the improvement of the conditions of working people under existing
forms of government, be that government monarchical, republican ... or
semi-social ... A trade union has to do with hours of labor, wages paid, and
rules of employment.' To accomplish this, craft unions sought to bring
together workers of all religious and political affiliations. All stripes and
colours of political interest were welcome, so long as they remembered that
'trade unions have not to do with political propaganda, but should have
workingmen vote, irrespective of party, for men and measures that in their
judgment will improve the conditions of workingmen.' This plea for toler-
ance, however, was followed by an assault on the class origins of socialists
that implied that their interests could be different from those of workers.
Together with the argument for keeping 'politics' out of the union, the article
was both a plea for 'pure and simple unionism' and a fight over who should
lead the working class. The author warned that socialism was 'a political
institution. It seeks to reform governments by levelling down and levelling
up the social inequalities.' Because of this, it was not an ideology that represented class interests. Instead, the author concluded, 'Socialism bears the
same relation to the student and philosopher that it does to the workingman.
In fact teachers of socialism have not usually come from the working class.'[15]

If this attack had some truth to it – indeed, it outwardly resembled later
arguments made by the Industrial Workers of the World against middle-class
socialists and intellectuals – it artfully dodged the question of the present
class position of the old-line labour leaders themselves. Few of those who
deplored the rise of socialism were still workers in the same way they had
been ten years earlier. The radical element of their populist, labourist ideology had been subtly altered over the years to blunt its edge, and the principles that had allowed them to build a union movement were now used to
justify moderation and cooperation with employers.

Nonetheless, the labour bureaucrats' charge that the socialists were not members of the working class had some merit. In principle, and in fact, the party made no attempt to limit membership to wage-earners. The famous socialist Phillips Thompson admitted that many prominent socialist theorists were 'extensive capitalists,' but argued that they were 'none the less trusted on that account ... No socialist ever dreamed of reading such men out of the party.' Local socialists supported this view by insisting that ideas, not class, were the most important criterion for party membership. 'This is not the time for dilly-dallying with non-socialists,' one asserted. 'We either want socialism or we do not. If we do, let's work and vote for it and it only. If others do not, let them remain outside our ranks until they make a study of the question ... Quality is more essential at this stage than quantity.' Party secretary Alex Lang made a 'Plea for Intolerance,' calling for a 'class-conscious party' that would abandon the 'broad road' of letting in 'sentimentalists.' E.T. Kingsley, the party's chief theorist from 1903 on, put the argument across most forcefully, insisting that 'the Socialist Party cannot depend on the support of members of trade unions unless they are to go back on union principles. The principles of unionism and socialism are antagonistic. To support one is to deny the other, no man can serve two masters.' And though he would later change his mind, in 1903 Parm Pettipiece argued that the party should 'stand firm; keep our organization iron-clad, aye, "narrow."'[16]

The insistence on party purity may have been essential to a new, struggling organization. Still, in making ideas rather than class the most important criterion for membership, the party attracted many supporters who were not from the working class. This gave some credence to the labour leaders' complaint that non-workers were trying to set the agenda for the union movement. Although certainly membership in the working class was no guarantee that one's policies and ideas would be correct, the labour bureaucrats were able to point to their own class experience and score points off the socialists. Each side used its own strengths in its attempt to become the legitimate leader for the working class: labour bureaucrats spoke of the necessity of experience and ties to the working class; socialists of the need for correct ideas that transcended class experience.[17]

The socialist party had to insist on the primacy of ideas, for many of its leaders were not from the working class. Ernest Burns, party secretary and treasurer, had worked for a time as a fisherman and served as the president of the fishermen's union. But by September 1900, he had already given up fishing to run a second-hand and junk store in Vancouver and 'as a result his activity in trade union circles has ceased.' Party organizer John Cameron, who worked in his father's planing mill in Ontario, came to Vancouver late in

1902 and started a tobacco shop and news-stand. Thomas Mathews combined a real estate office with a brokerage firm, offering in the pages of the *Canadian Socialist* 'Special Bargains in Real Estate' and the 'latest quotations' on mining stock. James Boult ran a news-stand for a time, then became a real estate agent himself. Fred Ogle, party candidate in 1903, left the Amalgamated Society of Engineers to come to Canada and take up work as a salesman and then as a party organizer, paid $2 a day for his services.[18]

While SPC editor and politician Parm Pettipiece was later to forge a career in the labour movement and would work as a compositor for Vancouver's daily press, his early years were spent as a publisher of newspapers. After two or three years of knocking about in jobs as a farm labourer, cattle hand, and labourer, Pettipiece went to work on the Calgary *Daily Herald* sometime between 1890 and 1892, when he went to the Edmonton *Bulletin*. In 1894, he purchased the Edmonton *Times* and started the *South Edmonton News*. Three years later, he bought the Edmonton *Herald* and began publishing the Revelstoke *Herald* in British Columbia. The year 1900 saw Pettipiece start up yet another paper, the Lardeau *Eagle*, which he continued until 1902, when he joined with another struggling publisher, Ontario socialist George Wrigley, to help put out the *Canadian Socialist*. Later that year, Wrigley went back to Ontario to start another paper, and Pettipiece became the sole owner of the British Columbia organ, retitled the *Western Socialist*. The difficulties of maintaining the party press forced Pettipiece to reorganize the company, and a joint stock company, the Western Socialist Publishing Company, was created in 1903. Capitalized at $10,000, in the form of 1,000 $10 shares, the company's first directors included Pettipiece, Kingsley, and Burns. Pettipiece continued as business manager, and George Dales, formerly with the Winnipeg *Voice*, was brought in as editor. Calling upon readers to purchase shares, the paper made it clear that it was not an investment in the usual sense of the word, for 'no dividends [are] to be paid; all profits go to spread socialism.' Eight months later, Pettipiece found that 'as his personal funds are now exhausted, he must seek a master from whom he can secure a subsistence wage.' But whatever his success rate may have been, it is clear that Pettipiece was not a printer who became a publisher, as Bartley had. Rather, he was an entrepreneur publisher who was later forced to learn a trade. Even then, he continued to work as an editor and business manager for the labour and socialist press and as a paid union officer. When he helped to launch attacks on the labour bureaucracy in 1902–3, however, he did so not as a rank-and-file worker but as a committed socialist from the petit bourgeoisie.[19]

James Hawthornthwaite, socialist MLA from 1901 to 1912, was another important party theorist who had no direct ties to the working class. A university graduate, real estate agent, mining promoter, and United States consular officer, he was perhaps the party's most successful politician, but like many others in the party, could hardly be said to be a producer in the sense the labourists meant the word. Similarly, Wallis Lefeaux was trained as a bookkeeper, then ran a clothing store and sold real estate before becoming a lawyer.[20]

To be sure, many socialists were workers and members of trade unions, although some, such as Allan Boag, augmented their wages with real estate speculation. Boag in fact was able to make some income from the socialist movement by renting one of his halls to the party for its meetings.[21] But the opposition to trade unions and trade unionists often came from those party members who were not active in the labour movement and were not employed as wage-earners. They formed part of the middle class, and as socialist spokesmen, functioned as intellectuals. Whatever the merits of their arguments, labour bureaucrats could, and did, point to these socialists to suggest that their theories did not reflect working-class experience and needs, and their accusations had some basis in fact.[22]

Certainly VTLC leaders maintained that a wide gulf separated them from the early socialists, based in part on the labourist distinction between productive and unproductive labour, although these were not the same as the Marxist categories. Indeed, such a distinction formed a core element of labourism. As a result, intellectuals of the left and the right alike were regarded with great suspicion. They were 'unmanly' somehow, unconnected with the important matters of life, more likely to create trouble for working men than to help them. Worse, intellectuals contributed nothing tangible to the economy; their existence meant that another layer of society skimmed the cream from the honest toilers. Intellectuals, never well defined, were the subject of jokes and pointed jibes in the *Independent*; often these were counterposed with remarks that reinforced the belief that practical men were of more value to society than those who sought 'pure' knowledge in any field. Not surprisingly, Thomas Edison was a favourite, and the labour paper reprinted an article by the inventor that summed up the labourist position well enough: 'I tell you I'd rather know nothing about a thing in science, nine times out of ten, than what the books would tell me; for practical purposes, for applied science, the best science, the only science, I'd rather take the thing up and go through with it myself. I'd find out more about it than anyone could tell me, and I'd be sure of what I know. That's the thing. Professor this or that will controvert you out of the books that it can't be so, though you have it right in the hollow of your hand all the time, and could break his spectacles with it.'[23] Anecdotes in the paper often took swipes at experts and professionals. '"I tell you sir,"' said the clergyman in one story, '"the trouble lies in the fact that there are too many lawyers." "There is where you are away off," replied the judge. "The real trouble is due to the fact that there aren't half enough clients."'[24] In another, 'a mining expert recently described a lode as traversing "a metamorphic matrix of a somewhat argilloarenaceous composition." This means literally "a changed mass of a somewhat clayey–sandy composition." This in turn may be translated into plain English as m-u-d.'[25]

The antipathy of trade unionists to intellectuals was further demonstrated when the VTLC opposed the creation of a university in Vancouver. Although the labourists believed that 'objective' science would aid their cause, universities were seen as parasites that fed off the producers and then bit the hand that fed them. 'When the universities and colleges are dependent upon the continued exploitation of labor,' the VTLC newspaper stormed, 'it is foolish to expect students to be taught impartial investigation into social problems.'[26] A lengthy resolution passed by the labour council put the labourist position well. The council made it clear that 'while protesting strongly against the granting of the public moneys or the lands of this province for such an object, we desire it to be distinctly understood that we are not opposed to education in any form; on the contrary, the council holds that education should be encouraged. But it must be evident that a university, established and conducted as similar institutions are in eastern parts of Canada and in European countries is, and of necessity must be, under present conditions, a purely class institution.' As a result, the council went on record as being opposed to the use of public funds for a university in British Columbia. Instead, the council maintained, money should be spent on technical schools and on free high school textbooks.[27]

The labourist critique of socialism borrowed from this traditional distrust of intellectuals and unproductive labour. One letter to the *Independent*, signed 'Reformer,' attacked those 'self-styled socialist leaders' who 'neither toil nor spin for their living, yet they would have you think that they were being robbed.' Pointing to an alleged inconsistency in the socialist position, the writer suggested that 'the doctrine of these so-called socialists is that if a man won't work neither shall he eat. Yet they decline to work but nevertheless eat and live high. I suppose they manage to exist by private subscription.'[28] The professional agitator who challenged the labour bureaucrat for the right to lead the working class was looked upon with especial suspicion. The *Independent* deplored the soap-box orator who complained that his efforts were 'never decently paid and never half appreciated.' The paper retorted, 'From our experience of these gentry, they don't deserve any more than they get. In most cases they are on a par with the common bum, so far as work goes, intolerant, spiteful, incompetent, and afflicted with the "green eye." Knocking union men is their long suit.'[30] When the socialist newspaper the *Liberator* denounced left-wing speakers who set out on lengthy speaking tours and were paid well for their efforts, the VTLC paper quoted it gleefully: 'It is a trifle inconsistent for us [socialists] to go on before the wage slaves of America with a propaganda that upholds the "iron law of wages," a "class conscious" program, expounded by ex-pulpiteers and other equally horny-handed sons of toil at $25 or $15 per diem.' The *Liberator* went on to call for socialist speakers to take only 'an existence wage' for their work, reminding them that 'on every coin that goes into the socialist movement there are drops of proletarian blood. The man who seeks to fatten his purse in the socialist movement is a human buzzard, no matter what his intellectual and oratorical accomplishments might be.' Commenting on the article, the *Independent* sniffed, 'Time works wondrous changes. Socialists used to be "Johnny on the Spot" with the reminder that a labor organizer or any other unionist who took pay for his work was a "grafter" and a "fakir." It now appears that labor unionists are not the only "fakirs" in the movement.'[30]

The labourists tended to see their campaigns against the socialists as moral crusades devoid of self-interest. Such charity was rarely extended to the socialists. The *Independent* printed with approval the sermons of a local social gospeller, who talked of the unity of Christianity and socialism but insisted that 'social changes can never be wrought by loud-mouthed and materialized agitators. Their shallow ignorance and tainted characters discredit the cause of reform.' These secular radicals 'rebel against poverty and work. They crave idleness and ease like their masters ... Give them money and they become worse men.' Instead, the cause would succeed only when led by those who brought 'high moral ideas into the agitation for change.'[31] Yet these labour leaders could steadfastly ignore their own status as business owners, politicians, and labour functionaries.

The importance of ideas to the socialists was also viewed with suspicion and was part of the labourist distrust of intellectuals in general. 'A would-be socialist with a little learning is a dangerous individual in the community,' the *Independent* warned. A parable cautioned those workers who might be taken in by the rhetoric of the left: 'A parrot and a dog were left in a room together. The parrot, out for mischief, said to the dog, "Sic him." The dog, seeing nothing else, went for the parrot and tore out about half his tail feathers before he escaped to his perch. The parrot, after reflecting a little, said, "Polly, you talk too damned much." There are many people, young and old, who would do well to remember this story.' Others suggested that 'some of our local champions of socialism talk too much. Socialism in their hands is just about as safe as a loaded gun in the hands of a lunatic.' Yet another remarked that he could 'smell a socialist.' 'Yes,' the editor responded, 'You can almost smell brimstone on some of them.' Other contributors argued that 'a stomach full of bread is of more practical benefit to a man on strike than a brain full of theories,' or that 'Socialism accomplished might prevent strikes, but preaching socialism will not settle a strike in progress.' To workers, the *Independent* warned, 'beware of demagoguery' and those 'adventurers' who used 'the inexperienced as stepping stones to vault would-be leaders into place.' Since the increased intervention of the state was inevitable, the author reasoned, 'The world will give ear even to socialism if properly presented. But demagogues and zealots can't accomplish anything. They only antagonize and disrupt ... The great work must now be started by rational men of long years of experience in the labor movement of this province.' Another writer in the same issue put it more succinctly: 'What between oppressive employers and luny [sic] socialists, the unions here are between the devil and the deep sea.' The net effect of this position was to paint socialists as impractical dreamers cut off from the reality of working life and as parasites who fed off the real toilers.[32]

Intellectualizing and zealotry were equally threatening to the labourists, for they undermined their position in the labour movement and the larger society. If correct ideology were the most important quality in labour leaders, they had little ability to compete with the sharp-tongued socialist upstarts who specialized in working with language. Nor could they match the zeal of the newcomers, for the labour bureaucrats had settled down in the community. They had businesses to run and important ties that they wanted to maintain to the larger society. Still progressive in their outlook, gradualism reflected their own class position and their long, steady work to build the city and their lives.

One indication of this is the difference in age and life stages between labourist leaders and socialist spokesmen. The important labourists tended to be significantly older than their socialist opponents, and they tended to have lived in the city considerably longer. Alvin Gouldner has suggested that age was an important factor in the battle between Karl Marx and Wilhelm Weitling over who would lead the Communist League, and a similar difference may have existed in Vancouver. Although figures are difficult to come by and samples are incomplete, a definite pattern does emerge. By 1903 the average age of the leading labourists such as Bartley, Watson, and Dixon was forty-three; that of the socialists, thirty-six. Averages, of course, are misleading, and direct comparisons may be more useful. George Bartley and Harry

Cowan of the *Independent* were thirty-six and thirty-four, respectively. Their counterparts on the socialist newspaper, Parm Pettipiece and George Wrigley, were both twenty-eight. When J.H. Watson came under attack by the socialist John Mortimer in the VTLC, he was forty-eight; his foe was thirty-two. When Francis Williams ran against Mortimer in the provincial election, the labourist gave away more than a worn-out ideology: he was fifteen years older than the socialist. Joseph Dixon, at forty-three, was the average age of the labourists, and was thirteen years older than Frank Rogers, the socialist organizer who was murdered by gun thugs during the UBRE strike against the Canadian Pacific Railway in 1903.[33]

Certainly the *Independent* suggested that differences in age could help explain differences in ideology in an article reprinted from the British journal *Nineteenth Century*:

Arrived at middle age, it is very possible that most of us will have been called to renounce a good deal. We started, probably, with the conviction that our heads would strike the stars and we have become strangely reconciled to the fact that they do not reach the ceiling. But it was no doubt better to start with the loftier idea; a man should allow a good margin for shrinkage in his visions of the future. And it is curious, it is pathetic, to see with what ease we may accomplish the gradual descent to the lower level, on which we find ourselves at last going along, if in somewhat less heroic fashion than we anticipated, yet on the whole comfortably and happily. We have accepted a good deal, we have learned how to carry our burden in the way that is easiest. We are no longer storm-tossed; we know pretty much, arrived at this stage, what we are going to do, those of us who considered they were going to do anything. The fact of taking life on a lower level of expectations makes it all the more likely that those expectations will be fulfilled. We have, with some easing of conscience, accepted certain characteristics and manifestations on our own part as inevitable, secretly and involuntarily cherishing a hope that where these do not fit in with those of our surroundings, it may yet be possible that other people should alter theirs.[34]

The labourists were also more established in the city, in part a function of age. Many had arrived ten years or more before the socialists. Dixon, Bartley, Watson, Williams, Browne, and others had all been in Vancouver for some years by 1903. In contrast, Pettipiece, Wrigley, and Mortimer arrived in 1902; George Dales, in 1903. Fred Ogle, who ran for the SPBC in 1903, had arrived so recently that he had to withdraw from the election as he did not meet the residency requirement. Thus, socialism was indicative not only of class differences. It was also the weapon of a younger generation, used to try to lever out older, more established unionists.[35]

Whether because of their age, community ties, class position, or adherence to labourism and producerism, labourists feared the overt grasping of political power that socialists called for. At bottom, they saw the socialists as having much in common with others from other classes who promised to legislate on behalf of the working class. 'The socialist party is a political party formed for the sole object of capturing the reins of government power,' the *Independent* warned. 'Just the same as the conservatives or liberals.'[36] And indeed, the socialist movement did threaten the position of these labour bureaucrats. The labourist appeal to reason, moderation, and gradualism reflected their own success in the city, their acceptance into the larger society. In their eyes, they had, by dint of hard work, helped to make both the city and their own lives into something of which they could be proud. The socialists were painted as interlopers and upstarts, as men with no ties to the community who would put ideological purity ahead of the lives and families of working people. Whether this is accurate is, of course, beside the point; but it does help explain the near-hysteria shown by many of the VTLC's more conservative union leaders when confronted with the spectre of socialism.

The study of the labour bureaucracy and the people who made it up suggests that the fight between labourists and socialists was more than a debate over ideology. The two groups were separated by age, occupation, their different ties to the community, even by their aspirations. The chief divisions, however, were those of class and culture. Many of the labour bureaucrats of the VTLC may have left the working class to become small businessmen, but they were usually still rooted in their craft; their businesses were the next logical progression of the journeyman to master. Many of the socialists, however, were, like Pettipiece, Wrigley, and Kingsley, intellectuals who started newspapers primarily to propagate ideas. Others, such as Ernest Burns and John Cameron, were small merchants. Neither group had an integral connection to the working class or its traditions; their vision of socialism was at odds with the vision of the labour leaders who had emerged through struggles and compromise with the employer on the job site. The relative newness to and status in the city of these socialists helped stoke the fire of revolution and made the VTLC leaders view the militants of the socialist party as a threat to all they had accomplished and stood for. Both sides could point to the inconsistencies of their opponents, but in fact socialists and labourists alike put forward programs and policies that spoke to their own class backgrounds and aspirations. What is most important to the study of bureaucracy is that neither side campaigned on the issue of increasing rank-and-file participation. In the struggle over who should lead the city's labour movement, neither was inclined to leave the matter in the hands of the working class itself.

8

Continuity, Change, and Resolution

The structure of the VTLC meant that the socialists would be kept from power for some time. Indeed, they could not exert much influence in the council until the labourists retired from the battlefield. The old patterns of officer selection, political compromise, and limited reformism dominated the council. The structures and traditions of the early bureaucrats ensured that continuity, not change, would remain the dominant feature of the council. When change in people and politics did occur, it was shaped and channelled by the bureaucracy.

While several historians have suggested that the years 1900 to 1903 saw a greater socialist influence in the VTLC, careful examination of the bureaucracy discounts this view.[1] If the socialist influence on the council were strong, one would expect to find this reflected in the membership of the VTLC itself. Presumably socialists would hold important positions on the executive and committees. Resolutions favouring left-wing policies would be another indicator, as would support for socialist politicians. Indeed, without such evidence in the historical record, it is difficult to know what difference a socialist presence would mean, or how it would differ from the labourist domination of the council's first ten years. But closer examination of the council suggests that despite the growth of the socialist party between 1900 and 1904, it had little effect on the VTLC.

One striking absence from the council is a significant number of socialists in positions of power or influence. Will MacClain of the IAM did serve one term as statistician in 1900, but his politics represented a relatively mild version of socialism. By April 1900 he had already led a faction out of the Socialist Labor Party to form the more moderate United Socialist Labor Party.[2] Even this less-strident political stance proved unpalatable to others in the labour council. When he denounced the Liberal–Labour politician Ralph Smith in October

1900, the Streetcar Railwaymen's Union unanimously insisted that the VTLC call for MacClain's resignation. If he were not removed, the union warned, it would withdraw its delegates from the council. The VTLC referred the issue back to the IAM on the grounds that the selection of delegates was a matter for each union to decide for itself. But the IAM did not back McClain either: in November, the union withdrew him as its delegate, and the following month, he was removed from his office as IAM local president.[3]

Ernest Burns was another socialist who took part in the VTLC in this period. Like MacClain, however, his influence was moderate and limited. A member of the council's parliamentary committee in 1902, his presence had no discernible socialist impact on the committee's recommendations, which held up the traditional labourist demands of an end to assisted immigration and prison labour, attacked the government's railway policy, and added the local concerns with the city hospital and ownership of the tide flats.[4]

Burns, an Englishman who had lived in the Pacific Northwest since 1890, was no impossibilist or radical. His socialist vision was coloured by his work with the Knights of Labor and the Populist Party in Washington state, and he urged reformism and gradualism, even while secretary of the Socialist Party of British Columbia.[5] In a letter to a Seattle paper, Burns announced that 'my socialism is of a more elastic quality than that of some ultra-orthodox comrades who have reduced socialism from a philosophy to a creed, and regard the slightest questioning of their tenets and dogmas as heresy of the most outrageous type ... [We] have to grow into socialism ... clearing away the rubbish of obsolete socialism on the one hand and laying the foundations for the temple of industrial democracy wherever we can find chance to work ... Constructive practical work is of far more service than revolutionary air fanning or unintelligent repetition of stock phrases of revolutionary jargon.'[6] Later, Burns would move even further to the right, splitting from the SPC to form the moderate Social Democratic Party in 1906. But his commitment to a reformist socialism was still at odds with the VTLC of 1902. As president of the fishermen's union, Burns sat as a council delegate, and was elected trustee in January 1902. But he failed in his bid for the vice-presidency the following term and was not even re-elected as trustee. Leaving the union to go into business with his father, Burns no longer played an active role in the council or the labour movement after his single term as trustee.[7]

Few other socialists served on the council in the alleged period of radicalism between 1900 and 1904. James McVety served a term as trustee in 1902 and continued as a delegate until 1905 when he became vice-president, and John Mortimer of the tailors was active in committee work and at meetings. Neither man, however, carried much weight in the council, and neither was elected to any significant office in this period. Instead, the council continued to select its officials much as it had in the past. Indeed, the council of 1900–1 resembled that of the previous ten years. Joseph Dixon served as president for three terms starting in January 1900. His vice-presidents included J.H. Watson, John Morton, and John Crow. None was a socialist. Watson was a careerist Liberal, while Morton and Crow were staunch labourists. Morton, born in Scotland in 1867, was a member of the Amalgamated Society of Carpenters and had arrived in Vancouver around 1892. In 1900 he became secretary of the VTLC's parliamentary committee and secretary of the labourist Independent Labour Party created by the council. Running as a labour candidate for municipal office, he was defeated in 1900 and 1902, but in 1903 served the first of six terms as alderman for the predominantly working class Ward Five.[8] Crow, an American, was a member of the cigarmakers union, and had arrived in Vancouver before the fire of 1886. Elected trustee of the VTLC in 1900, he then became vice-president and in 1901 succeeded Dixon as president. Like Morton, an aldermanic candidate in 1903, Crow ran on the labour ticket alongside perennial labourist politician Robert Macpherson, and he was on the executive committee of the Independent Labour convention in 1900.[9]

Nor did other officers come from the socialist tradition. C.R. Monck, who served in different positions in the 1890s, including three terms as president from July 1892 to 1893, resurfaced as treasurer in 1900 and announced his candidacy as a Liberal in 1903.[10] John Pearey, a delegate from the Streetcar Railwaymen's Union that had objected to MacClain sitting on the council, took over the presidency in the latter part of 1900. Pearey, a Scots immigrant, had already done stints as vice-president and president of the council in 1899, and in 1901 became treasurer of the Independent Labour Party as well as the VTLC.[11] Little is known of the first two men who served as secretary in 1900 and 1901. D.C. Harrison was elected secretary in the aftermath of the Deadman's Island dispute in 1899 and was re-elected later that year. Harrison, a member of the Streetcar Railwaymen's Union, was elected again in 1900, but resigned part way into his term, giving 'personal reasons' as the explanation. He was replaced by J.C. Marshall, who in turn resigned after two terms. No information on their political ideology has been found, but their repeated election to council posts during the reign of the labourist bureaucrats suggests they were not socialists.

Thus, in 1900 and 1901, the labour council resembled that of 1890; even many of the faces were the same. The two men credited with founding the council, Joseph Dixon and George Bartley, were still prominent, as Dixon led the council and Bartley controlled its newspaper. New blood had been brought in, and the Streetcar Railwaymen's Union now challenged the old crafts for positions on the council, but its politics were little different, and the union took to labourism as eagerly as the carpenters, printers, and other trades had. In 1902, however, the VTLC did undergo some significant changes. The elections of that year saw the temporary displacement of the dominance of the old craft unions in the council executive. W.J. Lamrick of the Retail Clerks Union succeeded Dixon and Crow as president; F.J. Russell of the Freighthandlers Union moved from the trustee position he had occupied in 1901 to the vice-presidency; T.H. Cross of the Postal Employees Union took over the secretary's job in late 1901 and continued in the position throughout 1902. This influx of workers from outside the traditional craft unions has been seen as part of a swing to socialism in British Columbia; historians such as Ross McCormack have suggested that 'dilution' of the old craft unions opened the way to more radical action, while the relatively unskilled workers who now came to the fore were more inclined to consider radical measures.[12]

There is, on the face of it, some evidence for this view. In July 1902 the council voted to allow the *Canadian Socialist* newspaper to report its proceedings, but refused a request to endorse the paper.[13] In the ensuing years the council upheld the principle of industrial unionism, broke with the Dominion Trades and Labour Congress (DTLC), and purged Watson. It even endorsed the American Labor Union, a radical industrial union that would soon form the nucleus of the syndicalist Industrial Workers of the World. Yet despite these actions, often interpreted as proof of the triumph of socialism, closer examination of the council's personnel and policies tends to confirm the strength of the bureaucracy to blunt the edge of radicalism.[14]

For example, though W.J. Lamrick has been credited with moving the VTLC to the left, it is not apparent that he was a socialist. Born in Ontario in 1856, he moved to Vancouver around 1896 and was first elected to the vice-presidency of the council in 1901. A member of the retail clerks local that had formed in 1899, Lamrick was appointed British Columbia organizer for the international two years later. In 1902 Lamrick was re-elected president of the VTLC and was selected by the council to represent it on the city's Tourist Association. In 1903 Lamrick was on the executive of the Vancouver Labour Party, an organization that ran Liberals such as Chris Foley and Francis Williams against socialist candidates in the provincial election. In his political outlook, then, Lamrick was no radical; nor did he represent much of a break with the council's labourist tradition. His politics reflected the successful merchant he would soon become rather than an unskilled proletarian.[15]

Other council executives also represented continuity rather than a break with the past, despite their occupations. T.H. Cross served as secretary under

Lamrick for three terms, and one term as trustee, and represented the Postal Employees Union. Cross emigrated from England in 1879. A veteran of the Riel Rebellion of 1885, he moved to Vancouver in 1896. Little is known of his politics. One key indicator, however, is his vote in January 1903 when he sided with Liberal supporters such as J.H. Watson, C.R. Monck, and Francis Williams. Cross supported their campaign to have the council endorse the machine candidate Macpherson over independent Liberal Chris Foley. It is likely that Cross's career in the post office was, like Watson's in the customs office, a patronage appointment, and insofar as his political views are known, he supported the mainstream Liberal party in the council.[16]

Other council executives fail to fit McCormack's description as well. A.N. Harrington of the Waiters Union appears to be a less skilled worker, and by McCormack's interpretation, one more likely to push for socialism. However, closer investigation suggests otherwise. Harrington served as council treasurer for three terms, from January 1903 to July 1904, always as a delegate of the waiters. But the city directories from 1901 to 1904 list him as being part of the Harrington Brothers Union Dye Works.[17] When secretary Eugene Harpur of the Barbers Union resigned part way through his term in 1903, his place was taken by C.T. Hilton of the Amalgamated Society of Carpenters. Hilton was re-elected in 1904, but had to withdraw, as he took up a government position. Hilton was another Liberal supporter: in 1906, he became financial secretary for the Liberal party and was able to put down the tools of his trade for the rest of his life when he was rewarded with a position in the customs office in 1909.[18]

Liberals and labourists continued to fill positions on the council in 1903. George Bartley sat on the label committee; A.E. Soper of the Team Drivers Union was sergeant at arms and member of the municipal committee, as well as secretary of the Vancouver Labor Party; John Crow served on the municipal committee; William George of the Civic Employees Union, who sat as a trustee in 1903 and then as vice-president in 1904, had been active in the VLP in 1900. F.J. Russell was a member of a 'new' union, the freighthandlers, that would become part of the militant UBRE in 1903. Elected a trustee of the council in 1901, he followed the typical pattern of promotion, becoming vice-president in 1902 and finally secretary in 1903. Although little is known of his political views, they did not deter newly elected Tory premier Richard McBride from appointing Russell to a government position to enforce the province's immigration act in the summer of 1903. The *Independent* lauded the appointment, and Russell left the council without seeking re-election.[19] The vice-president of the VTLC throughout 1903, George Dobbin, was the former president of the carpenters local.

Only two men who can be positively identified with the socialist movement appear in the so-called radical council of 1903. John Mortimer, a Scottish tailor and former president of the Winnipeg Trades and Labor Council, joined the Socialist Party in 1903 and was a member of the VTLC's parliamentary committee that same year. Ben Bates was another. A clerk in the city engineer's office, Bates was the chairman of the British Columbia Socialist Party in 1902, and in 1903 he sat on the auditing committee of the VTLC.[20]

If generalizations about the radicalism of the new organizations affiliated to the VTLC are misleading, so are arguments about their ability to 'dilute' the craft unionism and reformism of the council. While McCormack includes building labourers and longshoremen in this group of 'new' unions, both of these had long been members of the labour council. R. Cosgrove had served as a delegate from the building labourers and later its international union of hod carriers since 1891, and he held the council position of doorkeeper in 1891 and 1893, while Liberal and independent labourist Chris Foley was one of the union's delegates in 1903. Similarly, the longshoremen had organized as early as 1888. The Stevedores Union that evolved out of the Knights of Labor sent Colin McDonald to represent it and to serve as VTLC treasurer and vice-president from 1893 to 1897. Even if these delegates are counted and assumed to be radical, socialist, or left leaning, they formed only a minority of the council. At a roll call vote in January 1903 to select the council's candidate in an upcoming provincial election, the craft unions could put forward fifty-three delegates, the new unions only twenty-two. In a Labour Day edition of the same year, the *Independent* recorded that sixty-eight delegates came from old unions, twenty-eight from new. When unions such as the building labourers with their five delegates are counted as 'old' unions, and known labourists in others are subtracted, the ability of the new unions to shape the council was very limited indeed.[21] Whatever radicalism may have swept the province and the city in 1903 it was clearly not reflected in the personnel and unions of the Vancouver Trades and Labour Council.

Nor do the policies and politics of the council suggest that it was greatly influenced by the upsurge in socialism. In 1903 the council's principal political activity was the provincial by-election in the fall. Choosing the candidate to be endorsed by the council was a rancorous battle, second only to the Deadman's Island dispute of 1899 in its ability to divide the council. Once again, J.H. Watson was at the centre of the storm. But the conflict was not between socialists and labourists. On the contrary, it was a battle between Liberals such as Watson who plumped for the mainstream, Lib–Lab machine candidate Robert MacPherson and those labourists who insisted that labour needed an independent Liberal candidate, Chris Foley. At regular and special meetings called to discuss the endorsement, the council split into factions. Watson, aware that the mood of the council was against him, first sought to prevent the council from endorsing anyone. A motion that the council not endorse any candidate was made, and a roll-call vote insisted upon – probably the first in the council's history.[22] The voting pattern is illustrative. The 'nay' vote, that is, the vote to endorse a candidate, defeated the 'aye' vote by a margin of 2 to 1: 44 votes to 22. The following vote to endorse Foley was passed, 41 to 20. The only known socialist present, John Mortimer, cast his vote with Watson's faction, probably in the belief that if the council were not going to support the socialist party it should not put its resources behind either labourist candidate. From the two tallies, it is apparent that most voters preferred to field a candidate and that they wanted Foley to be that candidate.

Those unions that voted to endorse a candidate and presumably voted for Foley included most of the new unions. The retail clerks, led by council president Lamrick, the United Brotherhood of Railway Employees, with council secretary F.J. Russell and financial secretary J.T. Lilley in their ranks, and the building labourers, all voted alongside labourist stalwarts from the carpenters, iron moulders, barbers, cigarmakers, amalgamated carpenters, streetcar railwaymen, and the like to put forward Foley as a candidate. Of the 'new' unions only the postal employees sided with Watson and Mortimer. Since an 'aye' vote could be interpreted as either a vote for the mainstream Liberals or for the socialist position, it may be that some of those votes were indeed votes for the left. But the boilermakers' delegates led by Watson and the stonecutters' delegates led by C.R. Monck were undoubtedly votes for the Liberal party. Even the most generous interpretation of this episode illustrates clearly that the socialist influence on the VTLC was limited and weak. Politics continued in the labourist vein. The important issue in 1903 was not whether labourism should be replaced with socialism, but how best to carry the labourist message to the legislature.

Even the purge of Watson, considered by McCormack as a sign of socialist strength, reflected the disillusionment with the old Liberal party and Lib–Labism rather than any new radicalism. After the vote to endorse Foley, Watson refused to abide by the council's decision. At public meetings and in the press, Watson declared that the endorsement had been 'railroaded through,' for of the forty-six unions in the city, eighteen had voted for Foley, nine against, four had abstained, and fifteen were not represented at the meeting. Instead, Watson argued, a poll of all the members of all the unions in the city should have been taken. Watson's connections with the Liberal party and his patronage job in the customs office were well known and were seen as the real reason for his new-found concern for democracy. At one meeting, as Watson headed to the platform to speak, someone shouted out, 'Look out for your job, Joe!' Watson responded, 'That's all right, if I get bounced I can easily get another job.' Rejecting pleas in the *Independent* for harmony and unity in the upcoming election, Watson continued to fight hard for MacPherson and the mainstream Liberals led by Ralph Smith. Claiming that Foley was a 'liberal-tory-labor' candidate, Watson accused the independent labourists of selling out to the local Conservative party for support and induced his union, the boilermakers, to withdraw from the VTLC.[23]

Now he had gone too far. Delegates introduced a motion in the council to change the section of the constitution that outlined the qualifications for membership. The proposed amendment insisted that 'all delegates must be wage earners, and either actively employed at the trade or calling they are representing or acting as paid agents putting in their full time in the service of the respective unions.' This measure, which incidentally provided for the professionalization of delegates, was aimed squarely at Watson who had long ceased to be an active tradesman but continued to represent the boilermakers in the council.[24] Still Watson pressed his attack. Federal Union Number 23, organized by Watson and chartered directly to the DTLC, refused to send delegates to the Vancouver Trades and Labour Council, and condemned it for forcing Watson out and for 'allowing politics in the council.' A letter to the *Independent*, signed 'Fakir' and probably written by Watson or one of his supporters, objected to the new qualifications for delegates, asking, 'What is a labor representative? ... Many middle-class and professional men are more sincere than many of those who have felt the pinch of hunger. Are we to exclude middle-class and professional men from labor representation? Personally, I think it would be a narrow-minded and ill-advised policy.'[25] He was answered indirectly by the VTLC. The Iron Moulders Union supported the purge of Watson and suggested that 'in the future no Government Official be allowed to hold office.' On 19 March the council adopted the amendment tightening up delegates' qualifications and adopted a report by the parliamentary committee that outlined the charges against Watson. He was, the report maintained, a government official, not a worker. Contrary to the DTLC decision taken at the Montreal Congress in 1899, he was a representative of one of the 'old parties'; he was a 'disrupter' who granted DTLC charters to workers who came under the jurisdiction of the AFL's international unions; he made 'invidious comparisons between Canadian and American labor bodies' and induced the boilermakers to bolt the VTLC. Finally, he was attacked for his active and partisan participation in the by-election.[26]

The charges suggest that Watson was forced out of the council for reasons that any labourist or member of an international union could support. Willfully creating disunity, fostering dual unionism, and refusing to comply with democratic decisions made Watson undesirable to all but his most ardent supporters. Further allegations that he had supplied the CPR with scabs carrying Federal Union cards during the UBRE's fight with the railway added fuel to the fire, but again, no socialist content in the charges can be found.[27] Watson was quick to blame socialists, especially Mortimore, for his defeat in the council, claiming that the American Labor Union, which was supported by Mortimer, was the real disrupter in the union movement. Watson charged the socialists with placing their political creed before the interests of their union, an ironic and hypocritical complaint given his own political scheming. Finally, Watson attacked the socialists for their atheism and called for 'Christian principle' in the labour movement. But his red-baiting clouds the very real issues that led to his ouster, issues that cannot be categorized or dismissed as a sign of socialist strength.[28]

The endorsement of the ALU by some local unions does suggest some radical influence in the labour council. Socialists such as Mortimer and Ben Bates actively proselytized for the union, and in March 1903 the wholesale clerks sought a charter from the ALU. But the clerks maintained that they sought admission to the industrial union because no AFL union would take them in. Watson's suggestion that they affiliate directly to the DTLC was unlikely to be taken up, given the feuding that had just taken place over that very issue.[29] But in his defence of the ALU, Mortimer made it clear that socialists, even more than old-line unionists such as Watson, supported centralization and professionalism. Mortimer denounced the DTLC, for it could not enforce its mandates on subordinate unions, had no strike fund, and had no permanent executive. The ALU, however, could order its members out on a general strike. It had a significant strike fund, permanent headquarters, and a salaried executive 'devoting their whole time to the work of supervision and organization.' In short, Mortimer advocated the ALU because it functioned like a hierarchical business union, rather than as a loose federation that secured local autonomy.[30] In this instance at least, the socialists on the council were even less interested in rank-and-file control than the labourists.

If the labour council was relatively immune to the imprecations of the socialist movement, why then did the *Independent* spend so much time attacking the left? Clearly the labourists feared the growing support for socialism that was manifested not in the labour council but in the political arena. The socialist party was becoming increasingly powerful and was improving its electoral success. In 1902 the labourists had met with socialists to create a new party, the Provincial Progressive Party. Although the labourists, led by VTLC delegates such as Bartley and Watson, controlled the new party and fended off the socialists, the PPP stalled soon after. The socialist party proved that it was able to win votes and mobilize workers in the battle for the ballot.[31]

The defeat of Foley and the impotence of the PPP showed that the labourists were unable to accomplish much on the federal or provincial levels. The socialist party moved in to fill the vacuum, and labour bureaucrats feared that its political success would enable it to out-flank the labour council and become the de facto leader of the working class. In the provincial elections of 1903 the socialists gave proof that they could indeed threaten the dominance of the labourists. The Socialist Party of British Columbia (SPBC) elected three members to the legislature, and its ten candidates polled 9 per cent of the vote. In Vancouver the three labourist candidates lost, but even worse for the bureaucrats, two were out-polled by John Mortimer of the SPBC. A.E. Soper of the Labour party concluded that the working class had divided its vote between the Conservatives and the Socialists; the labourists simply dropped through the middle.[32] In the *Independent*, labourists announced their frustration and fear that workers would be gulled by the left. Deploring the disruption that helped defeat Foley and exposed the weakness of the labourists, one writer hoped that 'the alleged "mossbacks" in our various unions will get together again and talk over affairs and see what is the best thing to do in Vancouver under the circumstances.'[33]

Despite their setbacks at the polls in 1903, the same patterns of bureaucracy continued. With the collapse of the Retail Clerks Union, W.J. Lamrick left the council to take up work in the cooperative store it had established some years before.[34] George Dobbin moved up to become president, reasserting the dominance of the craft unions. C.T. Hilton, another carpenter, although a member of the Amalgamated Society, was made secretary. But some things had changed. The failure of the labourist political campaigns in 1903 led most of the old guard to resign from politics. The *Independent* reluctantly admitted in its editorial column that it might well be time to give the socialists a 'free hand to see what they can do' in the next election. The independent labourists had spent 'too much time and money' with little to 'show for their services except abuse, to want to thwart any new movement gotten up in the interests of labor.' On the critical issue of whether the VTLC paper would endorse socialists, Bartley wrote, 'That would depend entirely on who the candidates are.'[35] Some labourists such as Francis Williams, would stay with the VTLC, using his base there to pursue a political career on the city council. Others, such as Dixon, would devote their time to their businesses.

The socialists learned from their experience as well. Although the Socialist Party of Canada, the successor to the SPBC, still had an impossibilist, anti-union thread woven through its ideology, many of its members took a more moderate view. Pettipiece began to forge links with the labour movement, partly because his failure as a publisher forced him to learn the printing trade. Where previously he had called for the socialists to keep their party 'iron-clad, aye "narrow",' he now held up trade unions as essential organizations worthy of support.[36] James McVety returned to the VTLC's executive in 1905, and he quickly became adept at the rules of bureaucracy. Together, the two men would slowly bring the council to the left, although not to the revolutionary socialism of men such as Kingsley. For one lesson of 1903 may have been that while the bureaucracy would fight rapid changes, it could nonetheless be nudged to new positions. Bartley had hinted as much to his successors in 1903, when the *Independent* suggested that caution and an 'evolutionary movement' could win over the 'large numbers of working men who are in accord with the socialistic theory.'[37] Socialists such as McVety and Pettipiece took this counsel of patience. Pettipiece joined the VTLC's parliamentary committee, alongside oldtimers such as Charles Boardman and Bartley. Three years later he served with Lib–Lab Chris Foley on the parliamentary committee. Despite their past differences, Pettipiece had mellowed to the point where he could remark that he had never before worked on a committee 'where such harmony prevailed.' From there he began a steady climb through the bureaucracy.[38]

The council also took a more active role in larger political issues, perhaps a reflection of the influence of the SPC. In 1907, for example, the VTLC voted 18 to 11 to send money to the defence fund of Moyer, Pettibone, and Haywood, the Western Federation of Miners' officers who were on trial for murder in Colorado. The sum sent – $20 – was a token gesture, but one that previous councils had been loath to make in similar causes. The old patterns still showed through, however, in the close vote and in the subsequent failure to make the motion unanimous. Nor did the council reverse its earlier refusal to join with the IWW, the SPC, and the SLP in a committee to protest the prosecution of the three men.[39]

Other steps were taken to make the council more overtly political, and this too was a departure from the labourist position. In 1905 a motion was made to change the constitution to allow political discussions to take place during the meetings. An amendment to limit such discussions to twenty minutes was made, and another sought to limit them 'only to Labor matters.' All three failed, however, and the matter was laid to rest for nearly three years, when Pettipiece moved again to devote one hour of the last meeting of each month to be devoted to 'general matters pertaining to labour.' This time the motion passed.[40]

The socialist influence was also felt in the realm of culture, albeit negatively. In 1908 the annual discussion about Labour Day was taken up. The old craft unions, especially the carpenters, bricklayers, lathers, and cigarmakers, all voted to hold a parade. The socialists, however, insisted that 'election day [w]as the proper day to demonstrate the workers' strength,' and led by Pettipiece, they moved that the council take no action on a parade. With the motion supported by the IAM and the building laborers, the VTLC agreed to hold a picnic instead.[41] The following year the left took an even stronger stand against the traditional procession, denouncing it as a 'hollow sham so long considered a display of strength.' In contrast to the old generation typified by Dixon and others, 'the younger generation of trade unionists ... recognize the futility of parades ... and prefer to celebrate more quietly by holding picnics and the usual accompanying amusements, concluding the day's sport by listening to speakers, picked because of their ability to deliver the true message to the working class.' Again the socialists insisted that it was better to display 'the forces of labor on election day.'[42] The old craft union consciousness, exemplified for a time in the procession of the trades, even with its tendency towards accommodation with the larger society, had at least the benefit of stressing the contribution of the worker as a worker. But this core of labourism was diminished by the socialists; in its place was now the pale culture of electoral politics.

If the socialists broke with the craft traditions of the earlier council, they did not break with a more unseemly tradition, that of racism. The preeminence of the socialists in the labour council from 1907 onwards did little to change the attitude of organized labour or the actions of the council. In March 1907 the council endorsed the petition of the International Brotherhood of Electrical Workers that called for a $500 head tax to keep out would-be Chinese immigrants. The petition repeated the council's oft-stated belief that 'the Chinaman brings nothing to a white man's country that benefits it ... [and] is a menace to the morals, the health, and the prosperity of that community.'[43] Later that year, the council, on the motion of socialist Parmeter Pettipiece, voted to allow the Asiatic Exclusion League to meet in the union hall. The league also attracted council officers: vice-president A.W. Von Rhein of the Bartenders' Union, trustee J. Commerford of the building laborers, and Samuel Gothard, former council secretary and publisher of the VTLC paper the *BC Trades Unionist*, were all active in it. Von Rhein served as president for the league, and Gothard was one of its most virulent members.[44]

Socialists on the council were caught up in the anti-Asian fervour. Addressing the delegates, Pettipiece opined that 'the Japs were armed to the teeth' in Vancouver and that 'the time had come when the white population [must] look to protect themselves.' Nearly all the delegates present agreed that whites should 'look into this important question.'[45] Although Pettipiece would sometimes echo the socialist analysis that 'the importation of these Asiatics is but an incident to capitalist production,' on other occasions his writings would resemble those of any labourist. For example, in March 1908 Pettipiece wrote, 'In the fast-growing Oriental section of the city every conceivable sort of the rankest kind of "sweat shops" exist; or perhaps thrive would be the better term. And as a sort of refuge for the social garbage as a result of such economic conditions, the Chinese have provided the town with plenty of opium joints, where over 100 white women, social outcasts who have fallen to the last depths of degradation, are the imprisoned victims of these monstrous dens of iniquity.'[46] The editorial page of the council paper, which was overseen by a committee of Pettipiece, Von Rhein, and W.W. Sayer of the bricklayers, kept up the old line, announcing that 'there are no classes of people in the world that are more revoltingly dirty than an Oriental.' Deploring the number of Chinese employed in the restaurant business in the city, the paper complained of the inconsistency of those whose 'stomachs will revolt at the conditions in Chinatown,' yet would still 'patiently swallow the food prepared by the very class that in their native lairs horrifies us.'[47] When the VTLC voted to oppose the building of the Grand Trunk Pacific Railway with Chinese labour, the entire council, including socialist James McVety, supported the motion. Clearly socialism was no vaccine against racism.[48]

If the SPC had a better appreciation of the 'women's question' than many of the labourists, such concern was not well reflected in the labour council. While Bertha Burns, the wife of Ernest Burns, wrote a regular column for the *Western Clarion* under the name of Dorothy Drew, women in general remained unorganized and under-represented on the VTLC.[49] In 1905 Mrs Smith of the Laundry Workers' Union was seated as a delegate, and in 1907 three other women represented their unions on the council: Mrs Powell of the laundry workers, and Mrs Edwards and Mrs Walker from the United Garment Workers Union. Little is known of these delegates; they made no motions, served on no committees, and do not appear in the minutes apart from the notice of their initiations. Nor was their attendance exemplary: in 1909 the garment workers' delegates attended nine of forty-eight meetings. Without evidence, it is difficult to know, but it is likely that the women did not take an active role because they were continually outvoted and intimidated by men. Such was indeed the pattern in unions that organized women, such as the Waitresses and the Ladies' Auxiliary of the International Brotherhood of Electrical Workers, which functioned as a local of the IBEW and organized telephone operators.[50] The socialist council did little to correct the problem in this period.

If the left council represented the old racism and sexism, still the election of a significant socialist clique to the key positions of the VTLC from 1906 to 1909 did little to alleviate the distinction between leaders and led. Compulsory arbitration, for example, was not a tool of the labourists alone. Socialists in the council, such as James McVety, were equally quick to call for compulsory arbitration and to ignore the rank and file when quick settlements were deemed necessary. When McVety's fellow machinists and other trades struck the CPR in 1908 to resist wage cuts and to create a federation of railway trades for centralized bargaining, McVety was part of the delegation that hammered out an agreement in private sessions with the company. When rank-and-file unionists complained about the secret negotiations, McVety responded with words that might easily have come from labourists such as Joe Dixon or J.H. Watson. McVety defended the behind-the-doors settlement forcefully, arguing that despite outward appearances, the strikers were weakening, their financial resources stretched thin and solidarity beginning to unravel. The committee had to act quickly and without consulting with the rank and file, he insisted, to salvage whatever it could. Therefore, he wrote,

every offer of mediation was accepted gratefully, and when the last offer was presented we considered it very carefully from every standpoint ... Many times the question has been asked, 'Why did you not submit the proposition to the membership?' ... [The committee] decided it would be better to accept the terms offered and get the men back to their work ... It would have been a cowardly action to risk the employment of the men merely to save our own reputations, and bitter as the denunciations have been, I personally would act in the same way again if the circumstances were the same, in the belief that a good general should know when he is defeated and prepare to save as many of the rank and file as possible.[51]

McVety then came out in favour of compulsory arbitration, maintaining that the Lemieux Act, or the Industrial Disputes Investigation Act, that provided for compulsory investigation by the government but not compulsory arbitration, did not go nearly far enough. McVety argued that it was necessary to extend it to cover all industries, to make the government's awards and rulings compulsory, to extend the board members' tenure, and to allow adequate remuneration for witnesses. This would allow the act to become 'legislation of real importance,' he wrote.[52] Clearly the pressures of negotiations and the responsibility of keeping unionists on the job affected bureaucrats of every stripe. And when up against a corporate juggernaut like the CPR, calling on the state for help was a reasonable, if overly optimistic, tactic. Nonetheless, excluding the rank and file from the negotiating process drove a wedge between the leaders and the led, and socialists no less than labourists were inclined to act independently when a settlement was in sight.

Nor was socialism any guarantee of enthusiasm for meetings and council activities. In August 1907 the council adopted a motion to enforce attendance. Officers or standing committee members who missed three meetings 'without good and sufficient reasons,' which were 'sickness or absence from town,' would have their position declared vacant.[53] Six months later, however, the statistician complained that even with the passage of the strict attendance policy, less than 50 per cent of the delegates attended meetings and that he had been forced to send out twenty-eight notices of delinquency. Subsequent reports had similar dismal statistics to announce. The statistician concluded in July 1908 that 'delegates were not taking the interest in the Trades and Labor council that they should,' and he set about compiling an accurate tabulation of attendance. In the meantime, the council newspaper suggested that strengthening the VTLC by giving it the right to assess its affiliated members might help the attendance problem, for it would compel 'the rank and file to interest themselves in the central lodge's work – probably because they have to pay for it.'[54] When the report was published in February 1909, it revealed that not a single union had managed to have all its delegates present at every meeting; some unions had barely been represented at all. The figures were based on the past twelve meetings and each union's possible attendance was calculated by multiplying the number of its delegates by the number of meetings held. Thus, the bricklayers had five delegates, making a total of sixty possible attendances. They managed only thirty. Still, their record was better than that of the bartenders, who attended only eleven out of sixty. The cooks managed twenty-two of sixty, the printing pressmen two of twelve. Others did better: carpenters scored forty-four out of sixty, streetcar railwaymen forty out of sixty. Still, by August 1909 the council could not, on average, get even half its delegates to attend a meeting.[55]

The reasons for the apathy of delegates were not much considered, though the statistician's reports suggest that the summer months were a particularly bad time for attendance. But one reason may have been the constant flow of criticism levelled by the activists at those who were critical of the leadership. The editorial page of the BC Trades Unionist blazed away at the rank and file who protested against paying officials for their union work, arguing that 'there can be no objection to paying men for their services, providing they deliver the services. In fact, this is the least the rank and file can do, since they are unwilling or unfitted to do the job for themselves.'[56] An article reprinted from the *Miners Magazine* gave sarcastic tips on how to destroy the union movement and took aim at those who were critical of the leadership. Those who wanted to hurt organized labour, it suggested, should 'always hint or insinuate that those who do the work for the union are seeking an office or some glory. Be sure never to say anything good of labor agitators who work for the union when you are at the theatre, the saloon, or in bed.'[57]

Other articles in the labour press continued in a similar vein, defending professional and volunteer union bureaucrats against the sniping of the rank and file. One article, reprinted from the *Machinists' Journal* – the journal of council president James McVety's union – was a glowing tribute to salaried union officials:

What a much-abused person he is, the hardest worked and the poorest paid of men. The employer hates him and the fool workingman does not love him! He must know the trade of his craft and also be a philosopher. He must be a businessman and also a student of history and economics. He must be honest and yet be a diplomat.

He must be a fighter and yet be a strategist. He must be an organizer and an orator ...

To be a business agent one must be ready to make all sacrifices, to undergo all hardships and undertake the cause of humanity, to lead men to a better way of living. He is the last to vote for a strike, the first to enter its fight. The first to give up his best energies to its success, the last to surrender. If the strike is won he gets no credit. If the strike is lost he is deposed, and yet some men are born to be business agents.

Every man that ever raised his voice against the oppression of his class was a business agent. Moses was a business agent and so was Jesus.[58]

Although the militancy of the union leader was heralded in the article, another essay in the labour press painted a different picture of the role of the union leader, especially the business agent. Unpaid negotiating committees were unsatisfactory, it argued, for three reasons. First, fear of the employer meant the committee could not press as hard as an independent business agent. Second, experience was useful, and elected committees would not have the necessary background and practice that the professional would. Third, employers 'disliked to meet with new men on each occasion, preferring to meet with those familiar with the details of the last conference.' Continuity and experience were held to be more important than rank-and-file control. It was even, the article suggested, more important than militancy, for 'the good business agent' should be 'polite, diplomatic, and tactful in his dealings with the employer.'[59] Thus, the paper run by the socialist McVety maintained that cooperation was as important as confrontation for the labour movement and that leaders should act independently of the rank and file.

Accompanying this defence of leaders were attacks on union dissidents and 'knockers,' defined as 'the man who has a good word for nobody or anything,' and who insisted that 'no matter who takes a prominent part in any movement, that person ... is actuated by ulterior motives.'[60] The paper deplored the 'peculiar perversity possessing many union people that makes them knock the men they have elected to office.' Comparing the knockers to Indian men who abused their 'squaws,' the paper argued that complaining unionists piled 'all the work of the organizations on the shoulders of the officer and a heap of abuse on his head.'[61] In a full-page article by local carpenters' president P.W. Dowler, the paper printed the solution to the problem of dissidents. Since organized labor was on 'the firing line,' it was necessary to gather 'the stragglers into the organization.' More importantly, it was vital for members to 'uphold and assist your local and general officers in the management of the affairs of the organization.' These officers were, the article maintained, 'the nucleus upon which we repose our hopes for industrial freedom.'[62]

These articles and others like them appeared in a labour press that was controlled directly by socialists, such as Parm Pettipiece and James McVety, and indirectly by a labour council that had socialists elected to important executive positions. They suggest that whatever their political ideology was, socialists had no principled objections to the professionalization of the union leadership or to the divisions between leaders and led. Such objections would have been hypocritical, for in this period the council moved more forthrightly to professionalize its own leadership cadre. Under the leadership of the socialist faction, the council made it possible for its officers to become career union officers. The first step was taken in 1906, when Pettipiece 'in a few spirited remarks' urged that the council reaffiliate to the Dominion Trades and Labor Congress. This paved the way for his appointment to the position of DTLC organizer six months later.[63] Pettipiece then called on the council to recommend to the DTLC and the AFL that local men should be appointed as organizers. Subsequently, the council's executive board, headed by President McVety, nominated Pettipiece for both jobs and suggested that 'funds be placed at his disposal for carrying on the work.' Both recommendations were approved by the council as a whole.[64] Thus, by February 1908 Pettipiece had managed to become the successor to the now discredited J.H. Watson as the British Columbia representative of the Canadian and

American trade union centrals. The chief difference was that while Watson had had to depend on his patronage job for an income, Pettipiece could depend on the labour movement itself.

Other measures were taken to professionalize the bureaucracy of the VTLC. On Pettipiece's motion, the salary of the secretary was doubled to $10 per month, the first raise ever given to the job. No doubt long overdue, still the labourist council had resisted the move. In 1907 the council considered appointing a permanent secretary so he could 'devote his whole time to the work of the council.' When the permanent paid position was created, Pettipiece was appointed to the job.[65]

The paid positions seemed to forge unlikely alliances in the council. In 1908 Parm Pettipiece argued successfully to have the election for secretary postponed, so that his fellow ITU member Harry Cowan could run for the job. The fact that Cowan had always been a strong Liberal and labourist seemed unimportant. Later that year Cowan was also appointed as business agent for the council to help sign up unions that were unaffiliated to the VTLC. Pettipiece's support for an apparent political foe is puzzling, but it may be that political differences were often overcome in the interests of the labour movement, craft solidarity, and the stability of the bureaucracy.[66]

The VTLC institutions of the labour hall and the newspaper continued to reinforce the separation between union leaders and the rank and file under the reign of the socialists. In 1905 the council took steps to tighten control over the hall, voting to create a board of trustees to administer it separately 'from the legislative affairs of the Trades and Labor Council.' The trustees then could operate with greater autonomy from the council delegates: once elected, they could make decisions without reference to the general membership. At the same time, the positions of secretary and treasurer were combined. The new job was given responsibility for overseeing the money received from the sale of stock in the hall, rents, per capita taxes, and other revenue. Finally, a committee was struck to investigate the possibility of finding new accommodations.[67]

Two years later, the secretary-treasurer position was combined with that of hall caretaker. The new job was paid $60 per month, and the council voted to give it permanently to delegate A.R. Burns. A member of the ITU, born in Ontario and in Vancouver since 1903, Burns was in his early fifties when he was given the job, and he held it for two years.[68]

Moving and re-organizing the hall became an important concern of the council in the middle of 1909. The executive spent several meetings drawing up new financial schemes to pay for the move, and created separate books for the labour temple to keep its accounting apart from that of the VTLC.[69] In

September, McVety, who now held positions as business manager for the council paper and as a member of the labour hall committee, received unanimous assent to form a joint stock company to control the new building. The new hall was justified to the membership on the grounds that the union movement had outgrown the old one and that the recent real estate boom had increased both the old hall's value and its taxes. No reason for the creation of a company separate from the council was given, although members were reassured that the unions, 'through their delegates' would control it. The fact that these delegates, already one step removed from the rank and file, would control the company only indirectly, through the selection of board members, was not stressed. But the new company, instead of being directly accountable to the delegates at council meetings, could now operate like any other joint stock company, with shareholders able to exert little control over its day-to-day affairs.[70]

The new company was organized under the Joint Stock Companies Act, instead of the Benevolent Societies Act as the previous hall had been. Capitalized at $100,000 in $1 shares, half of the shares were given to the VTLC for purchase of the old hall by the new company. The remainder were for sale to the public. Shares in the old hall could be redeemed at the rate of one old share for two new ones. While this seemed a generous offer, it was in fact a way to avoid paying interest on the old shares. The shares in the old hall were, strictly speaking, not shares but interest-bearing debentures. If they were cashed in, the council had to pay the accrued interest on them. Exchanging them for new shares cost the council nothing and limited the amount that might be paid out to investors in the future, for the new shares paid no interest. Instead, stockholders would be paid only when the company decided to declare a dividend.[71] Thus, the socialists proved adept at mastering the intricacies of corporate capitalism.

The new corporate structure also allowed James McVety to give up his job as a machinist. While he remained a member of the IAM, he gave up his trade to become the paid manager of the labour hall at the age of twenty-eight. Some years later, he became a civil servant, working in federal and provincial employment service positions.[72]

The council's newspaper also allowed some bureaucrats to polevault out of the working class. With the demise of the *Independent* in 1904, the council had no official organ. Instead, a privately owned paper, the *BC Trades Unionist and Label Bulletin,* was put out by Samuel J. Gothard. A Vancouver resident and ITU member since 1895, Gothard served as ITU secretary from 1901 to 1903, and as vice-president in 1903 and 1905. He had helped raise subscriptions for the *Independent* for a time and gave support to the UBRE strikers in 1903. Along with Pettipiece, Gothard moved that ITU local 226 'heartily endorse' the railway union in its fight with the CPR. When the ITU considered its own strike action to enforce its demands later that year, Gothard tried to press for more militant action. When a motion was made to consult with the international on the possibility of striking, Gothard tried to have it amended. Instead of slowly grinding through the rules of the international, Gothard proposed that the local simply declare that it would automatically go on strike if its demands were not met by 1 May. Although his amendment was defeated, Gothard had established himself as a firebrand.[73]

The paper was independent of the council, but the VTLC did endorse it in 1905. In 1906, when Gothard became secretary of the council, the paper took on a quasi-official status. The council created a press committee, headed by Pettipiece, to oversee the newspaper's contents. The relationship caused some friction, however, In October the paper printed an article that the press committee found objectionable, and Pettipiece moved that the VTLC's endorsement be removed. In 1907, however, the council turned again to Gothard and his paper. This time Gothard was to surrender all editorial control to the press committee; he would, however, continue as business manager and would handle all the revenues and expenditures.[74]

Now an official publication of the VTLC under the editorial guidance of Parm Pettipiece, the paper called upon Vancouver workers to support it, and lambasted those who did not. To those who complained that the newspaper was not worthy of support, the editors retorted that 'if the *Trades Unionist* is not what it should be it's the fault of no one but Vancouver Union men themselves. Like begets like.' Workers who disagreed with the paper should purchase it in any case, for 'they are not compelled to think as the paper thinks; but they can be taught by reading the paper that unionism is a real live issue.' It was also, workers were reminded, an important part of union culture and solidarity. The *Trades Unionist* pointed out that 'to be a worthy member of a working-class movement requires something more than wearing a red tie'; it also meant sacrifice and support for the movement's institutions.[75] In an article printed in boldface, the newspaper announced its view of the role of workers in supporting the union press:

Union men – Try, for your own sake, to realize that you are the most benighted people, even with your progress in existence [*sic*].

What we want you to do –

We want you, first of all, to subscribe to the paper. That is the first requisite. The Trades and Labor Council needs a paper. THIS is the paper. Therefore it is up to you to patronize it.[76]

Apathy was not the only problem the newspaper faced. Gothard continued to create trouble, launching several unauthorized and shady money-raising schemes and calling for boycotts that opened the council to libel suits.[77] By January 1909 the council had had enough. Delegates voted to end the arrangement with Gothard and to start a new paper that would be under the complete control of the council. James McVety was appointed business manager of the new VTLC organ, and Harry Cowan was given the post of editor, even though both held executive positions on the council: McVety was president and Cowan secretary. The Tailors Union protested the two editing and publishing the paper while sitting on the executive board, and threatened to withhold its per capita payments until the situation was corrected. In venerable bureaucratic fashion, the rest of the council voted to file the tailors' letter and thus ensured that the paper would reflect the wishes of the executive board. While Cowan would resign from the executive a month later, McVety stayed on, and his comrade Pettipiece would take over the secretary position.[78]

The council organized the *Western Wage Earner* on a different basis from the old *Independent*. Both Bartley and Cowan had made a living from the labourist newspaper, but their income was generated from the printing jobs done by the Independent Printing Company. Putting out the paper was part of their work, but their salaries were not guaranteed by the council. When McVety became business manager of the new paper, however, the council voted to pay him directly a salary of $100 per month. The money was good by working-class standards: carpenters averaged around $90, labourers about $65. Machinists such as McVety would do well to earn his new salary.[79] Unlike Bartley, McVety was not responsible for actually composing or printing the paper; production was contracted out to the socialist E.T. Kingsley and his non-union shop.[80]

For the first time in the council's history, it was possible for some of its officials to hold down permanent, full-time, and well-paid jobs as functionaries. That this took place under the auspices of a socialist-led council strongly suggests that professionalism in the labour bureaucracy is no easy guide to ideology. It also suggests that workers who come to the bureaucracy from unions that do not allow for easy advancement into small businesses may be more inclined to use the labour movement to escape the working class. Men such as Bartley and Dixon could move with little trouble into the petit-bourgeois world of publishing and contracting. Men such as Watson and McVety had, as CPR employees, no such opportunity; for them, the labour and socialist movements offered their best chance to get off the shop floor. The ascension of socialists who were not craft workers helped push the labour council towards a paid bureaucracy and hierarchy that the old labourists could scarcely imagine.

The bitter squabbling of 1903 had resulted in some changes over time. Six years later socialists controlled the labour council and its important institutions. Yet the rank and file was no closer to the structure of command, and it was now possible to use the VTLC directly as a way to leave the working class. Changes in political action were slow in coming; racism was much the same, and women fared little better in the council.[81] The old pressures of compromise for the sake of unity, middle-class aspirations, and resolving union disputes worked to soften the impact of the socialists on the rest of the labour movement. The left did call for new organizations, and in 1910 the British Columbia Federation of Labour was formed. While the new organization appeared to resemble the dream of the One Big Union, in fact it was a way to centralize authority and command. With no provision for rank-and-file control, the creation of another layer of bureaucrats made it even more difficult for the voice of the workers to be heard. Stalwarts such as McVety and Pettipiece staffed the new labour body, and the VTLC, still under their domain, became less important as the players moved to the provincial arena. The socialists themselves would soon come under attack by radicals who upheld shop-floor democracy and direct action as the ideology of syndicalism and the Industrial Workers of the World began to be heard in the province. In 1907 Parm Pettipiece, who had led the assault on the labourists only four years earlier, was denounced by the IWW organizer Joe Ettor as a 'counterfeit wearing the buttons of the SP and the AF of L on his coat collar,' and clashes between the VTLC and the SPC on the one side and the IWW on the other became common.[82] The labourists had been displaced and the rhetoric was different, but the issue of bureaucracy in the union movement did not go away; it simply donned a pink cloak.

Conclusion

To a large extent, the Vancouver Trades and Labour Council reflected Michels's maxim, 'who says organization says bureaucracy.' Never directly accountable to the rank and file of the labour movement, the council steadily increased its autonomy over time. From its shaky start in 1889, when it was loath to support political action for fear of alienating the affiliated unions, the council had by 1909 established itself as an independent body that purported to speak for the entire labour movement. By the end of its second decade, the VTLC was dominated by a small cadre of professional labour leaders who largely determined the direction of the city's unions, at least in the public sphere of political action and propaganda.

This dominance was accompanied, and accomplished, by putting in place many of the mechanisms described by Weber and his 'ideal-type' bureaucracy. While their avowed intent was to make the labour movement more efficient and effective, these measures also separated the leadership from the rank and file. Thus, the council established strict rules for the handling of finances, centralized the decision-making process, set up codes of behaviour for officers and unionists, staffed positions with experts, established specific areas of authority for its officers, and created paid staff positions. Each of these measures made action by the labour movement more streamlined, but each also was another building block in the wall of bureaucracy. Both the right and the left were responsible for the creation of the labour bureaucracy. Although labourists had started the VTLC, the socialists were quick to make use of the early bureaucracy and to strengthen it. Indeed, one of the most important facets of bureaucracy, the payment of officials, was most pronounced under the socialist tenure. Nor were socialists opposed to centralization, as they consolidated the labour hall and newspaper into a few hands, using legal stratagems to remove them from the control of the council at large. In this sense, bureaucracy may be seen as being removed from ideology, for conservatives and radicals alike worked to preserve and extend the labour bureaucracy.

This similarity between left and right labour leaders makes it difficult to distinguish between them in many regards, especially when the exigencies of trade unionism tend to push them towards similar policies. For this reason, using ideology to define the labour bureaucrat is not particularly useful. More useful is defining the bureaucrats by the power they exert over those they administer. The power of the labour bureaucrat was limited, but still it existed. Men such as Joe Dixon, George Bartley, James McVety, and Parm Pettipiece could make decisions that affected scores of unionists. These decisions ranged from dues assessments to political programs to the content of the labour press, even to the establishment of the press itself. With time and the development of rules and procedures, these leaders were further removed from the control of the rank and file and their delegates to the council itself. As spokesmen – the masculine term is appropriate and illustrative – these leaders also ensured that their voices alone were heard, and this too carried important consequences for the labour movement. It meant the exclusion of the unskilled, of Asians, and of women from the mainstream of the labour council; it meant that those who best understood and played by the rules the bureaucracy had itself created would present labour's message as filtered through their own experience. Whether the particular bureaucrats were of the left or the right, this power to make decisions and to speak on behalf of all workers separated them from the rank and file.

The examination of the Vancouver Trades and Labour Council from its beginning in 1889 until the heyday of the socialists in 1910 provides other suggestions for the debate on the labour bureaucracy. First, it suggests that the ideology of the bureaucrats is not determined primarily by their positions in the bureaucracy itself. Other causes – class, occupation, mobility, race, gender, even age – are more direct and influential and more likely to shape the political outlook of the labour leader. The council had two generations of leaders. The first was firmly rooted in the craft traditions of labourism, the second in the political traditions of the socialist movement. Both generations forged their ideologies outside the VTLC, yet managed to push the council in the direction they favoured, with different consequences for the labour movement. In this respect, the bureaucracy reflected the politics of the leaders; it did not create them.

At the same time, the bureaucracy did create its own political demands. The need for organization, for self-defence, for consolidating the demands and gains of the labour movement, forced unionists to create structures of control and authority. These in turn drove a wedge between the leaders and the led, as the council moved to limit dissent, create paid positions, and set up rules and regulations to conduct its business. Leaders were quick to defend their actions and to see those who challenged them as disrupters and as bad unionists. This distinction was sometimes based on ideology, as labourists and socialists quarrelled. But both generations held similar opinions about the rank and file, regardless of ideology. The pressure of bureaucracy, of the very difference between leaders and led, affected left and right and became a subtle ideology of its own.

The very nature of unionism in this period also carried some implications for ideology and bureaucracy. For both generations of leaders, the success of the movement depended on some semblance of unity. But the significant differences between the various unions and the personnel of the council meant that agreement on any issue was difficult. To preserve its fragile consensus, labourists and socialists alike had to learn to compromise. The labour council was the place for such compromise, and as a result, changes in structure and policy were often slow in coming. It took the socialists four years to replace the labourists; starting in 1903, they were not successful until 1906, when James McVety ascended to the presidency. Once in power – indeed, to take power – the left had to work for consensus and moderation. Other delegates might be cajoled into supporting particular issues, but they could rarely be coerced, and thus concessions had to be made. The responsibility for the jobs and even the lives of other men also had to be considered once one had taken power, and this weighed on both the left and the right. If socialists often talked more radical lines, in practice they too had to come to an agreement with the employer. James McVety was no slower in cutting a deal with the CPR than any of his predecessors on the council, and the pressure of deciding what was best for others contributed to this.

Thus, it may be that the answer to the question to 'why is there no socialism?' cannot be laid directly on the door of the labour bureaucracy, at least in the traditional sense that bureaucrats are automatically reactionary. Many of the bureaucrats of the council – often those who were the professional bureaucrats of the socialist movement – held progressive ideas in advance of the rank and file. But as Marx remarked, men may make their own history, but not in circumstances of their own choosing. In the absence of revolutionary situations, even socialists could do little. In the face of apathy and repression, they could not press on blindly; they had to consider the consequences of their actions. At the same time, it should be noted that by the time they had ascended to the ranks of the bureaucracy, their own revolution, as Michels put it, had been accomplished. Labourists and socialists alike profited from their positions in the labour movement. Labourists consolidated ties with the city's elite, in part because their class position as artisans and the accompanying ideology carried no sharp distinctions between journeyman and master; the producer mentality allowed them to forge links across class lines. Socialists, however, often came from the petit bourgeoisie and learned to use the labour movement to their advantage, securing white-collar work as editors, business managers, and politicians. While the two generations tangled on many issues, both had few qualms about profiting from their experience on the labour council, although in different ways. What does remain constant for labour bureaucrats is the desire to promote and protect their own self-interest. For it is this different self-interest that separates them from the rank and file, not any particular left or right position. As leaders, labour bureaucrats have interests that are significantly different from those of the membership, for they wish to maintain their positions. The saga of Cincinnatus is as rare in the history of bureaucracy as it is in the history of Rome. What we should expect from labour bureaucrats as a group is not a consistent platform of incorporation or radicalism, for this will change according to how they perceive their interests. What may be found is a consistent ideology that presents the particular interests of this group as the universal interests of the working class.

The use of bureaucracy as an analytical tool with which to approach the labour movement may also shed some new light on earlier generalizations. By assuming that the leadership of the labour movement does form a discrete body worthy of investigation in its own right, we learn, for example, that the alleged radical upsurge of 1903 made barely a ripple in the VTLC. The particular nuances of class are made more apparent by an investigation of the men who filled the positions in the council, and clues about ideology, militancy, and radicalism may be gleaned. In this way, the debate over the labour bureaucracy may serve a similar function as the labour aristocracy discussions of the 1950s did: as a profitable way to start digging into other questions about working-class life.

Bureaucracy is not a question of this or that tactical manoeuvre, this or that position. It is a fundamental belief in the inability of the masses to rule themselves. In the more subtle sense of perpetuating this belief, the bureaucracy may be said to perform its function of incorporation into private and state capitalism. In the age of monopoly capitalism, efficiency and boundless production have become the rationale for capitalism, and this ideology has been extended to and taken in by the labour movement. The reformism of the union bureaucracy lies precisely in its efforts to convince the working class, by example, ideology, and, on occasion, repression, that some such form of leadership is inevitable and in the best interests of the working class. Therefore, while the leadership may oppose specific abuses and turns of capitalism, and may or may not represent the articulated wishes of the rank and file, it is by its very nature committed to the rule by an elite in labour, industry, and society. If bureaucracy is to be eliminated, it will only be done when a revolutionary movement decides to do so, as part of a larger movement against economic and political oppression. History suggests that such a prospect may be unlikely. But there are precedents: the anarchist movement, the Industrial Workers of the World, the student protest movements of the 1960s, the resurgence of left-wing politics in the former Soviet Union, all show that it is possible.

Notes

INTRODUCTION

1 In 'Struggling with Class Struggle: Marxism and the Search for a Synthesis of U.S. Labor History,' *Labor History* 28 (1987), Michael Kazin has argued that it is a mistake to look for socialism in the working class. Those who believe it is possible to find a culture of resistance in the American working class include Paul Buhle, *Marxism in the USA from 1870 to the Present Day* (London: Verso 1987); David Montgomery, *Workers Control in America* (Cambridge: Cambridge University Press, 1984) and *The Fall of the House of Labor: The Workplace, the State, and American Labor Activism, 1865–1925* (Cambridge: Cambridge University Press, 1987); Herbert Gutman, *Work, Culture, and Society in Industrializing America* (New York: Vintage, 1977) and *Power and Culture: Essays on the American Working Class*, ed. Ira Berlin (New York: Pantheon, 1987).

2 See, for example, Mike Davis, *Prisoners of the American Dream: Politics and Economy in the History of the U.S. Working Class* (London: Verso, 1986); Michael Goldfield, *The Decline of Organized Labor in the United States* (Chicago: University of Chicago Press, 1987); Bryan Palmer, *Solidarity: The Rise and Fall of an Opposition in British Columbia* (Vancouver: New Star Books, 1987); and Kim Moody, *An Injury to All: The Decline of American Unionism* (London: Verso, 1988).

3 For an elaboration of this argument, see Adam Przeworski, *Capitalism and Social Democracy* (Cambridge: Cambridge University Press, 1985), 2.

4 See Ch. 1 for an examination of this argument.

5 James Naylor delivers a powerful blow to western exceptionalism in *The New Democracy: Challenging the Social Order in Industrial Ontario, 1914–1925* (Toronto: University of Toronto Press, 1991).

6 Mark Leier, *Where the Fraser River Flows: The Industrial Workers of the World in British Columbia* (Vancouver: New Star Books, 1990).

7 John Kelly, *Trade Unions and Socialist Politics* (London: Verso, 1988), 178.

8 Thomas Bramble points out the paucity of work in this area by labour historians and provides an important step forward, in 'Conflict, Coercion, and Co-option: The Role of Full-Time Officials in the South Australian Branch of the Vehicle Builder Employees' Federation, 1967–80,' *Labour History* 63 (1992), 135–54.

9 Bryan D. Palmer, *Working Class Experience: Rethinking the History of Canadian Labour, 1800–1991* (Toronto: McClelland and Stewart, 1992); Craig Heron, *The Canadian Labour Movement: A Short History* (Toronto: Lorimer, 1989); Ian McKay, *The Craft Transformed: An Essay on the Carpenters of Halifax, 1885–1985* (Halifax: Holdfast Press, 1985). Bill Freeman's *1005 – Political Life in a Union Local* (Toronto: Lorimer, 1982) is another examination of the effect of bureaucracy in the late twentieth century. Warren Van Tine examines the earlier years in *The Making of the Labor Bureaucrat: Union Leadership in the United States, 1870–1920* (Amherst: University of Massachusetts, 1973), but concentrates on national labour leaders and the differences between the Knights of Labor and the 'new generation' of Samuel Gompers and business unionism. For an examination of bureaucracy in the AFL, see Elizabeth Jones-Wolf and Ken Jones-Wolf, 'Rank-and-File Rebellions and AFL Interference in the Affairs of National Unions: The Gompers Era,' *Labor History* 35 (1994), 237–59.

10 Though I define the bureaucracy in terms of power, I do not explicitly use the work of Michel Foucault to do so. This is for several reasons. First, Foucault's work is difficult to assess. Historians and literary theorists cannot even agree on what Foucault actually means in many of his works, or on the importance of his theoretical concerns, let alone the implications for subjects, such as the labour bureaucracy, that he did not address. Second, I do not believe that Foucault has said much that is new, though it may be new to readers who do not know much about left-wing thought. Foucault's critique of social institutions was foreshadowed by anarchist thinkers, and his ideas on power have been expressed more clearly, succinctly, and powerfully by writers in the anarchist tradition, such as Michael Bakunin, and by Marxists such as Alvin Gouldner. It should be noted that Foucault himself explicitly denied that he was an anarchist, though some anarchists have found his work useful. See Peter Marshall, *Demanding the Impossible: A History of Anarchism* (London: Fontana, 1993), for an anarchist critique of Foucault. Finally, it is apparent that whatever Foucault may have thought, his work is vulnerable to being interpreted to defend liberal democracy. My colleague Tina Loo, in her excellent essay 'Dan Cranmer's Potlatch: Law as Coercion, Symbol, and Rhetoric in British Columbia, 1884–1951,' *Canadian Historical Review* 73 (1992), 125–65, seems to me to use Foucault to defend a kind of liberal pluralism in rather the way Ralf Dahrendorf did. The point is not that Foucault is responsible for later

interpretations of his work, but that his ambiguities and turbidity make such interpretations apparently consistent with his writings. Such interpretations are not possible from the works of anarchist and critical Marxist thinkers, and thus I have relied instead on them.

11 For a brief informative look at this debate, see Christopher Moore, 'Men at Work,' *The Beaver* 72 (1992), 60–2. See Palmer, *Working Class Experience*, 417, for a bibliography of the most important shots fired in the debate.

12 See, for example, J. Carroll Moody and Alice Kessler-Harris, eds., *Perspectives on American Labor History: The Problems of Synthesis* (DeKalb, Ill.: Northern Illinois University Press, 1989). Melvyn Dubofsky's review of this book sets out the problems of synthesis in 'Lost in a Fog: Labor Historians' Unrequited Search for a Synthesis,' *Labor History* 32 (1991), 295–300. See also Howard Kimeldorf, 'Bringing Unions Back In (Or Why We Need a New Old Labor History),' and responses from several labour historians, in *Labor History* 32 (1991), 91–129. Ian McKay has echoed the call for a 'new institutionalism' in 'The Three Faces of Canadian Labour History,' *History Workshop* 24 (1987), 172–8.

13 Lizabeth Cohen, 'Reflections on the Making of *Making a New Deal*,' *Labor History* 32 (1991), 598. Hexter's earlier description of historians as lumpers and splitters is cited in John Cannon, ed., *The Historian at Work* (London: George Allen and Unwin, 1980), 3.

14 For a more sophisticated and eloquent discussion of class and class experience, see Palmer, *Working Class Experience*. David Montgomery refutes the 'no revolution–no class' argument in 'Class, Capitalism, and Contentment,' in 'A Symposium on *The Fall of the House of Labor*,' *Labor History* 30 (1989), 125–37. The quote from Ralph Miliband is from *Divided Societies: Class Struggle in Contemporary Capitalism* (New York: Oxford University Press, 1989), 6.

CHAPTER 1 Bureaucracy and the Labour Movement

1 Charles Ashleigh, 'The Voyage of the Verona,' reprinted in *Rebel Voices: An IWW Anthology*, ed. Joyce L. Kornbluh (1964; reprint, Ann Arbor: University of Michigan Press, 1972), 107–12.

2 *New York Times*, 21, 22 May 1986. Recent events have revealed that Presser was also an active FBI plant before and after the convention. In 1991 new elections supervised by the U.S. government replaced the old-guard leadership with the reform slate of Ron Carey.

3 Robert Michels, *Political Parties: A Sociological Study of the Oligarchical Tendencies of Modern Democracy*, trans. Eden and Cedar Paul (1915; reprint, Glencoe: Free Press, 1948); Jonathan Zeitlin, 'Trade Unions and Job Control: A Critique of

"Rank and Filism,"' *Bulletin of the Society for the Study of Labour History,* 46 (1983), 6–7.

4 Selig Perlman, *A Theory of the Labor Movement* (1928; reprint, New York: Augustus M. Kelley, 1970); Gregory Zinoviev, 'The Social Roots of Opportunism,' in *Lenin's Struggle for a Revolutionary International – Documents, 1907–1916: The Preparatory Years,* ed. John Riddell (New York: Monad Press, 1984), 486.

5 Raymond Williams supplies the etymology of bureaucracy in *Keywords: A Vocabulary of Culture and Society* (Glasgow: Fontana, 1976), 40–1.

6 *From Max Weber: Essays in Sociology,* ed. H.H. Gerth and C. Wright Mills (New York: Oxford University Press, 1946), 196–204.

7 For evaluations of Marx's contribution to the theory of bureaucracy, see Eva Etzioni-Halevy, *Bureaucracy and Democracy: A Political Dilemma* (London: Routledge and Kegan Paul, 1983), 9–13, 23–6, 74–84; and András Hegedus, 'Bureaucracy,' in *A Dictionary of Marxist Thought,* ed. Tom Bottomore (Cambridge, Mass.: Harvard University Press, 1983), 57–9. For a brief discussion of Weber's notion of the 'ideal-type,' see Frank Parkin, *Max Weber* (Chichester: Ellis Horwood, 1982), 28–39. Max Weber, 'Bureaucracy,' reprinted in *Critical Studies in Organization and Bureaucracy,* ed. Frank Fischer and Carmen Sirianni (Philadelphia: Temple University Press, 1984), 24–39. Warren Van Tine, *The Making of the Labor Bureaucrat* (Amherst: University of Massachusetts Press, 1973), x.

8 Weber, 'Bureaucracy,' 24–33.

9 Wolfgang J. Mommsen, 'Max Weber and Roberto Michels: An Asymmetrical Partnership,' *European Journal of Sociology* 22 (1981), 110. Weber is cited on 108. The quote on Weber and the SPD is on 107. See also Fischer and Sirianni, 6–10, and Parkin, 104–8. See Etzioni-Halevy, 27–40, for Weber's ambivalence towards bureaucracy.

10 Mommsen, 105–6. For the Mannheim Congress, see Carl E. Schorske, *German Social Democracy, 1905–1917: The Development of the Great Schism* (1955; reprint, Cambridge, Mass. Harvard University Press, 1983), 49–53. Michels's definition of democracy is in Michels, 28, 31–2. The quote is adapted from David Beetham, 'Michels and His Critics,' *European Journal of Sociology* 22 (1981), 85.

11 Michels, 30–47.

12 Ibid., 47, 96, 33–6.

13 Beetham, 85–9, addresses this argument succinctly and makes many of the same points; a substantial part of the following discussion is based on his outline. Michels, 199, 291, 319–21, 364.

14 It is at this point that Michels's critique separates from the syndicalist analysis, a concept that will be taken up in the last section of this chapter. As Beetham notes, Michels combines left- and right-wing arguments to bolster his claim that oligarchy is inevitable. Michels's disdain of the masses was an important cause of his

pessimism and was no doubt part of the reason he embraced Mussolini's fascism in the 1920s; see Beetham, 84–5. For Michels's conversion to fascism, see Mommsen, 114–16. Michels, 47, 56–7, 73.

15 Michels, 402–9, 420–2.

16 The quote is from ibid., 422. It is Michels's view of the inability of the 'masses' to effect change that is most often challenged by authors such as Thomas Bramble. As explained earlier, however, this is not the issue that this study concentrates on.

17 See Beetham for an outline of the debates and criticisms of Michels.

18 Selig Perlman, ix.

19 Ibid., 239.

20 Ibid., 4, 156, 290, 304–18.

21 Michels, 326; Perlman, 154–214.

22 Karl Marx, *Capital* (Moscow: Progress Publishers, 1971), vol. 1, 712.

23 Reeve Vanneman and Lynne Webber Cannon, *The American Perception of Class* (Philadelphia: Temple University Press, 1987).

24 For an overview of the competing and conflicting consciousness of the working class in America, see David Montgomery, *The Fall of the House of Labor: The Workplace, the State, and American Labor Activism, 1865–1925* (Cambridge: Cambridge University Press, 1987). See also Sidney M. Peck, *The Rank and File Leader* (New Haven: College and University Press Services, 1963), for a dated but interesting study of working-class consciousness in America in the 1950s. The study indicates a much higher level of consciousness than many commentators have assumed.

25 Seymour Martin Lipset, Martin A. Trow, James S. Coleman, *Union Democracy: The Internal Politics of the International Typographical Union* (Glencoe: Free Press, 1956), 3. Obviously, a huge literature along the lines of Perlman and Lipset et al. exists. Talcott Parsons and Daniel Bell are two of the more prominent observers who have put forward the liberal position. Perlman remains the most insightful and interesting of these defenders of the status quo.

26 Lipset et al., 3–16, 80. It should be noted that the methodology of Lipset et al. is open to question. Despite its alleged objectivity, the questions given to unionists allowed only a narrow range of responses. No margin is left for the impact of the questioners – all professionals – on the respondents, or for the cultural milieu of McCarthyism, which may have evoked tamer responses.

27 Ibid., 79.

28 See Beetham, 89, for this argument. Several other liberal works fit this model, among them William M. Leiserson, *American Trade Union Democracy* (New York: Columbia University Press, 1959). Leiserson holds that union democracy must be representative for unions to play their proper role as agents of reform

within capitalism. See also Larry James, *Power in a Trade Union: The Role of the District Committee in the AUEW* (Cambridge: Cambridge University Press, 1984), for a discussion of 'Polyarchy,' or a system of checks and balances. This view holds the same problems as do other liberal views.

29 Karl Radek, 'The SPD: Unity or Split?,' in *Lenin's Struggle*, 462–3. Similarly, Lenin argued that British imperialism, through '1) vast colonies and 2) monopoly profits (due to her monopoly position in the world market)' was responsible for 'the (temporary) victory of opportunism in the English labour movement.' The superprofits of imperialism allowed the capitalists to 'devote a part (and not a small one, at that!) of these superprofits to *bribe their own workers* to create something like an alliance ... between the workers of the given nation and their capitalists against the other countries.' Lenin, 'Imperialism and the Split in Socialism,' *Collected Works* (Moscow: Progress Publishers, 1981), vol. 23, 112–14.

30 Zinoviev, 'The Social Roots of Opportunism,' 484. See 486–96 for an appraisal similar to Radek's. For a Trotskyist version that is virtually identical, see Tom Kerry, *Workers, Bosses, and Bureaucrats: A Socialist View of Labor Struggles since the 1930s* (New York: Pathfinder Press, 1980).

31 Lenin, vol. 23, 38.

32 Ibid., 50–2.

33 Nikolai Bukharin, *Historical Materialism: A System of Sociology* (1921; reprint, Ann Arbor: University of Michigan Press, 1969), 304–7. This book was long considered a Marxist and Bolshevik classic.

34 Ibid., 310–11.

35 Ibid., 309–11.

36 Ibid., 309.

37 Michels, 399. A great deal has been written on the precise role of the manager and other white collar workers. Two collections are helpful: *The New Working Class: White Collar Workers and Their Organizations*, ed. Richard Hyman and Robert Price (London: Macmillan Press, 1983), and *Between Labor and Capital*, ed. Pat Walker (Montreal: Black Rose Books, 1978). For an interesting discussion of the convergence of Marxism with radical elite theory, see Frank Parkin, 'Social Stratification,' in *A History of Sociological Analysis*, ed. Tom Bottomore and Robert Nisbet (New York: Basic Books, 1978), 599–632. Unlike the structural–functionalist argument, or the 'authority' argument of Ralf Dahrendorf, some elite theory starts with the concept of class and sees it as fundamental. The debate is in some ways similar to the one on the autonomy of the state, and it has similar consequences for Marxism, in that both suggest fundamental cleavages in society apart from that of class. See Frank Parkin, *Marxism and Class Theory: A Bourgeois Critique* (London: Tavistock, 1979). For the need to bring together Weberian

and Marxist insights to fully understand bureaucracy, see David Beetham, *Bureaucracy* (Minneapolis: University of Minnesota Press, 1987).

38 Michels, 405–6.

39 Clearly there is some self-interest in their argument. But we can be as charitable to the Bolsheviks as Zinoviev was to the SPD and assume that they too labour under the self-deception that the party's interests are the same as those of the working class. They may likewise believe that they are sacrificing themselves for the common good in taking up the reins of power. This is not, however, the same as democracy.

There has been no mention of the antidemocratic practices in 'actually existing socialism,' but there is no shortage of evidence to indicate that the Bolsheviks were consistent with their theory. Two examples are indicative: in 1918, before the exigencies of the civil war, Lenin called for workers to learn 'iron discipline while at work, with unquestioning obedience to the will of a single person, the Soviet leader.' Lenin, 'The Immediate Tasks of the Soviet Government,' *Collected Works*, vol. 27, 237–77. See also Trotsky's praise of one-man management in *Terrorism and Communism* (Ann Arbor: University of Michigan Press, 1970); on page 170, he notes approvingly that 'no organization except the army has ever controlled man with such severe compulsion as does the [Soviet] state organization of the working class.' Trotsky did of course denounce the Soviet bureaucracy after he was dumped from its ranks. But his earlier writings, and, more importantly, his actions while in power, show his later polemics to be little more than sour grapes. Trotsky's about-face is perhaps best explained by the observation of Max Nomad, who suggested that 'a fallen dictator's abhorrence of tyranny is as permanent as a sick tiger's aversion to meat' (in a *A Skeptic's Political Dictionary and Handbook for the Disenchanted* [New York: Bookman, 1953], 121).

40 C. Wright Mills, *The New Men of Power: America's Labor Leaders* (New York: Harcourt, Brace, 1948), 7–9, 224–9, 239–65.

41 But because of its links to organized crime, the Teamsters' Union hampers our understanding of the labour bureaucracy, for corruption and bureaucracy are not at all the same thing. It is important to see union bureaucracy and corruption as two separate issues. The two may be related in the sense that control of the union by a small group may be a necessary condition for corruption. Such control, however, is not a sufficient condition. Efforts to equate bureaucracy and corruption obscure the nature of both. As an example of the analytical mistake of arguing that corruption and bureaucracy are the same thing, see Sylvester Petro, *Power Unlimited: The Corruption of Union Leadership* (New York: Ronald Press, 1959). Petro, once a CIO activist, goes further to suggest that the closed shop and the secondary picket are examples of union dictatorship and corruption that have as their

end the destruction of American society. Union activity that secures wages higher than those the market establishes is seen in the same light. A more balanced assessment of union corruption and the links of corruption to bureaucracy is given in *Autocracy and Insurgency in Organized Labor*, ed. Burton Hall (New Brunswick: Transaction Books, 1972). Unfortunately, its authors' preoccupation with specific cases and crimes, such as the murder of United Mine Workers of America dissident Jock Yablonski by the agents of union president Tony Boyle, prevents their formulating a theoretical framework beyond suggesting that labour leaders have formed an alliance with the state to suppress dissidents.

42 Stan Weir, 'The Conflict in American Unions and the Resistance to Alternative Ideas from the Rank and File,' in *Workers' Struggles, Past and Present: A 'Radical America' Reader*, ed. James Green (Philadelphia: Temple University Press, 1983), 251–68. *Radical America* has advanced a number of variations of this theme in its pages. Staughton Lynd has made similar arguments, most recently in 'Trade Unionism in the USA,' *New Left Review* 184 (1990), 76–87.

43 Gabriel Kolko, *The Triumph of Conservatism* (New York: Free Press, 1964). James Weinstein, *The Corporate Ideal in the Liberal State* (Boston: Beacon Press, 1968). For a Canadian analysis along similar lines, see Alvin Finkel, *Business and Social Reform in the Thirties* (Toronto: Lorimer, 1979). See Peter Novick, *That Noble Dream: The 'Objectivity Question' and the American Historical Profession* (Cambridge: Cambridge University Press, 1990), 439, for a critique.

44 For an overview of the attack on workers and unions in Canada, see Craig Heron, *The Canadian Labour Movement: A Short History* (Toronto: Lorimer, 1989), 120–46, and Bryan D. Palmer, *Working Class Experience: Rethinking the History of Canadian Labour, 1800–1991* (Toronto: McClelland and Stewart, 1992), 340–416.

45 Zeitlin, 'Trade Unions,' 7; John Bodnar, *Workers' World: Kinship, Community, and Protest in an Industrial Society, 1900–1940* (Bloomington: Indiana University Press, 1982).

46 For accounts of the battles between left and right in the CIO and especially in the Canadian Congress of Labor, see Irving Abella, *Nationalism, Communism, and Canadian Labour: The CIO, the Communist Party, and the Canadian Congress of Labour, 1935–56* (Toronto: University of Toronto Press, 1973). Bryan D. Palmer, ed., *Jack Scott: A Communist Life* (St John's, Nfld.: Committee on Canadian Labour History, 1988), 101. In arguing that the whites did gain some support, I do not mean to play down the role of the state in purging the left, or to suggest that these unions enjoyed a complete democracy that merely reflected the will of the workers. As Jerry Lembcke and William Tattam have demonstrated in *One Union in Wood: A Political History of the International Woodworkers of America* (Vancouver: Harbour Publishing, 1984), capital and the state conspired to purge the

left. Nevertheless, the rank and file did not oppose this to any great degree, and I suggest that the temporary success of the left-wing slate cannot be interpreted as mass support for the political program of the CPC. Stephen Gray demonstrates that the red bloc in the IWA was no less susceptible to the pressures of incorporation and bureaucracy than the white bloc, despite its left agenda; see Gray's 'Woodworkers and Legitimacy: The IWA in Canada, 1937–1957,' PhD thesis, Simon Fraser University, 1989. The labour lawyer John Stanton, who worked for the left leadership of the IWA and Mine-Mill, makes similar observations in *Never Say Die! The Life and Times of John Stanton, A Pioneer Labour Lawyer* (Ottawa: Steel Rail Press, 1987), 197–208, and *My Past Is Now: Further Memoirs of a Labour Lawyer* (St John's: Canadian Committee on Labour History, 1994), 100–35.

47 James Hinton, *The First Shop Stewards' Movement* (London: George Allen and Unwin, 1973), and *Labour and Socialism: A History of the British Labour Movement, 1867–1974* (Amherst: University of Massachusetts Press, 1983); Richard Price, *Masters, Unions, and Men: Work Control in Building and the Rise of Labour, 1830–1914* (New York: Cambridge University Press, 1980).

48 Tony Adams, 'Leadership and Oligarchy: British Rail Unions, 1914–1922,' *Studies in History and Politics* 5 (1986), 23–45; Zeitlin, 'Trade Unions.' See also Jonathan Zeitlin, 'Shop Floor Bargaining and the State: A Contradictory Relationship,' in *Shop Floor Bargaining and the State: Historical and Comparative Perspectives*, ed. Steve Tolliday and Jonathan Zeitlin (Cambridge: Cambridge University Press, 1985).

49 Zeitlin, 'Trade Unions,' 7.

50 Ibid.

51 Richard Hyman, *Industrial Relations: A Marxist Introduction* (London: Macmillan, 1975), 64–93; and 'The Politics of Workplace Trade Unionism: Recent Tendencies and Some Problems for Theory,' *Capital and Class* 8 (1979), 54–67. The block quote may be found on 61. Zeitlin, 'Trade Unions,' 7. See also Richard Hyman, 'Officialdom and Opposition: Leadership and Rank and File in Trade Unions,' *Bulletin of the Society for the Study of Labour History* 46 (1983), 7. For an excellent summary of much of the debate, see John Kelly, *Trade Unions and Socialist Politics* (London: Verso, 1988), esp. Ch. 7; Jonathan Zeitlin, '"Rank and Filism" in British Labour History: A Critique,' *International Review of Social History* 34 (1989), 42–102; Richard Price, '"What's in a Name?" Workplace History and "Rank and Filism,"' *International Review of Social History* 34 (1989), 62–77; James E. Cronin, 'The "Rank and File" and the Social History of the Working Class,' *International Review of Social History* 34 (1989), 78–88; Jonathan Zeitlin, '"Rank and Filism" and Labour History: A Rejoinder to Price and Cronin,' *International Review of Social History* 34 (1989), 89–102; Richard Hyman, 'The

Sound of One Hand Clapping: A Comment on the "Rank and Filism" Debate,'
International Review of Social History 34 (1989), 309–26.

52 Hyman, 'Officialdom and Opposition'; Hyman, *Industrial Relations, passim*.

53 This argument draws upon the anarchist critique of power, especially that of
Michael Bakunin. It does so not to abandon historical materialism, as liberals
often do, but to extend it. Alvin Gouldner and John Clark have argued that Bakunin was the first critical, post-Marxist, while Anthony D'Agostino has shown that
the doctrines of Marxism and anarchism have never been 'hermetically sealed
compartments.' Alvin Gouldner, *Against Fragmentation: The Origins of Marxism
and the Sociology of Intellectuals* (Oxford: Oxford University Press, 1985), esp.
Ch. 6 and 7. Gouldner argues that 'Bakuninism and Marxism cannot be understood as two adversaries,' 187. John Clark, 'Marx, Bakunin, and the Problem of
Social Transformation,' *Telos* 42 (1979–80), suggests that libertarian Marxists
'whether they call the result Marxism or not ... reach a position that seems in
many ways more in the spirit of Bakunin than Marx,' 97. Anthony D'Agostino,
Marxism and the Russian Anarchists (San Francisco: Germinal Press, 1977), Ch.
1. Since many writers have erroneously believed that Bakunin held to a doctrine
of pure free will and disliked historical materialism, it is necessary to point out
that Bakunin himself criticized Marx for being 'too metaphysical' and for abandoning materialism when he talked of dialectics. Bakunin saw himself as following
in Marx's footsteps and acknowledged his intellectual debt to him.

54 Michael Bakunin, *God and the State* (New York: Dover, 1970), 35, 41–2.

55 Saul D. Alinsky, *Rules for Radicals: A Practical Primer for Realistic Radicals*
(New York: Vintage, 1972), 27–8.

56 G.P. Maximoff, ed., *The Political Philosophy of Bakunin: Scientific Anarchism*
(New York: Free Press, 1964), 328.

57 Hyman addresses the special position of shop stewards in 'The Politics of Workplace Trade Unionism' and in *Strikes* (Glasgow: Fontana, 1977), 45–7.

58 Thus did Bakunin point out, 'We of course are all sincere Socialists and revolutionists, and still were we endowed with power, even for a short duration of a few
months, we would not be what we are now. As Socialists we are convinced, you
and I, that social environment, social position, and conditions of existence are
more powerful than the intelligence and will of the strongest and most powerful
individual, and it is precisely for this reason that we demand not natural but social
equality of individuals as the condition for justice and the foundation of morality.
And that is why we detest power, all power, just as the people detest it' (in Maximoff, 249).

59 Hyman, 'Politics of Workplace Unionism,' 61.

60 Bakunin, *Bakunin on Anarchy*, ed. Sam Dolgoff (Montreal: Black Rose Books,
1980), 245.

CHAPTER 2 VTLC: Early Structure and the Beginning of Bureaucracy

1 G.P. Maximoff, ed., *The Political Philosophy of Michael Bakunin* (New York: Free Press), 207.

2 Norbert MacDonald, *Distant Neighbors: A Comparative History of Seattle and Vancouver* (Lincoln: University of Nebraska Press, 1987), 9–31, and 'The Canadian Pacific Railway and Vancouver's Development to 1900,' in *British Columbia: Historical Readings*, ed. W.P. Ward and R.A.J. McDonald (Vancouver: Douglas and McIntyre, 1981), 396–425; Margaret Ormsby, *British Columbia: A History* (1958; reprint, Toronto: Macmillan, 1976), 295–7; Alan Morley, *Vancouver: From Milltown to Metropolis* (Vancouver: Mitchell Press, 1961), 60–70; Eric Nicol *Vancouver* (Toronto: Doubleday, 1970), 44–51; Robert Chodos, *The CPR: A Century of Corporate Welfare* (Toronto: Lorimer, 1973), 53–6; Martin Robin, *The Rush for Spoils: The Company Province, 1871–1933* (Toronto: McClelland and Stewart, 1972), 57–62; MacDonald, *Distant Neighbors*, 11; Ormsby, 296.

3 Ormsby, 304.

4 R.A.J. McDonald, 'Victoria, Vancouver, and the Economic Development of British Columbia, 1886–1914,' in Ward and McDonald, *Historical Readings*, 396; McDonald, 'City-Building in the Canadian West: A Case Study of Economic Growth in Early Vancouver, 1886–1893,' *BC Studies* 43 (1979), 3–28; MacDonald, *Distant Neighbors*, 30–5, and 'The CPR and Vancouver's Development'; McDonald, 'Working Class Vancouver, 1886–1914: Urbanism and Class in British Columbia,' *BC Studies* 69/70 (1986), 33–69.

5 MacDonald, 'The CPR,' 404–5, and *Distant Neighbours*, 37; Ormsby, 300.

6 George Bartley, 'Twenty-five Years in the BC Labor Movement,' *BC Federationist*, 27 Dec. 1912; Paul Phillips, *No Power Greater: A Century of Labour in BC* (Vancouver: BC Federation of Labour, Boag Foundation, 1967), 12–18.

7 Bartley, 'Twenty-five.' Though the story of the Italian muckers was reported by Bartley, it is more likely that it was apocryphal. Archie Green, in *Wobblies, Pile Butts, and Other Heroes: Laborlore Explorations* (Urbana: University of Illinois Press, 1993), has collected several similar tales, ranging from 1875 to 1946 and from Great Britain to California and even another variant from BC. Because of its widespread telling, the story is more likely to be folklore, a proletarian version of the so-called urban legend. As Green points out, these 'shovel stories point in many directions: moral judgments of botched work, ethnic rankings within laboring crews, transference of sabotage from job action to rhetorical performance to ritual act,' 334. I would add the case of the Vancouver workers also points to the bureaucratization of the labour movement, for the tale does harken back to an earlier age when workers used direct action rather than negotiation and formal organization to solve their problems.

The storyteller and the group of whom the story is told are significant. Bartley was a Canadian of British descent, a skilled worker, a member of the labour aristocracy and the labour bureaucracy. As such, the direct action of shortening the shovel was not a tactic he could employ. Bartley did not work with a shovel; his trade had a tradition of unionization that stretched back two hundred years; as a citizen, he could fight with the ballot, the union, the strike, and the newspaper. The anecdote reinforces the differences in work between the two ethnic groups as well as the difference between the rough and the respectable workers. In his appreciation of the direct action of the shovel shortening, Bartley may well have been reflecting on the simplicity of a bygone age in labour relations.

8 *Daily News–Advertiser,* 22 Nov. 1889; Vancouver Trades and Labor Council Minutes (hereafter VTLCM), 21 Nov. 1889.

9 VTLCM, 6, 27 Dec. 1889; McDonald, 'Working-Class Vancouver,' 43.

10 Population and language figures are from MacDonald, *Distant Neighbours,* 38–9; the figures on religious affiliation are from Patricia E. Roy, *Vancouver: An Illustrated History* (Toronto: Lorimer, 1980), 170.

11 See, for example, A. Ross McCormack, *Reformers, Rebels, and Revolutionaries: The Western Canadian Radical Movement, 1899–1919* (Toronto: University of Toronto Press, 1979), 19; Jean Barman, *The West beyond the West: A History of British Columbia* (Toronto: University of Toronto Press, 1991), 207; Carlos Schwantes, *Radical Heritage: Labor, Socialism, and Reform in Washington and British Columbia, 1885–1917* (Vancouver: Douglas and McIntyre, 1979), 14; Robert H. Babcock, *Gompers in Canada: A Study of American Continentalism before the First World War* (Toronto: University of Toronto Press, 1974), 55, 115, 165–6; George Woodcock, *British Columbia: A History of the Province* (Vancouver: Douglas and McIntyre, 1990), 175.

12 The information in this paragraph has been assembled from *Province,* 4 Jan. 1943; *Sun,* 2, 5 Jan. 1943; ITU roll book, Vancouver City Archives (VCA), add. ms. 381, vol. 15, file 3, 1889; Bartley, 'Twenty-five.' See Ron Verzuh, *Radical Rag: A Pioneer Labour Press in Canada* (Ottawa: Steel Rail Publishing, 1988), 103, for McVety and the *Voice.* City directories give the same address for the two men, with Bartley as the owner, Cowan as boarder, 1901. For the marriage of Harry Cowan and Connie Bartley, see *Independent,* 5 April 1902. Mastheads of the paper indicate that Bartley was editor and Cowan, business manager. The two Canadians, who played such important roles in the life of the council, were united even in death: Cowan, his wife, and Bartley were buried in the Cowan plots in the Mountain View Cemetery.

13 For Dixon's career, see *Province,* 16 Sept. 1926; *Sun,* 16 Sept. 1926; McDonald, 'Working Class Vancouver.' The *Independent's* support for Dixon may be found throughout the paper in 1900; for one example, see 19 May 1900.

14 *Province*, 23 Aug. 1902, contains a description of Watson's early years. Bartley, in 'Twenty-five,' outlines his work with the VTLC, the Nationalist party, and the ARU. See Martin Robin, *Radical Politics and Canadian Labour, 1880–1930* (Kingston: Industrial Relations Centre, Queen's University, 1968), 48–50, for the Nationalist party, and Thomas R. Loosmore, 'The British Columbia Labour Movement and Political Action, 1879–1906,' MA thesis, University of British Columbia, 1954, 70–110.

15 VTLCM, 16 April, 22 May 1896; *Independent*, 3 May 1902; Bartley, 'Twenty-five'; Eugene Forsey, *Trade Unions in Canada, 1812–1902* (Toronto: University of Toronto Press, 1982), 492; Robert H. Babcock, *Gompers in Canada: A Study in American Continentalism before the First War* (Toronto: University of Toronto Press, 1974), 41; *World*, 21 Jan. 1899.

16 Though the records do not shed light on this, it is likely that Watson's short term as president was because he had taken up the new job and thus was ineligible to hold the office. See Bartley, 'Twenty-five,' for Watson's contributions as organizer; Babcock, 48, 237, n 34; Samuel Gompers Letterbooks, Gompers to Watson, 23 April, 29 May 1901; Gompers Papers, microfilm; *Independent*, 2 Nov. 1901; see 9 Nov. 1901 for Draper's letter. For Draper and the AFL, see Babcock, *passim*, but esp. ch. 6; Babcock, 74–6.

17 VTLCM, 15, 19 Jan. 1903; *Province*, 26 Jan. 1903; *World*, 26 Jan. 1903; *Independent*, 14 Feb. 1903.

18 *Western Socialist*, 31 Jan. 1903; *World*, 22 May 1908; *Daily News–Advertiser*, 23 May 1908.

19 Records for most of the unions affiliated to the VTLC no longer exist. The *Independent*, 5 Sept. 1903, lists union officers and VTLC delegates and shows that most delegates were officers or former officers of their unions. VTLC minutes, and those for ITU Local 226 and Carpenters and Joiners Local 452 also confirm that most delegates were union officers.

20 VTLCM, 17 June 1892. See McDonald, 'Working Class Vancouver,' for the class mobility of many union workers, and ch. 4 of this work.

21 VTLCM, 19 May, 16, 23 June 1893. For clashes between the Knights and the ITU in Ontario, see G.S. Kealey and Bryan D. Palmer, *Dreaming of What Might Be: The Knights of Labor in Ontario, 1890–1900* (Toronto: New Hogtown Press, 1987), 156, 158, 164, 262, 370; VTLCM, 27 Oct. 1893.

22 VTLCM, 14, 28 Sept., 12 Oct. 1894. It has not been possible to determine what Bartley's job was.

23 VTLCM, 14 Feb. 1896.

24 James Hinton, in *Labour and Socialism* (Amherst: University of Massachusetts, 1983), and *The First Shop Stewards' Movement* (London: George Allen and Unwin, 1973), and Richard Price, in *Masters, Unions, and Men* (New York:

Cambridge University Press, 1980), argue that centralization was an integral element of a conservative, right-leaning bureaucracy. Tony Adams, in 'Leadership and Oligarchy,' *Studies in History and Politics* 5 (1986), 23–45, suggests that in the British railway unions, centralization was more likely to be a project of the left wing. This view is the more accurate one of the VTLC.

25 Kealey and Palmer, 128–31, 54. See Allen Seager, 'Workers, Class, and Industrial Conflict in New Westminster, 1900–1930,' in *Workers, Capital, and the State in British Columbia,* ed. Rennie Warburton and David Coburn (Vancouver: University of British Columbia Press, 1988), 119, for the tendency of unionists to conflate 'unskilled' and 'foreigner.' VTLCM, 27 March, 3, 10 April 1891, outlines the hod carriers' dispute.

26 Kealey and Palmer, 202, 130, 125–6; Philip Foner, *History of the American Labor Movement,* vol. 2, *From the Founding of the AF of L to the Emergence of American Imperialism* (New York: International Publishers, 1975), 78–9, 132–4; Bruce Laurie, *Artisans into Workers: Labor in Nineteenth-Century America* (New York: Noonday Press, 1989); Richard Jules Oestreicher, *Solidarity and Fragmentation: Working People and Class Consciousness in Detroit, 1875–1900* (Urbana: University of Illinois Press, 1989), 187–214. Kealey and Palmer, 159–65. As Kealey and Palmer have argued, the split between the middle-class and working-class elements in the Knights may well have been exaggerated, and none of the above is intended to argue that factionalism was the only element in the decline of the Knights. It does suggest that the VTLC may have had some good reasons for the federalist scheme of organization besides protecting the positions of the union leaders.

27 Bartley, 'Twenty-five.'

28 VTLCM, 20 May, 20 June, 21 Aug., 14 Nov. 1890; 9 Sept., 23 Sept. 1892; 3 Dec. 1897; *World,* 2 Sept. 1899.

29 *World,* 13 Sept. 1890.

30 VTLCM, 11 Dec. 1891; 21 Oct., 2 Dec. 1892; 24 March 1893.

31 Nicol, 40, 108. W.C. McKee, 'The Vancouver Park System, 1886–1929: A Product of Local Businessmen,' *Urban History Review* 3 (1978), 33–49.

32 Nicol, 114–15; McKee, 42–3.

33 For the VTLC's crusades for parks, see McDonald, '"Holy Retreat" or "Practical Breathing Spot"? Class Perceptions of Vancouver's Stanley Park, 1910–13,' *Canadian Historical Review* 65 (1984), 127–53; Bartley, 'Twenty-five'; *World,* 4 March 1899.

34 *World,* 3, 31 Aug. 1895; VTLCM, 6 Dec. 1895, 8 May 1896, 17, 31 July 1896, for Watson's earlier pro-park position; *World,* 4 March 1899; Bartley, 'Twenty-five.'

35 *World,* 1 April, 4 March 1899; *Province,* 1 April 1899; *World,* 28 Feb. 1899.

36 *Daily News–Advertiser,* 3 Feb. 1900; *World,* 17 Feb. 1900; *Independent,* 19 May 1900.

37 *World,* 29 April, 16 Sept., 9 Dec. 1899; *Daily News–Advertiser,* 7 Jan. 1900; *World,* 9 Jan. 1900; Robin, *Radical Politics,* 77–8; Paul Phillips, *No Power Greater: A Century of Labour in British Columbia* (Vancouver: BC Federation of Labour, the Boag Foundation, 1967), 33, 42; Loosmore, 156–72.

38 VTLCM, 14 Aug. 1891; 21 Dec. 1894; 5 June 1896; 23 Sept. 1892; 7 Oct. 1892; 18 Nov. 1892.

39 VTLCM, 9 Oct., 6 Nov. 1896; 27 Sept. 1895; 26 Feb. 1892.

40 VTLCM, 14, 25 Feb. 1890 for Hallam's appointment. See his complaints on the tardiness of union reporting, VTLCM, 25 Feb. 1890, 27 Feb. 1891, 25 March, 13 Aug. 1892. See VTLCM, 11 Dec. 1891, for a request for the secretary to bring in a detailed report of unions in arrears, and 11 March 1892 for the request for statistics. VTLCM, 15 Jan. 1892, notes that the Tinners were in arrears; VTLCM, 10 Nov., 24 Nov., 22 Dec. 1893, 1 March 1895.

41 VTLCM, 31 Jan., 14 Feb. 1890; 8 May, 11 Sept. 1891; 26 Feb. 1892; 25 Sept. 1891.

42 VTLCM, 21 Aug. 1890.

43 VTLCM, 15 Jan., 20 May, 2, 15 July 1892.

44 VTLCM, 6 Nov., 5 Sept. 1890; 9 Jan., 13 Feb., 27 March 1891; 6 May 1892; 2, 8 Dec. 1893.

45 VTLCM, 12 Dec. 1890; 23 Jan., 1891; 31 Jan. 1890; 23 Jan., 31 July 1891; 20 May 1892.

46 VTLCM, 27 Sept., 11, 25 Oct. 1895; 14 Feb., 22 May 1896. Bishop did return to Vancouver and started his own business as a master painter. He advertised regularly in the VTLC newspaper and was on its list of fair employers. This suggests he made restitution or had not stolen the money. Nonetheless, the episode pointed out the utility of stricter procedures in the handling of council funds.

47 VTLCM, 29 April 1899.

48 Data for this section have been compiled from VTLC minutes. When such minutes were not extant, newspaper reports were used.

CHAPTER 3 The Development of Institutions and Formal Bureaucracy

1 VTLCM, 14 Nov. 1890.

2 Michael Kazin, *Barons of Labor: The San Francisco Building Trades and Union Power in the Progressive Era* (Urbana: University of Illinois Press, 1989), 102. Sidney Lens has argued that the walking delegates were the precursors of the professional business agent; see *The Crisis of American Labor* (New York: Perpetua, 1961), 46–50.

3 VTLCM, 13 Feb., 19 June, 24 April, 8 May 1891. The dispute with the stonecutters is in the *World,* 16 May 1891. The vote to keep Irvine is from VTLCM, 22 May 1891.

4 *World,* 18, 19, 20 Aug. 1891; *Daily News–Advertiser,* 19, 20 Aug. 1891; VTLCM, 14 Aug., 25 Sept., 9 Oct., 18 Dec. 1891; 8 Jan., 12, 26 Feb. 1892, for the details of fundraising and the issue of retaining an attorney. The quote on changing the law to aid the union movement is from VTLCM, 20 Nov. 1891.

5 Paul Phillips, *No Greater Power: A Century of Labour in British Columbia* (Vancouver: BC Federation of Labour, Boag Foundation, 1967), 22.

6 *World,* 18, 19, 20 Aug. 1891; *Daily News–Advertiser,* 19, 20 Aug. 1891.

7 VTLCM, 6 May 1892. No further mention can be found of this scheme, but the motion indicates that the hiring of officials to carry out policy was not in itself a hindrance to some kinds of militancy and class-conscious action.

8 VTLCM, 4 Dec. 1891; 3 June, 2 July 1892.

9 VTLCM, 19 May 1893.

10 VTLCM, 4 Aug. 1893.

11 VTLCM, 3 Dec. 1897.

12 VTLCM, 13 Oct. 1893.

13 VTLCM, 27 Oct. 1893.

14 VTLCM, 10 Nov. 1893; 3 Dec. 1897.

15 George Bartley, 'Twenty-five Years in the BC Labor Movement,' *BC Federationist,* 27 Dec. 1912; VTLCM, 30 July 1897; *World,* 1 April, 27 May, 24 June, 5 Aug. 1899. For an examination of the fight for legal intervention in safety matters in Ontario, see Eric Tucker, *Administering Danger in the Workplace: The Law and Politics of Occupational Health and Safety Regulation in Ontario, 1850–1914* (Toronto: University of Toronto Press, 1990).

16 VTLCM, 5, 19 Nov. 1897.

17 James Hawthornthwaite Papers, Don Stewart Collection. Dixon was probably especially hampered by the 1906 amendment to the act that changed the wording 'engineer' to 'a certified engineer' throughout.

18 VTLCM, 28 Sept. 1894.

19 *Independent,* 21 April 1900.

20 Ibid., 31 March 1900.

21 Ibid., 14 April 1900.

22 Ibid., 30 June 1900.

23 Ibid., 14 July 1900.

24 In this, the Vancouver council resembled the DTLC. See Paul Craven, *'An Impartial Umpire': Industrial Relations and the Canadian State, 1900–1911* (Toronto: University of Toronto Press, 1980), Ch. 5 and 6. See also Robert H. Babcock, *Gompers in Canada: A Study in American Continentalism before the First World War* (Toronto: University of Toronto Press, 1974), 82–8, 92–4. The ideology of the VTLC is examined more fully in the next chapter.

25 *Independent,* 19 May 1900.

26 Ibid., 30 June 1900.
27 Ibid., 9 March 1901.
28 Ibid., 19 Oct. 1901.
29 Ibid., 15 June 1901.
30 Ibid., 29 June 1901.
31 Ibid., 17 Aug. 1901.
32 Ibid., 27 July 1901.
33 VTLCM, 7 May 1903.
34 *Independent*, 20 July, 2 Nov. 1901; Martin Robin, *Radical Politics and Canadian Labour, 1880–1930* (Kingston: Industrial Relations Centre, Queen's University, 1968), 53–6.
35 VTLCM, 24 Oct. 1890.
36 Ibid., 13, 27 March 1896.
37 *World*, 15 April, 13 May 1899.
38 Ibid., 10 June 1899.
39 *Independent*, 31 March 1900.
40 *World*, 5 Aug. 1899.
41 Ibid., 2 Sept. 1899.
42 *Independent*, 31 March 1900. For a discussion on plumbing in the city see Margaret Andrews, 'Sanitary Conveniences and the Retreat of the Frontier: Vancouver, 1886–1926,' *BC Studies* 87 (1990), 3–22.
43 *Independent*, 31 March 1900. It may be that workers' own financial troubles prevented them from taking up shares; $2.00 was nearly a half-day's pay for a unionized worker. But this too suggests that the council was out of step with the rank and file.
44 *Independent*, 31 March 1900.
45 Ibid., 21 April 1900.
46 Ibid., 21 April, 13 Oct. 1900; emphasis added.
47 Ibid., 13 Oct. 1900.
48 VTLCM, 21 Aug., 17 July, 4 Sept., 6 Nov. 1902; 1 Jan., 7 May, 21 May 1903; 21 May, 4 June 1903; 7 April 1904
49 *Independent*, 13 Oct. 1900.
50 Ibid., 24 Aug. 1901.
51 Ibid., 28 Sept. 1901.
52 Ibid., 24 Aug. 1901.
53 Ibid., 31 March 1900.
54 Ibid., 16 Nov. 1901.
55 Ibid., 29 Sept. 1900.
56 Ibid., 5 Oct. 1901.
57 Ibid., 26 Oct. 1901.

58 Ibid., 12 Oct. 1901.

59 Ibid., 17 Aug. 1901.

60 The estimate of 1/3 is based on projections given in 1892 and again in 1904 that the paper could survive if 400–500 subscriptions could be guaranteed. Presumably the failure of the *Independent* means that such a number of subscribers was not forthcoming. VTLCM, 23 Sept., 7 Oct., and 18 Nov. 1892, 19 May 1904. The estimate of 1,600 VTLC affiliated members is in the *Independent*, 31 March 1900.

61 VTLCM, 5 Nov. 1903.

62 Ibid., 15 Jan., 5 Feb. 1903.

63 The politics of the dispute are not clear. Several council delegates were working to remove J.H. Watson, and this was the opening shot in their battle, described further on. It may be that the same members wanted to displace Cowan and Bartley, seeing them as allies of Watson, but dropped the issue in the face of their strong support in the council. It is not apparent that this was primarily a fight of socialists against labourists, for the attack on Watson crossed several political lines.

64 VTLCM, 19 Nov. 1903.

CHAPTER 4 Labourism, Bureaucracy, and the Labour Aristocracy

1 Though early work on BC's labour movement suggested that it was exceptional for being radical and socialist, more recent work has debunked this view. Pockets of radicalism did exist, as they did in other provinces, but the Vancouver Trades and Labour Congress itself was, in its first decade, committed to labourism rather than socialism. For accounts of western exceptionalism, see Martin Robin, *Radical Politics and Canadian Labour, 1880–1930* (Kingston: Industrial Relations Centre, Queen's University); A.R. McCormack, *Reformers, Rebels, and Revolutionaries* (Toronto: University of Toronto Press, 1979); Paul Phillips, *No Power Greater* (Vancouver: BC Federation of Labour, Boag Foundation, 1967). For the critique of western exceptionalism, see Allen Seager, 'Workers, Class, and Industrial Conflict in New Westminster, 1900–1930,' in *Workers, Capital, and the State in British Columbia*, ed. R. Warburton and D. Coburn (Vancouver: University of British Columbia Press, 1988), 117–40; Jeremy Mouat, 'The Genesis of Western Exceptionalism: British Columbia's Hard-Rock Miners, 1895–1903,' *Canadian Historical Review* 71 (1990), 317–45; James Naylor, *The New Democracy: Challenging the Social Order in Industrial Ontario, 1914–1925* (Toronto: University of Toronto Press, 1991). The best analysis of the ideology of the Vancouver labour movement is R.A.J. McDonald, 'Working Class Vancouver, 1886–1914,' *BC Studies*, 69–70 (1986), 33–69; I have drawn liberally from this last, though Professor McDonald and I disagree on causes of labourism.

2 McDonald, 34. See Craig Heron, 'Labourism and the Canadian Working Class,'

Labour / Le Travail 13 (1984) for an extended definition and analysis of labourism. Bryan Palmer also examines it in *Working Class Experience: Rethinking the History of Canadian Labour, 1800–1991* (1983; 2nd rev. ed., Toronto: McClelland and Stewart, 1992), 177–80. McCormack devotes Ch. 5 to Winnipeg labourism in *Reformers, Rebels, and Revolutionaries*. For an insightful look at socialism and labourism outside Vancouver, see Gordon Hak, 'The Socialist and Labourist Impulse in Small-Town British Columbia: Port Alberni and Prince George, 1911–33, *Canadian Historical Review* 70 (1989), 519–42.

3 *Independent*, 14 July, 14 April 1900.

4 Ibid., 12 May 1900.

5 Ibid., 5 May 1900.

6 VTLCM, 2 Dec. 1893; 30 March, 28 Sept. 1894; 6 Dec. 1895.

7 *Independent*, 7 April 1900; VTLCM, 8 Nov. 1895.

8 *World*, 19 Jan. 1891; VTLCM, 7 April, 1 Sept., 10 March, 24 March 1893; 22 June 1894.

9 VTLCM, 19 May 1893; 15 Feb. 1895.

10 *Independent*, 28 April 1900.

11 For other calls for day labour, see VTLCM, 14 Feb., 18 June 1897.

12 *Independent*, 31 March 1900.

13 VTLCM, 14 Feb. 1890.

14 Thomas Loosmore, 'The British Columbia Labour Movement and Political Action, 1879–1900,' MA Thesis, University of British Columbia, 1954, 45.

15 VTLCM, 7 Oct. and 2 Dec. 1892. It has not been possible to determine when aldermanic salaries were first paid. City council minutes' indices make no mention of the issue, and only an in-depth examination of the minutes would turn up the dates. VTLCM, 7 Dec. 1894; 31 Jan. 1896; 11 Nov. 1899.

16 VTLCM, 6 Dec. 1895; 4 Jan., 2 Feb. 1894.

17 Loosmore, ii, 37, 40, 45; Craig Heron, 'Labourism and the Canadian Working Class,' 51, 54, 74; see G.S. Kealey and B.D. Palmer, *Dreaming of What Might Be* (Toronto: New Hogtown Press, 1987), 301–11, for the Knights' brainworkers. See also Russell Hann, 'Brainworkers and the Knights of Labor: E.E. Sheppard, Phillips Thompson, and the *Toronto News*, 1883–1887,' in *Essays in Canadian Working Class History*, ed. Gregory S. Kealey and Peter Warrian (Toronto: McClelland and Stewart, 1976), 35–57.

18 Louis Aubrey Wood, *A History of Farmers' Movements in Canada: The Origins and Development of Agrarian Protest, 1872–1924* (1924; reprint, Toronto: University of Toronto Press, 1975), 114–15.

19 Cited in S.E.D. Shortt, 'Social Change and Political Crisis in Rural Ontario: The Patrons of Industry, 1889–1896,' in *Oliver Mowat's Ontario*, ed. Donald Swainson (Toronto: Macmillan and Company, 1972), 216.

20 Cited in Russell Hann, *Farmers Confront Industrialism: Some Historical Perspectives on Ontario Agrarian Movements* (Toronto: New Hogtown Press, 1975), 12.
21 For the experience of women on the farm, see Marjorie Griffin Cohen, *Women's Work, Markets, and Economic Development in Nineteenth Century Ontario* (Toronto: Univeristy of Toronto Press, 1988), and Pauline Rankin, 'The Politicization of Ontario Farm Women,' in *Beyond the Vote: Canadian Women and Politics,* ed. Linda Kealey and Joan Sangster (Toronto: University of Toronto Press, 1989), 309–32.
22 H. Clare Pentland, *Labour and Capital in Canada, 1650–1850* (Toronto: Lorimer, 1981), 58–9; Gavin Wright, 'American Agriculture and the Labor Market: What Happened to Proletarianization?' *Agricultural History,* 62 (1988), 192. For information on Bartley, see *Province,* 4 Jan. 1943, *Sun,* 21 Nov. 1939; Dixon was the son of a Cumberland County, England, farmer.
23 Wright, 201.
24 Gordon Darroch, 'Class in Nineteenth-Century Central Ontario: A Reassessment of the Crisis and Demise of Small Producers during Early Industrialization, 1861–1871,' in *Class, Gender, and Region: Essays in Canadian Historical Sociology,* ed. G.S. Kealey (St John's: Committee on Canadian Labour History, 1988), 64, 68.
25 Shortt, 226–9; Ramsay Cook, 'Tillers and Toilers: The Rise and Fall of Populism in Canada in the 1890s,' *Historical Papers* (1984), 5–8. See Kealey and Palmer, 387–91, for connections between the Knights and the Patrons of Industry. Similarities also existed between the U.S. populist and labour movements. See, for example, Lawrence Goodwyn, *The Populist Moment* (Oxford: Oxford University Press, 1978), esp. Ch. 4. Norman Pollack, in *The Populist Response to Industrial America* (Cambridge: Harvard University Press, 1962), goes so far as to suggest that the farmers' protest was the most important resistance to capitalism, overshadowing the efforts of the labour movement. VTLCM, 24 March 1893; 12 Oct. 1894. Reference to co-operation with farmers in the Nationalist Party may be found in VTLCM, 7 Dec. 1894.
26 See Hann, 21; Cook, 19–20, for Wrigley et al.; the assessment of the *Eagle* as a 'booster paper' may be found in Jeremy Mouat, 'The Context of Conflict: The Western Federation of Miners in British Columbia, 1895–1903,' unpublished paper, University of British Columbia, 1986, 44. For the paper's support of Chris Foley, see *Independent,* 10 Nov. 1900.
27 VTLCM, 31 July 1891, gives the salary of the secretary.
28 See Stan Weir, 'The Conflict in American Unions and the Resistance to Alternative Ideas from the Rank and File,' in *Workers' Struggles, Past and Present: A 'Radical America' Reader,* ed. James Green (Philadelphia: Temple University Press, 1983), 251–68, and Ch. 1 for a discussion of this argument.
29 Heron, 'Labourism and the Canadian Working Class'; McDonald, 'Working Class

Vancouver.' For my own objections to the urbanism argument, see 'Rethinking Vancouver's Labour Movement: Ethnicity, Urbanism, and the Labour Aristocracy,' *Canadian Historical Review* 74 (1993), 510–34.

30 Marx, 'Inaugural Address of the Workingmen's International Association,' in Marx and Engels, *Selected Works* (Moscow: Progress Publishers, 1976), vol. 2, 14–15; Engels, 'Preface to The Condition of the Working Class in England,' in Marx and Engels, *Selected Works*, vol. 3, 446–8; Engels, 'Trades Unions,' in Marx and Engels, *Articles on Britain* (Moscow: Progress Publishers, 1971), 378.

31 Eric Hobsbawm, 'The Labour Aristocracy in Nineteenth-Century Britain,' in *Labouring Men: Studies in the History of Labour* (New York: Anchor Books, 1967), 322–3; Robert Michels, *Political Parties* (Glencoe: Free Press, 1948), 283–4. E.P. Thompson, 'The Peculiarities of the English,' in *The Poverty of Theory and Other Essays* (New York: Monthly Review Press, 1978), 281. Richard Price gives a useful reappraisal of the labour aristocracy argument in 'The Segmentation of Work and the Labour Aristocracy,' *Labour / Le Travail* 17 (1986), 267–72.

32 Bartley, 'Twenty-five'; VTLCM, 25 Feb., 28 March 1890. For the rates of printers in 1908, see *BC Trades Unionist*, March 1908. The rates of other workers have been taken from McDonald, 'Working Class Vancouver,' 38. His figures are taken from the Census of Canada figures for 1911. For the rates of women in the garment industry and the calculation that most women earned about half the wage of their male counterparts, see James Conley, 'Class Conflict and Collective Action in the Working Class of Vancouver, British Columbia, 1900–1919,' PhD thesis, Carleton University, 1986, Ch. 9, esp. 420; the rate for domestic service in 1911 is from McDonald, 38. See also Star Rosenthal, 'Union Maids: Organized Women Workers in Vancouver, 1900–1915,' *BC Studies* 41 (1979), 41, 46. McDonald, 41–2, also examines the wage rates of Asian and women workers to conclude that they were paid 40 to 50 per cent less than white males.

33 *Independent*, 31 March, 7 April 1900; 25 May 1901. For Pleming, see Vancouver *Sun*, 1 April 1952; for Hepburn, *Sun*, 22 Aug. 1940. City directories list him as a contractor by 1904. Cowan and Bartley may be traced in the city directories. See *Independent*, 22 Feb. 1902, for the well-wishes for Dixon. For Bishop, see *Independent*, 7 Nov. 1903.

34 *Independent*, 11 May, 31 Aug. 1901. Lamrick's career is outlined in *Province*, 2 March 1926. Lee's business is outlined in the city directories, beginning in 1908. See McDonald, 'Working Class Vancouver,' 66–7, for the 'upward mobility' of the union leadership.

35 R.Q. Gray, 'Styles of Life, the "Labour Aristocracy," and Class Relations in Later Nineteenth-Century Edinburgh,' *International Review of Social History* 18 (1973), 428–9. The counter-argument to the culturalist position is advanced in Hobsbawm, 'Debating the Labour Aristocracy,' 220–1, and 'The Aristocracy of

Labour Reconsidered,' 238–9, both in *Worlds of Labour: Further Studies in the History of Labour*. The quote may be found on page 238.

36 Michael Kazin, *Barons of Labor: The San Francisco Building Trades and Union Power in the Progressive Era* (Urbana: University of Illinois Press, 1989), 281. Michael Piva, in 'The Aristocracy of the English Working Class: Help for an Historical Debate in Difficulties,' *Histoire Sociale* 7 (1974), 276, and Henry Pelling in 'The Concept of the Labour Aristocracy,' in *Popular Politics and Society in Late Victorian Britain* (London: Macmillan, 1968), 56, make the same argument. Hobsbawm counters it in 'Debating the Labour Aristocracy,' 222–3, and 'The Aristocracy of Labour Reconsidered,' 238–9, where he suggests that 'there really is no denying that the labour aristocrats, so long as their privileged position lasted, were not aiming at the overthrow of capitalism.' The quote in the text is from the latter article, 244.

   I have not discussed the argument of John Foster, who prefers to define the labour aristocracy by its 'authority in industry.' That is to say that labour aristocrats were those workers who were 'pacemakers and taskmasters'; these people, and subcontractors, not the 'highly paid, autonomous craft elite' are, in his argument, the real aristocrats. John Foster, *Class Struggle and the Industrial Revolution* (London: Weidenfeld and Nicolson), 1974. Bryan Palmer makes a similar argument in *A Culture in Conflict: Skilled Workers and Industrial Capitalism in Hamilton, Ontario, 1860–1914* (Montreal: McGill-Queen's University Press, 1979), 239–41. For a critique of this view, see Gareth Stedman Jones, 'Class Struggle and the Industrial Revolution,' in *Languages of Class: Studies in English Working Class History, 1832–1982* (Cambridge: Cambridge University Press, 1983), 25–75. Hobsbawm, in 'Debating the Labour Aristocracy,' 216, also rejects Foster's formulation.

37 Ian McKay demonstrates the dichotomy between skilled and unskilled workers in 'Class Struggle and Merchant Capital: Craftsmen and Labourers on the Halifax Waterfront, 1850–1902,' in *The Character of Class Struggle: Essays in Canadian Working-Class History 1850–1985*, ed. Bryan D. Palmer (Toronto: McClelland and Stewart, 1986), 17–36. For an outline of printers' ability to defend their trade, see Gary Marks, *Unions in Politics: Britain, Germany, and the United States in the Nineteenth and Early Twentieth Centuries* (Princeton: Princeton University Press, 1989). See esp. Ch. 4 here. For Canadian printers, see Gregory S. Kealey, *Toronto Workers Respond to Industrial Capitalism, 1867–1892* (Toronto: University of Toronto Press, 1980), Ch. 6, 'Printers and Mechanization'; G.S. Kealey, 'Work Control, the Labour Process, and Nineteenth-Century Canadian Printers,' in *On the Job: Confronting the Work Process in Canada*, ed. Craig Heron and Robert Storey (Montreal and Kingston: McGill-Queen's University Press, 1986), 75–101. See also Sally Zerker, *The Rise and Fall of the Toronto Typographical*

Union, 1832–1972: A Case of Foreign Domination (Toronto: University of Toronto Press, 1982). For the difficulties faced by cigarmakers and tailors in Vancouver, see Conley, 'Class Conflict and Collective Action,' and Irene Howard, *The Struggle for Social Justice in British Columbia: Helena Gutteridge, the Unknown Reformer* (Vancouver: University of British Columbia Press, 1992). Conley has also described the movement of some trade unions to more militant politics in 'Frontier Labourers, Crafts in Crisis, and the Western Labour Revolt: The Case of Vancouver, 1900–1919,' *Labour / Le Travail* 23 (1989). For similar evolutions in other cities, see G.S. Kealey, '1919: The Canadian Labour Revolt,' *Labour / Le Travail* 13 (1984), 11–44; Craig Heron and Bryan D. Palmer, 'Through the Prism of the Strike: Industrial Conflict in Southern Ontario, 1901–14,' *Canadian Historical Review* 58 (1977), 423–58. For an examination of labour aristocrats under attack on their relative privilege, see Ian McKay, *The Craft Transformed: An Essay on the Carpenters of Halifax, 1885–1985* (Halifax: Holdfast Press, 1985). Useful studies on the fragmented response of Canada's skilled metalworkers may be found in Craig Heron, 'The Crisis of the Craftsman: Hamilton's Metal Workers in the Early Twentieth Century,' *Labour / Le Travailleur* 6 (Autumn 1980), 7–48, and Wayne Roberts, 'Toronto Metal Workers and the Second Industrial Revolution, 1889–1914,' *Labour / Le Travailleur* 6 (1980), 49–72.

CHAPTER 5 Culture and Community

1 See David Montgomery, *The Fall of the House of Labor: The Workplace, the State, and American Labor Activism, 1865–1925* (Cambridge: Cambridge University Press, 1987.), 13, 17–20, 105–6, 148, 180, 204–6, for the creation of workers' codes of ethics and militancy; Hobsbawm, 'Trends in the British Labour Movement,' in *Labouring Men: Studies in the History of Labour* (New York: Anchor, 1967.) 379, for the appreciation that 'the labour aristocrat might wear a top-hat ... but when the pickets were out against the boss, he knew what to do.'
2 The preference of the VTLC leaders for the Sept. celebration is in itself some evidence of their desire to unite workers while making sure their actions were not interpreted as revolutionary.
3 *World*, 8 Sept. 1890.
4 VTLCM, 21 July, 29 Sept. 1893; George Bartley, 'Twenty-five Years in the BC Labor Movement,' *BC Federationist*, 27 Dec. 1912.
5 VTLCM, 20 July, 3, 31 Aug. 1894; Bartley, 'Twenty-five.'
6 VTLCM, 31 Aug. 1894; *World*, 3, 6 Sept. 1898.
7 *World*, 2 Sept. 1899; 4 Sept. 1897.
8 VTLCM, 16 Feb. 1894; *Independent*, 14 April 1900.
9 Ibid., 16 April 1903; 18 Feb. 1904; 18 Aug. 1904. On this last date, the bill

remained unpaid and was referred to the executive officers. It has not been possible to determine if it was ever paid. The looseleaf bill was slipped into the pages of the minutes.

10 Ibid., 21 Dec. 1894; *Independent*, 21 Sept. 1901.
11 *Independent*, 31 March 1900.
12 VTLCM, 14 Feb. 1890; 26 Feb. 1892.
13 *Independent*, 12 May 1900.
14 Ibid., 28 April 1900.
15 VTLCM, 1 Feb., 31 Aug. 1895.
16 *Independent*, 31 March 1900.
17 VTLCM, 3 April, 15 May 1902.
18 Ibid., 21 July 1904; 3 April 1902. See James Conley, 'Class Conflict and Collective Action in the Working Class of Vancouver, BC, 1900–1919,' PhD thesis, Carleton University, 1986, 435–7, for the problems of unions and the label campaign.
19 *Independent*, 7 April 1900; VTLCM, 25 Sept. 1896.
20 *Independent*, 12 May 1900.
21 R.A.J. McDonald, 'Working Class Vancouver 1886–1914,' *BC Studies* 69–70 (Spring–Summer 1986) 45; see also Peter W. Ward, 'Class and Race in the Social Structure of British Colmbia, 1870–1939,' *BC Studies* 45 (1980), 17–35, for union membership. Paul Phillips, *No Power Greater: A Century of Labour in British Columbia* (Vancouver: BC Federation of Labour, Boag Foundation, 1967), 169, estimates the province's unionization rate at 12 per cent in 1911. The strength of construction and streetcar railway unions probably accounts for the higher rate in the city.
22 VTLCM, 14 March 1890; 7 Dec. 1894.
23 *Independent*, 23 June 1900.
24 Ibid., 23 Nov. 1901; emphasis added.
25 Bartley, 'Twenty-five'; McDonald, 'Working Class Vancouver,' 62; *Independent*, 21 Dec. 1901; 4 Jan. 1902; 1 Jan., 20 June 1903; VTLCM, 7 Dec. 1894, 31 Jan. 1896.
26 Dominion Day Celebration Committee, Vancouver City Archives, add. ms. 47, vol. 1, file 2, minute books. Bartley's own long service with the committee is indicated by the fact that he donated the minute books and records to the archives. His identification with the community rather than the labour movement is suggested by the absence of any other archival deposits in his name; it appears that at the end of his life, Bartley held this connection to be among the most important. *Independent*, 30 June, 8 Sept. 1900; 8 June 1901.
27 VTLCM, 7 June 1895; *Independent*, 7 July 1900; VTLCM, 8 May 1897; Bartley, 'Twenty-five.' See Robert Michels, who suggested that when placed in this heady environment, the labour leader's 'manners become gentler and more refined. In his daily association with persons of the highest birth he learns the usages of good

society and endeavors to assimilate them,' in *Political Parties* (Glencoe: Free Press, 1948), 283–4.

28 *Independent,* 31 Aug. 1901; the poem is from *Independent,* 7 Sept. 1901.

29 Ibid., 16 March 1901.

30 Ibid., 31 March 1900.

31 *World,* 3, 31 Aug. 1895; VTLCM, 6 Dec. 1895; 8 May 1896; 17, 31 July 1896. R.A.J. McDonald '"Holy Retreat" or "Practical Breathing Spot"? Class Perceptions of Vancouver's Stanley Park, 1900–13 *Canadian Historical Review* 64 (1984), 127–53, outlines the VTLC's concern with parks in some detail. *World,* 15 Oct. 1898. W.C. McKee, 'The Vancouver Park System, 1886–1929: A Product of Local Businessmen,' *Urban History Review* 3 (1978), 44–5, argues that wealthier areas of the city received parks long before working class areas did.

32 *Independent,* 7 April 1900. See Alan Metcalfe, *Canada Learns to Play: The Emergence of Organized Sport, 1807–1914* (Toronto: McClelland and Stewart, 1987), esp. Ch. 6, for a discussion of lacrosse and professionalism.

CHAPTER 6 Relations of Race and Gender

1 For a discussion of the prevalence of racism in the working class of Vancouver see W. Peter Ward, *White Canada Forever: Popular Attitudes and Public Policy toward Orientals in British Columbia* (Montreal: McGill-Queen's Press, 1978), and Patricia E. Roy, *A White Man's Province: British Columbia Politicians and Chinese and Japanese Immigrants, 1858–1914* (Vancouver: University of British Columbia Press, 1989); R.A.J. McDonald, 'Working Class Vancouver, 1886–1914,' *BC Studies* 69/70 (1986), 33–69.

2 W. Peter Ward, 'Class and Race in the Social Structure of British Columbia, 1870–1939,' *BC Studies* 45 (1980), 29.

3 Gillian Creese, 'Class, Ethnicity, and Conflict: The Case of Chinese and Japanese Immigrants, 1880–1923,' in *Workers, Capital, and the State in British Columbia: Selected Papers,* ed. Rennie Warburton and David Coburn (Vancouver: University of British Columbia Press, 1988), 73, 80. See also Rennie Warburton, 'Race and Class in British Columbia: A Comment,' *BC Studies* 49 (1981), 79–85. Earlier labour historians, in the main, also attributed racism to the acceptance of low wages and long hours by Chinese workers, and their inability to read and understand safety regulations printed in English; see Thomas R. Loosmore, 'The British Columbia Labour Movement and Political Action, 1879–1900,' MA thesis, University of British Columbia, 1954, 19; Paul Phillips, *No Greater Power: A Century of Labour in British Columbia* (Vancouver: BC Federation of Labour, Boag Foundation, 1967), 8, 10. Ward's positive arguments for the primacy of race hinge on a more subtle definition of race than he extends to class. In effect, he argues that

race was an experienced phenomenon while class was an idealistic, intellectual one. But it is difficult to imagine a cannery worker, a coal miner, a store clerk, a carpenter, a railway navvy, or a fisher not bumping up against the living reality of class every day. A class-conscious, socialist critique of the type preferred by Ward may not have followed from their daily lives, but surely workers could not have missed the observation that they were employees, and because of that lived lives very different from those of the Bell-Irvings, the Dunsmuirs, the Woodwards, or the Hays. Pointing out, quite correctly, that Asians were often denied membership in white clubs, groups, and institutions, Ward neglects to add that working people were not eligible to join the Chamber of Commerce and were unlikely to be found in the ranks of the Terminal Club in this period. Ward's evidence that intermarriage between racial groups was rare prompts the question, how many workers married into the bourgeoisie? Taken together, Ward's arguments depend on special pleading, unrealistic yardsticks for measuring class consciousness, and a calculated refusal to consider culture as an element of class. Ward's assertion that class was less significant than race remains unproven.

Creese, however, has suggested that racism was a sign of 'developing, but not yet mature, working-class consciousness,' 80. I believe this argument has a Whiggish, idealist whiff about it, for it assumes that consciousness is progressive and evolutionary, and thus not directly related to the material conditions workers faced. More 'mature' class consciousness did not end racism in the working class; the need to organize all workers in certain industries did. Furthermore, the argument strongly implies that workers could have, and should have, had a different consciousness than they did. This assumption blurs our understanding of how and why racism was expressed, for it downplays the statements and actions of the labour activists themselves.

4 As Engels noted in an oft-quoted passage, 'According to the materialist conception of history, the *ultimately* determining element in history is the production and reproduction of real life. More than this neither Marx nor I have ever asserted. Hence if somebody twists this into saying that the economic element is the only *determining* one, he transforms the proposition into a meaningless, abstract, senseless phrase. The economic structure is basis but the various elements of the superstructure ... constitutions, political, philosophical, juristic theories, religious views ... also exercise the influence upon the course of the historical struggles and in many cases preponderate in determining their *form* ... Otherwise the application of the theory to any period of history would be easier than the solution of a simple equation of the first degree' (Frederick Engels, Letter to J. Bloch, 21 Sept. 1890, in Marx and Engels, *Selected Works* [Moscow: Progress Publishers, 1977] vol. 3, 487).

There is, of course, a huge literature on historical materialism and the precise role that the productive forces play in determining ideas. Marxists themselves are divided and do not even agree on what Marx believed to be the appropriate relationship. I do not pretend to be able to solve the debate. But in examining the labour leadership in BC, it is clear that the leaders themselves put a great deal of stock in their opposition to Asians and that their opinions are not explained by a simple economic equation.

5 Alexander Saxton, *The Indispensable Enemy: Labor and the Anti-Chinese Movement in California* (Berkeley: University of California Press, 1971), 2, 6, 14–16, 154.

6 Michael Kazin, *Barons of Labor: The San Francisco Building Trades and Union Power in the Progressive Era* (Urbana: University of Illinois Press, 1989), 146, 145–76.

7 VTLCM, 14, 25 Feb. 1890; Vancouver City Archives (hereafter VCA), add. ms. 132, William Pleming Collection, typescript, 21.

8 VTLCM, 16 Dec. 1892.

9 *World*, 16 Sept. 1899. The story was mentioned in other papers, but always as an item brought forward at the VTLC meeting. It was not covered as an actual story, which suggests that it was apocryphal. Phillips, *No Power Greater*, 14. See also Mariana Valverde, *The Age of Light, Soap, and Water: Moral Reform in English Canada, 1885–1925* (Toronto: McClelland and Stewart, 1991), Ch. 5, for the racist sexual fears of whites in this period.

10 *Independent*, 31 March, 1900, 28 April 1900.

11 Ibid.

12 Ibid., 7 April 1900.

13 Ibid., 24 May, 5 April 1902.

14 Ibid., 21 April 1900.

15 Ibid., 9 March 1901.

16 Ibid., 14, 21, 28 April 1900.

17 Ibid., 7 April 1900. See Kazin, 168–70, for a similar attitude among the San Francisco building trades council. Kazin argues that this 'hands across the ocean' stance was based on the need of labour leaders 'to explain their actions as derived from economic and political principles which were unselfish,' 168. American workers also put together a 'nationalist version of workers' rights,' 196, that closely resembled the VTLC's concept of a British Canada. Clearly 'class consciousness' of a fairly sophisticated type could easily incorporate racism.

18 VTLCM, 6, 20 May, 3 June 1892; Loosmore, 62–3, 80–2; *World*, 4 Feb., 15 April, 10 June, 27 May 1899.

19 See Saxton for a discussion of the national and local industries and the ability to withstand wage battles. Gwendolyn Mink, *Old Labor and New Immigrants in American Political Development: Union, Party, and State, 1875–1920* (Ithaca:

Cornell University Press, 1986), 71–80, makes similar arguments. For the struggles of the cigarmakers and tailors in Vancouver, see VTCLM, *passim*; *World*, 6 Aug. 1898; 5 Aug. 1899. See *World*, 5 Aug. 1899, for notice of a resolution to prohibit union members from smoking nonunion cigars, and 10 and 24 June 1899 for the union label as a device to prevent Chinese labour. See *World*, 15 April 1899 for VTLC support of the tailors' strike. VTLCM, 3 April 1902.

20 *Independent*, 2 June 1900.
21 Ibid., 23 June 1900; 16 Feb. 1901.
22 Ibid., 15 Sept. 1900.
23 Ibid.
24 Ibid., 29 Sept. 1900.
25 Ibid., 8 June 1901.
26 See, for example, the *Independent*, 3 May 1902.
27 Ibid., 28 Sept. 1900.
28 Ibid., 15 Sept. 1900.
29 Ibid., 22 Sept. 1900.
30 Ibid., 28 Sept. 1901.
31 Ibid., 29 Sept. 1900.
32 Ibid., 21 Jan. 1903.
33 Ibid., 6 July 1901.
34 Ibid., 5 April 1902.
35 Ibid., 27 Dec. 1902.
36 Ibid., 31 March 1900.
37 Ibid., 27 April 1901.
38 Ibid., 29 June 1901.
39 Ibid., 19 Oct. 1901.
40 BC did not pass a Factory Act until 1908; VTLCM, 15 Dec. 1904. For the problems of gender-specific factory legislation, see Mary Lynn Stewart, *Women, Work, and the French State: Labour Protection and Social Patriarchy, 1879–1919* (Montreal, Kingston: McGill-Queen's University Press, 1989); Paul Phillips and Erin Phillips, *Women and Work: Inequality in the Labour Market* (Toronto: Lorimer, 1983), 18–21.
41 *Independent*, 8 Aug. 1903.
42 Ibid., 21 April 1900, 14 Feb. 1903, 26 April 1902, 5 April 1902. For a fascinating look at the notion of masculinity and the iconography of the male as unionist, see Elizabeth Faue, *Community of Suffering and Struggle: Women, Men, and the Labor Movement in Minneapolis, 1915–1945* (Chapel Hill: University of North Carolina Press, 1991), esp. Ch. 2 and 3.
43 *World*, 17 Feb. 1900. *Independent*, 31 March, 7 April, 11 Aug., 22 Sept., 23 June 1900.

44 *Independent,* 17 Aug. 1900, 17 Aug. 1901. VTLC, 4 Dec. 1902; Elaine Bernard, *The Long Distance Feeling: A History of the Telecommunications Workers Union* (Vancouver: New Star Books, 1982), 26.

45 Marie Campbell, 'Sexism in British Columbia Trade Unions, 1900–1920,' in *In Her Own Right: Selected Essays on Women's History in BC,* ed. Barbara Latham and Cathy Kess (Victoria: Camosun College, 1980), 183. Marjorie Griffin Cohen has argued that even in the farm economy, 'non-market-oriented activity ... was more central to women's economic activity than was their market-oriented activity,' in her *Women's Work, Markets, and Economic Development in Nineteenth-Century Ontario* (Toronto: University of Toronto Press, 1988), 41. Star Rosenthal, 'Union Maids: Organized Women Workers in Vancouver, 1900–1915,' *BC Studies* 41 (1979), 40–1; Jean Barman, *The West beyond the West: A History of British Columbia* (Toronto: University of Toronto Press, 1991), Table 11, 369, for provincial figures.

46 Rosenthal, 41, 44. VTLCM, 4 Jan. 1902; 21 July 1904. In making the distinction between 'productive' and 'unproductive' labour, I do not wish to imply that some work was unnecessary or useless. Nor do I believe that the distinctions between the two are illustrative of differences in class or ideology. The difference between productive and unproductive labour was acknowledged by Adam Smith and used by Marx. Briefly, the distinction is not based on the kind of work that is done but on whether the work produces surplus value for the employer. In Marx's formulation, unproductive labour is that which is 'not exchanged with capital, but directly with revenue ... An actor, for example, or even a clown ... is a productive labourer if he works in the service of a capitalist ... while a jobbing tailor who comes to the capitalist's house and patches his trousers for him, producing a mere use-value for him, is an unproductive labourer. The former's labour produces a surplus value; in the latter's, revenue is consumed.' Domestic service clearly falls into this category. The work of servants creates use-value for their employer, but no exchange or surplus value. Wages paid to the employer's factory hands are taken from the products these workers create, but the wages of the servant are paid out of the employer's own pocket. Wage hikes to the factory employee can be passed on to the consumer in the form of higher prices. Higher wages paid to the servant mean less money for the employer. Thus, my suggestion that capitalists are more reluctant to grant wage increases to unproductive workers than productive workers. See Marx, *Theories of Surplus Value* (Moscow: Progress Publishers, 1972), vol. 1, 157. For an examination of the problems of the tailors' union in a later period, see Irene Howard, *The Struggle for Social Justice in British Columbia: Helena Gutteridge, The Unknown Reformer* (Vancouver: University of British Columbia Press, 1992).

CHAPTER 7 The Clash with Socialism: Intellectuals versus Artisans

1 For the SLP and STLA's sectarianism, see A.R. McCormack, *Reformers, Rebels, and Revolutionaries: The Western Canadian Radical Movement, 1899–1919* (Toronto: University of Toronto Press, 1979), 20–1, and Carlos Schwantes, *Radical Heritage: Labour, Socialism and Reform in Washington and British Columbia, 1885–1917* (North Vancouver: Douglas and McIntyre, 1979) 81–4. The attacks on the labourists are from the *Independent*, 23 June 1900; 21 April 1900.

2 *Independent*, 9 June 1900.

3 Martin Robin, *Radical Politics and Canadian Labour, 1880–1930* (Kingston: Industrial Relations Centre, Queen's University, 1968), 32–5; McCormack, 20–3; Schwantes, 97–102.

4 McCormack, 25–31.

5 Ibid., 26.

6 *World*, 15 Jan. 1898. VTLC minutes for this period are missing, and it is not possible to tell from newspaper accounts who Bartley is referring to. In any case, his Philippic against hotheads is the standard response of the challenged official. His enjoinder against those who favoured 'monopoly' may plausibly be interpreted as an attack on industrial unionism or an attack on socialist orthodoxy.

7 Paul Phillips, *No Greater Power: A Century of Labour in British Columbia* (Vancouver: BC Federation of Labour, Boag Foundation, 1967), 31–7; McCormack, 21–2; Robin, *Radical Politics*, 51–2; Schwantes, 97–100.

8 For the splits in the IAM, see David Montgomery, *Workers' Control in America: Studies in the History of Work, Technology, and Labor Struggles* (Cambridge: Cambridge University Press, 1984), 48–90; Mark Perlman, *The Machinists: A New Study In American Trade Unionism* (Cambridge, Massachusetts: Harvard University Press, 1961), 17–23; Wayne Roberts, 'Toronto Metal Workers and the Second Industrial Revolution, 1889–1914,' *Labour / Le Travailleur* 6 (1980), 49–72; and John H.M. Laslett, *Labor and the Left: A Study of Socialist and Radical Influences in the American Labor Movement, 1881–1924* (New York: Basic Books, 1970), Ch. 5, 'Populism, Socialism, and the International Association of Machinists.' The deskilling of the craft throughout North America is given as one explanation for the number of socialists in the IAM.

9 *Independent*, 23 June 1900. More on the fishermens' union may be found in J.K. Ralston, 'The 1900 Strike of Fraser River Sockeye Salmon Fishermen,' MA thesis, University of British Columbia, 1965.

10 *Independent*, 26 May 1900.

11 Ibid., 31 March 1900.

12 Ibid., 7 April 1900.

13 Ibid., 5 May 1900. This diatribe was probably intended more for the followers of

the STLA and its leader, Daniel DeLeon, than the more pragmatic and flexible socialists such as MacClain and Rogers. The STLA was widely attacked as a 'dual union,' and the remark about 'dispensations' and 'apostles' was likely a swipe at DeLeon, who was often characterized as the 'red pope.'

14 Ibid., 12 May 1900.

15 Ibid., 7 April 1900.

16 Thompson's remarks may be found in *Canadian Socialist*, 23 Aug. 1902; *Western Socialist*, 20 Sept. 1902; Lang, *Western Socialist*, 31 Jan. 1903; Kingsley, *Western Clarion*, 26 Dec. 1903. Cited in R.A. Johnson, 'No Compromise – No Political Trading: The Marxian Socialist Tradition in British Columbia,' PhD dissertation, University of British Columbia, 1975, 172. Kingsley's anti-union stance is also documented in McCormack, 31, 56; *Western Clarion*, 15 Oct. 1903; cited in Johnson, 170.

17 For an examination of this theory, see Alvin Gouldner, *Against Fragmentation: The Origins of Marxism and the Sociology of Intellectuals* (Oxford: Oxford University Press, 1985), 116.

18 *Western Socialist*, 14 Feb. 1902; 14 Feb. 1903; *Canadian Socialist*, 9 Aug. 1902; city directories, 1899–1904; city directories, 1901–2; *Western Clarion*, 17 June 1903.

19 Details of Pettipiece's early career may be found in the *Western Clarion*, 5 Nov. 1903. For a discussion of the role of journalists in European socialism, see Lenore O'Boyle, 'The Image of the Journalist in France, Germany, and England, 1815–1848,' *Comparative Studies in Society and History* 10 (1968), 290–317. See also her analysis of the attraction of professionals to socialism, in 'The Problem of an Excess of Educated Men in Western Europe, 1800–1850,' *Journal of Modern History* 42 (1970), 471–95. See *Western Socialist*, 20 Sept. 1902, for his purchase of the paper from Wrigley, and 17 Jan. 1903 for the creation of the Western Socialist Publishing Company. Its 'no dividend' share offer appears in *Western Socialist*, 21 Feb. 1903. Pettipiece's need to find employment was printed in *Western Clarion* (the name for the merger of the *Western Socialist* and the Nanaimo *Clarion*). E.T. Kingsley headed the new socialist paper. Una Larsen, Pettipiece's daughter, has recalled that her father did not become a printer until the family moved to Vancouver in 1902 and believes that he sought work in the trade as an apprentice at the age of 27, for his newspaper adventures could not support the family (Una Larsen, interview with author, Vancouver, Feb. 1989).

20 For Hawthornthwaite, see Robin, *Radical Politics and Canadian Labour*, 41; McCormack, 69; for Lefeaux, see Daisy Webster, *Growth of the NDP in British Columbia, 1900–1970*, np, nd., 50–1.

21 *Western Socialist*, 7 March 1903.

22 Such divisions between labour leaders and socialist theorists were hardly unique

to Vancouver's labour movement. Similar battles were fought throughout North America in this period and had been fought even earlier in Europe. Indeed, the struggle between artisans and intellectuals may be traced back to 1846 and Marx's purging of Wilhelm Weitling from the Communist League. See Leier, 'Workers and Intellectuals: The Theory of the New Class and Early Canadian Socialism,' *Journal of History and Politics* 10 (1992), 87–108, for a short account of the contemporary theoretical discussion of the rise of intellectuals and their class interests.

23 *Independent*, 15 Sept. 1900.
24 Ibid., 14 Sept. 1901.
25 Ibid., 3 May 1902.
26 Ibid., 20 July 1901.
27 Ibid., 22 Aug. 1904.
28 Ibid., 13 Oct. 1900.
29 Ibid., 30 May 1903.
30 Ibid., 25 July 1903.
31 Ibid., 7 Dec. 1902.
32 Ibid., 23 May, 20, 13 June, 30 May, 1903; 24 Aug. 1901. The long excerpt is from *Independent*, 30 May 1903.
33 The figures were collected from obituaries and newspaper stories in the daily and labour press and records at the Mountain View Cemetery in Vancouver. The twelve labourists and their dates of birth are John Pearey, 1839; T.H. Cross, 1847; J.H. Watson, 1855; W.J. Lamrick and Francis Williams, both 1856; Joseph Dixon, 1860; C.T. Hilton, 1863; George Bartley and John Morton, both 1867; Harry Cowan, 1869; A.N. Harrington and J.H. Browne, ITU member and VTLC statistician in 1902, both 1870. The socialists were George Dales, 1847; Allan Boag, 1858; John Mortimer, 1871; Frank Rogers, 1873; Parm Pettipiece and George Wrigley, both 1875; A.R. Stebbing, SPBC candidate with Mortimer in 1903, 1869; John Cameron, SPBC organizer, 1866. See Gouldner, *Against Fragmentation,* for the suggestion that age and particular phase of the life cycle may influence ideology.
34 *Independent*, 14 April 1900.
35 For Mortimer, see *Independent*, 12 April 1902; for Dales, *Western Socialist*, 21 Feb. 1903; for Ogle's aborted election attempt, see *Western Clarion*, 17 June 1903.
36 *Independent*, 23 May 1903.

CHAPTER 8 Continuity, Change, and Resolution

1 Phillips, *No Power Greater: A Century of Labour in British Columbia* (Vancouver: BC Federation of Labour, Boag Foundation, 1967), 43; A.R. McCormack,

Reformers, Rebels, and Revolutionaries: The Western Canadian Radical Movement, 1899–1919 (Toronto: University of Toronto Press, 1979), 48; John T. Saywell, 'Labour and Socialism in British Columbia: A Survey of Historical Development before 1903,' *British Columbia Historical Quarterly* 15 (1951), 148.

2 McCormack, 21–2.

3 *Independent*, 20 Oct., 17 Nov. 1900. The union directory published in the paper lists MacClain as IAM president in November, but he is not so listed in December.

4 George Bartley, 'Twenty-five Years in the BC Labour Movement,' *BC Federationist*, 27 Dec. 1912.

5 Carlos Schwantes, *Radical Heritage* (North Vancouver: Douglas and McIntyre, 1979), 109.

6 Reprinted in *Independent*, 1 Feb. 1902.

7 *Independent*, 4 Jan., 1902; VTLCM, 19 June 1902.

8 Ibid., 28 April, 12, 26 May, 28 July, 11 Aug., 22 Dec. 1900; Bartley, 'Twenty-five'; *Independent*, 11 Jan. 1902.

9 Ibid., 21 July 1900; Bartley, 'Twenty-five'; *Independent*, 19 May 1900, 3 Jan. 1903.

10 *Independent*, 26 Sept. 1903.

11 Ibid., 26 Jan. 1901 lists Pearey as financial secretary of the ILP. *Sun*, 17 March 1925 gives biographical information.

12 McCormack, 48.

13 VTLCM, 17 July 1902.

14 McCormack, 48.

15 *Province*, 2 March 1926; *Independent*, 9 Nov. 1901; 18, 25 July 1903.

16 VTLCM, 19 Jan. 1903.

17 There is little doubt that it is the same A.N. Harrington. The obituary in the *Province*, 18 March 1918, lists him as a 'longstanding member of the VTLC,' while his full name – Adoniran Nehemiah – is listed in the directory.

18 *Province*, 8 Jan. 1946; city directories list his jobs with the Liberal party and the customs office.

19 *Independent*, 20 June 1903.

20 Ibid., 26 May 1900, 25 July 1903, and *Province*, 23 Nov. 1900 list members and officers of the Vancouver Labor Party and the Independent Labor Party. Details on John Mortimer are in the *Independent*, 12 April 1902 and *BC Trades Unionist*, Jan. 1909. Bates's chairing of the BCSP is in the *Western Socialist*, 29 Nov. 1902.

21 VTLCM, 19 Jan. 1903; *Independent*, 5 Sept. 1903.

22 I have been unable to find a previous roll call vote, but minutes for 1898–1901 are missing, and though newspaper accounts make no mention of a roll call vote, this is not conclusive.

23 *Province*, 26 Jan. 1903. Watson's count of the unions appears to include those that

were not affiliated with the VTLC at the time; *World*, 26 Jan. 1903. *Independent*, 7 Feb. 1903 called for unity; Watson's angry reply is in *Independent*, 14 Feb. 1903. VTLCM, 5 Feb. 1903 notes the withdrawal of the Boilermakers from the council.

24 VTLCM, 5 Feb. 1903.

25 Ibid., 19 Feb. 1903; *Independent*, 21 Feb. 1903.

26 VTLCM, 19 March 1903; *Independent*, 21 March 1903. The parliamentary committee was composed of representatives from several unions, and included craft unionists such as G.F. Pound of the Printing Pressmen, E. Harpur of the Cigarmakers, and Francis Williams, the Tailors delegate who had run with Joseph Dixon as an independent labour candidate in 1900. It does not appear to be a particularly radical committee, though John Mortimer did serve on it.

27 VTLCM, 16 April 1903, contains the letter from the UBRE secretary alleging that Watson brought scabs to Revelstoke. Watson denied the charges in the *Independent*, 25 April 1903, and then launched into an attack on the UBRE. I have not been able to find conclusive proof for the allegations, though they seem plausible enough. But Watson would have been purged in any case for his other actions.

28 *Independent*, 18 April, 6 June 1903.

29 Ibid., 21 March, 4 April 1903.

30 *Independent*, 11 April 1903.

31 McCormack, 28–30; Martin Robin, *Radical Politics* (Kingston: Industrial Relations Centre, Queen's University, 1968), 57–60; Phillips, *No Power Greater*, 38–42.

32 McCormack, 32; *Independent*, 3 Oct. 1903.

33 *Independent*, 30 May, 1903

34 VTLCM, 6 April 1905; for the collapse of the union see *Independent*, 21 June 1904.

35 *Independent*, 20 June 1903.

36 *Western Clarion*, 15 Oct. 1903. See McCormack, 56–7, for his subsequent stand.

37 *Independent*, 27 June 1903.

38 VTLCM, 18 Aug. 1904, 1 May 1907. For an analysis of the U.S. labour movement that documents a similar swing from revolution to reform, see Erik Olssen, 'The Case of the Socialist Party that Failed, or Further Reflections on an American Dream,' *Labor History* 29 (1988) 416–49.

39 VTLCM, 7 Feb. 1907; 5 April 1906.

40 Ibid., 3 Aug. 1905; 19 March 1908.

41 Ibid., 16 April, 7 May, 18 June 1908.

42 *Western Wage Earner*, Sept. 1909.

43 VTLCM, 21 March 1907.

44 Ibid., 1, 15 Aug. 1907. For the activities of Gothard and Von Rhein in the League, see Patricia E. Roy, *A White Man's Province: British Columbia Politicians and*

Chinese and Japanese Immigrants, 1858–1914 (Vancouver: University of British Columbia Press, 1989), Ch. 8, *passim*.

45 VTLCM, 2 Jan. 1908.

46 *BC Trades Unionist*, Feb. 1908, March 1908.

47 Ibid., March 1908.

48 *Western Wage Earner*, Oct. 1909.

49 For more on the activity of Bertha Burns, see Linda Kealey, 'Women in the Canadian Socialist Movement, 1904–1914,' in *Beyond the Vote: Canadian Women and Politics*, ed. Linda Kealey and Joan Sangster (Toronto: University of Toronto Press, 1989), 172, 176, 186. Dorothy G. Steeves, *The Compassionate Rebel: Ernest Winch and the Growth of Socialism in Western Canada* (Vancouver: Boag Foundation, 1977), 28.

50 VTLCM, 21 Dec. 1905; 20 June 1907, 14 Dec. 1907. The figures on attendance are from the *Western Wage Earner*, Feb. and Aug., 1909. For sexism and intimidation in other unions, see Marie Campbell, 'Sexism in BC Trade Unions,' 168–71 esp.; for the women in the IBEW, see Elaine Bernard, *The Long Distance Feeling* (Vancouver: New Star Books, 1983).

51 *BC Trades Unionist*, Dec. 1908.

52 Ibid., Jan. 1909.

53 VTLCM, 15 Aug. 1907.

54 *B.C. Trades Unionist*, Dec. 1908.

55 Ibid., Feb. 1908; VTLCM, 2 July 1908; *Western Wage Earner*, Feb. 1909, Aug. 1909.

56 *BC Trades Unionist*, June 1908.

57 Ibid.

58 Ibid., Sept. 1908.

59 *Western Wage Earner*, March 1909.

60 Ibid.

61 Ibid., April 1909.

62 Ibid.

63 VTLCM, 5 Sept. 1906, 21 March 1907.

64 Ibid., 20 June 1907; VTLC Executive Board Minutes, 2 July 1907; VTLCM, 4 July 1907.

65 VTLCM, 16 May 1907; McCormack, 62.

66 Ibid., 16 Jan., 5 March 1908; VTLC Executive Board Minutes, 4 March 1908. Though there is no record of a salary for the business agent being paid, the title itself strongly suggests that it was a salaried position.

67 VTLCM, 18 May 1905.

68 Ibid., 21 Feb. 1907; *Province*, 5, 7 May 1929. It is possible that Burns was given the job as a compensation for illness or injury, though there is no record of this.

69 VTLC Executive Board Minutes, 26 Aug., 1, 9, 15 Sept. 1909.

70 *Western Wage Earner*, Oct. 1909.

71 Ibid., Nov. 1909.

72 *Province*, 5, 6 Jan. 1943.

73 ITU Minutes, VCA, add. ms. 381, vol. 8, 25 Feb. 1900; vol. 9, 15 March 1903, 27 April 1903. The ITU rolls list Gothard from 1895 on.

74 VTLCM, 21 Dec. 1905; 16 Aug, 18 Oct., 1 Nov. 1906; 6 June 1907; *BC Trades Unionist*, Dec. 1908; VTLC Executive Board Minutes, 7 June 1907.

75 *BC Trades Unionist*, Jan. 1908.

76 Ibid., Feb. 1908.

77 Ibid., Jan. 1909, *Western Wage Earner*, Feb. 1909.

78 *Western Wage Earner*, Feb., March, April 1909.

79 For McVety's salary, see *Western Wage Earner*, Feb. 1909. For wage rates of other workers, see R.A.J. McDonald, 'Working Class Vancouver,' *BC Studies* 69/70 (1986), 38. It has proved difficult to calculate the wages of machinists. As A CPR employee, he would have been paid less than those who worked in other shops, and in 1907 his rate would have been between 42 and 45 cents per hour. Based on a nine-hour day and a six day work week, this would give a top monthly rate of about $97. See H.A. Logan, *Trade Unions in Canada: Their Development and Functioning* (Toronto: Macmillan, 1948), 146, for the CPR rates. James Conley blames the 'size and power' of the CPR for the lower rates of its machinists, but does not supply the figures in 'Class Conflict and Collective Action in the Working Class of Vancouver, British Columbia, 1900–1919,' PhD dissertation, Carleton University, 1986, 325–6.

80 VTLC Executive Board Minutes, 19 May 1909. No record of Kingsley appears on the membership rolls of the ITU local.

81 See Marie Campbell, 'Sexism in British Columbia Trade Unions,' and Linda Kealey, 'Women in the Canadian Socialist Movement, 1904–1914,' in *Beyond the Vote: Canadian Women and Politics* (Toronto: University of Toronto Press, 1989), 189–90.

82 See my *Where the Fraser River Flows: The Industrial Workers of the World in British Columbia* (Vancouver: New Star Books, 1990), esp. Ch. 3 and 4. The quote from Ettor may be found in the IWW newspaper, the *Industrial Union Bulletin*, 17 Aug. 1907.

References

PRIMARY SOURCES

I Manuscripts

Angus MacInnis Memorial Collection. Special Collections, University of British Columbia.
Dominion Day Celebration Committee. Vancouver City Archives, Additional Manuscripts 47.
James Hawthornthwaite Papers. Don Stewart private collection, Vancouver, BC.
Samuel Gompers Papers. Letterbooks, microfilm, 1890–1901.
Vancouver Trades and Labour Council, Executive Board Minutes. Special Collections, University of British Columbia.
Vancouver Trades and Labour Council, Minutes. Special Collections, University of British Columbia.
Vancouver Typographical Union Records. Vancouver City Archives, Additional Manuscripts 381.
William Pleming Collection. Vancouver City Archives, Additional Manuscripts 132.

II Newspapers and Magazines

BC Trades Unionist and Label Bulletin (Vancouver), 1907–9.
Canadian Socialist (Toronto and Vancouver), 1902.
Daily News–Advertiser (Vancouver).
Independent (Vancouver), 1900–4.
Industrial Union Bulletin (Chicago), 1906–9.
Industrial Worker (Spokane), 1909–13.
Province (Vancouver).

World (Vancouver).
Western Clarion (Vancouver), 1903–18.
Western Socialist (Vancouver), 1902–3.
Western Wage Earner (Vancouver), 1909–11.

III Interviews

Una Larsen (née Pettipiece), interviewed by the author, Vancouver, February 1989.

SECONDARY SOURCES

I Books

Abella, Irving Martin. *Nationalism, Communism, and Canadian Labour: The CIO, the Communist Party, and the Canadian Congress of Labour, 1935–1956.* Toronto: University of Toronto Press, 1973.
Alinsky, Saul D. *Rules for Radicals: A Practical Primer for Realistic Radicals.* New York: Vintage, 1972.
Avery, Donald. *'Dangerous Foreigners': European Immigrant Workers and Labour Radicalism in Canada, 1896–1932.* Toronto: McClelland and Stewart, 1980.
Babcock, Robert. *Gompers in Canada: A Study of American Continentalism before the First World War.* Toronto: University of Toronto Press, 1974.
Bakunin, Michael. *God and the State.* New York: Dover, 1970.
– *Marxism, Freedom, and the State,* trans. and ed. K.J. Kenafick. London: Freedom Press, 1984.
– *Statism and Anarchy,* ed. Marshall Shatz. Cambridge: Cambridge University Press, 1990.
Baldelli, Giovanni. *Social Anarchism.* Chicago: Aldine Atherton, 1971.
Barman, Jean. *The West beyond the West: A History of British Columbia.* Toronto: University of Toronto Press, 1991.
Beetham, David. *Bureaucracy.* Minneapolis: University of Minnesota Press, 1987.
Bendix, Reinhard. *Work and Authority in Industry: Ideologies of Management in the Course of Industrialization.* New York: Harper Torchbooks, 1956.
– *Max Weber: An Intellectual Portrait.* New York: Anchor Books, 1962.
Bernard, Elaine. *The Long Distance Feeling.* Vancouver: New Star Books, 1982.
Bodnar, John. *The Transplanted: A History of Immigrants in Urban America.* Bloomington: Indiana University Press, 1985.
– *Workers' Worlds: Kinship, Community, and Protest in an Industrial Society, 1900–1940.* Bloomington: Indiana University Press, 1982.
Bottomore, Tom, ed. *A Dictionary of Marxist Thought.* Cambridge, Mass.: Harvard University Press, 1983.

– and Robert Nisbet, eds. *A History of Sociological Analysis*. New York: Basic Books, 1978.

Braverman, Harry. *Labor and Monopoly Capitalism: The Degradation of Work in the Twentieth Century*. New York: Monthly Review Press, 1974.

Brown, Robert Craig, and Ramsay Cook. *Canada 1896–1921: A Nation Transformed*. Toronto: McClelland and Stewart, 1974.

Buhle, Mari Jo. *Women and American Socialism, 1870–1920*. Urbana: University of Illinois Press, 1983.

Buhle, Paul. *Marxism in the USA, from 1870 to the Present Day*. London: Verso, 1987.

Bukharin, Nikolai. *Historical Materialism: A System of Sociology* (1921, reprint) Ann Arbor: University of Michigan Press, 1969.

Cannon, John, ed. *The Historian at Work*. London: George Allen and Unwin, 1980.

Castoriadis, Cornelius. *Political and Social Writings*, volumes 1 and 2. University of Minnesota Press, 1988.

Cherwinski, W.J.C., and G.S. Kealey, eds. *Lectures in Canadian Working-Class History*. Toronto: Committee on Canadian Labour History and New Hogtown Press, 1985.

Chodos, Robert. *The CPR: A Century of Corporate Welfare*. Toronto: Lorimer, 1973.

Cohen, Marjorie Griffin. *Women's Work, Markets, and Economic Development in Nineteenth-Century Ontario*. Toronto: University of Toronto Press, 1988.

Craven, Paul. *'An Impartial Umpire': Industrial Relations and the Canadian State, 1900–1911*. Toronto: University of Toronto Press, 1980.

Cunningham, Frank. *Democratic Theory and Socialism*. Cambridge: Cambridge University Press, 1987.

D'Agostino, Anthony. *Marxism and the Russian Anarchists*. San Francisco: Germinal Press, 1977.

Dahrendorf, Ralf. *Class and Class Conflict in Industrial Society*. Stanford: Stanford University Press, 1966.

Davis, Mike. *Prisoners of the American Dream: Politics and Economy in the History of the US Working Class*. London: Verso, 1986.

den Otter, Andy A. *Civilizing the West: The Galts and the Development of Western Canada*. Edmonton: University of Alberta Press, 1982.

Djilas, Milovan. *The New Class*. New York: Praeger, 1962.

Dolgoff, Sam, ed. *Bakunin on Anarchism*. Montreal: Black Rose Books, 1980.

Etzioni-Halevy, Eva. *Bureaucracy and Democracy: A Political Dilemma*. London: Routledge and Kegan Paul, 1983.

Faue, Elizabeth. *Community of Suffering and Struggle: Women, Men, and the Labor Movement in Minneapolis, 1915–1945*. Chapel Hill: University of North Carolina Press, 1991.

Finkel, Alvin. *Business and Social Reform in the Thirties*. Toronto: Lorimer, 1979.

Fischer, Frank, and Carmen Sirianni, eds. *Critical Studies in Organization and Bureaucracy*. Philadelphia: Temple University Press, 1984.

Foner, Phillip S. *The History of the Labor Movement in the United States, Volume 3: The Policies and Practices of the AFL, 1900–1909*. New York: International Publishers, 1964.

– *History of the American Labor Movement, Volume 2: From the Founding of the AF of L to the Emergence of American Imperialism*. New York: International Publishers, 1975.

Forsey, Eugene. *Trade Unions in Canada, 1812–1902*. Toronto: University of Toronto Press, 1982.

Foster, John. *Class Struggle and the Industrial Revolution*. London: Weidenfeld and Nicolson, 1974.

Freeman, Bill. *1005 – Political Life in a Union Local*. Toronto: Lorimer, 1982.

Galbraith, John Kenneth. *The Anatomy of Power*. Boston: Houghton Mifflin, 1983.

Gerth, H.H., and C. Wright Mills, eds. *From Max Weber: Essays in Sociology*. London: University of Oxford Press, 1946.

Giddens, Anthony. *A Contemporary Critique of Historical Materialism*. Berkeley: University of California Press, 1987.

Ginzberg, Eli. *The Labor Leader – An Exploratory Study*. New York: Macmillan, 1948.

Goldfield, Michael. *The Decline of Organized Labor in the United States*. Chicago: University of Chicago Press, 1987.

Goodway, David, ed. *For Anarchism: History, Theory, and Practice*. London: Routledge, 1989.

Goodwyn, Laurence. *The Populist Moment*. Oxford: Oxford University Press, 1978.

Gordon, David M., Richard Edwards, and Michael Reich. *Segmented Work, Divided Workers: The Historical Transformation of Labor in the United States*. Cambridge: Cambridge University Press, 1982.

Gouldner, Alvin W. *The Future of Intellectuals and the Rise of the New Class*. Oxford: Oxford University Press, 1979.

– *Against Fragmentation: The Origins of Marxism and the Sociology of Intellectuals*. Oxford: Oxford University Press, 1985.

Green, Archie. *Wobblies, Pile Butts, and Other Heroes: Laborlore Explorations*. Urbana: University of Illinois Press, 1993.

Green, James, ed. *Workers' Struggles, Past and Present: A 'Radical America' Reader*. Philadelphia: Temple University Press, 1983.

Guerin, Daniel. *Anarchism*. New York: Monthly Review Press, 1970.

Gutman, Herbert. *Work, Culture, and Society in Industrializing America: Essays in American Working-Class and Social History.* New York: Vintage, 1977.

– *Power and Culture: Essays on the American Working Class,* ed. Ira Berlin. New York: Pantheon, 1987.

Hall, Burton H., ed. *Autocracy and Insurgency in Organized Labor.* New Brunswick: Transaction Books, 1972.

Hann, Russell. *Farmers Confront Industrialism: Some Historical Perspectives on Ontario Agrarian Movements.* Toronto: New Hogtown Press, 1975.

Haskell, Thomas L., ed. *The Authority of Experts: Studies in History and Theory.* Bloomington: Indiana University Press, 1984.

Heron, Craig. *The Canadian Labour Movement: A Short History.* Toronto: Lorimer, 1989.

Hinton, James. *The First Shop Stewards' Movement.* London: George Allen and Unwin, 1973.

– *Labour and Socialism: A History of the British Labour Movement, 1867–1974.* Amherst: University of Massachusetts, 1983.

Hobsbawm, E.J. *Labouring Men: Studies in the History of Labour.* New York: Anchor, 1967.

– *Worlds of Labour: Further Studies in the History of Labour.* London: Weidenfeld and Nicolson, 1984.

Howard, Irene. *The Struggle for Social Justice: Helena Gutteridge, the Unknown Reformer.* Vancouver: University of British Columbia Press, 1992.

Hyman, Richard. *Industrial Relations: A Marxist Introduction.* London: Macmillan, 1975.

– *Strikes,* 2nd rev. ed. Glasgow: Fontana, 1977.

– and Robert Price, eds. *The New Working Class: White Collar Workers and their Organizations.* London: Macmillan, 1983.

Jacoby, Russell. *Dialectic of Defeat: Contours of Western Marxism.* Cambridge: Cambridge University Press, 1981.

Jacoby, Sanford. *Employing Bureaucracy: Managers, Unions, and the Transformation of Work in American Industry, 1900–1945.* New York: Columbia University Press, 1985.

James, Larry. *Power in a Trade Union: The Role of the District Committee in the AUEW.* Cambridge: Cambridge University Press, 1984.

Johnson, Walter. *The Trade Unions and the State.* Montreal: Black Rose Books, 1978.

Kaufman, Stuart Bruce. *Samuel Gompers and the Origins of the AFL, 1848–1896.* Westport, Conn.: Greenwood, 1973.

Kautsky, Karl. *Selected Political Writings,* ed. and trans. Patrick Goode. New York: St Martin's Press, 1983.

Kazin, Michael. *Barons of Labor: The San Francisco Building Trades and Union Power in the Progressive Era.* Urbana: University of Illinois Press, 1989.

Kealey, G.S. *Toronto Workers Respond to Industrial Capitalism, 1867–1892.* Toronto: University of Toronto Press, 1980.

– ed. *Class, Gender, and Region: Essays in Canadian Historical Sociology.* St John's, Nfld.: Committee on Canadian Labour History, 1988.

– and B.D. Palmer. *Dreaming of What Might Be: The Knights of Labor in Ontario, 1880–1900.* Toronto: New Hogtown Press, 1987.

– and Peter Warrian, eds. *Essays in Canadian Working Class History.* Toronto: McClelland and Stewart, 1976.

Kealey, Linda, and Joan Sangster, eds. *Beyond the Vote: Canadian Women and Politics.* Toronto: University of Toronto Press, 1989.

Kelly, John. *Trade Unions and Socialist Politics.* London: Verso, 1988.

Kerry, Tom. *Workers, Bosses, and Bureaucrats: A Socialist View of Labor Struggles since the 1930s.* New York: Pathfinder, 1980.

Kolko, Gabriel. *The Triumph of Conservatism.* New York: Free Press, 1964.

Kornbluh, Joyce L., ed. *Rebel Voices: An IWW Anthology.* (1964, reprint) Ann Arbor: University of Michigan Press, 1972.

Lasch, Christopher. *The New Radicalism in America, 1889–1963.* London: Chatto and Windus, 1965.

Laslett, John H.M. *Labor and the Left: A Study of Socialist and Radical Influences in the American Labor Movement, 1881–1924.* New York: Basic Books, 1970.

– and S.M. Lipset, eds. *Failure of a Dream? Essays in the History of American Socialism.* New York: Anchor Books, 1974.

Latham, Barbara, and Cathy Kess, eds. *In Her Own Right.* Victoria: Camosun College, 1980.

Laurie, Bruce. *Artisans into Workers: Labor in Nineteenth-Century America.* New York: Noonday Press, 1989.

Laycock, David. *Populism and Democratic Thought in the Canadian Prairies, 1910–1945.* Toronto: University of Toronto Press, 1990.

Leier, Mark. *Where the Fraser River Flows: The Industrial Workers of the World in British Columbia.* Vancouver: New Star Books, 1990.

Lieserson, William M. *American Trade Union Democracy.* New York: Columbia University Press, 1959.

Lembcke, Jerry, and William Tattam. *One Union in Wood: A Political History of the International Woodworkers of America.* Vancouver: Harbour Publishing, 1984.

Lenin, V.I. *Collected Works,* vol. 27. Moscow: Progress Publishers, 1965.

– *What Is to Be Done?* Peking: Foreign Languages Press, 1978.

– *Collected Works,* vol. 23. Moscow: Progress Publishers, 1981.

Lens, Sidney. *The Crisis of American Labor.* New York: Perpetua, 1961.

Levy, Carl, ed. *Socialism and the Intelligentsia, 1880–1914*. London: Routledge and Kegan Paul, 1987.

Lipset, Seymour Martin, Martin A. Trow, and James S. Coleman. *Union Democracy: The Internal Politics of the International Typographical Union*. Glencoe: Free Press, 1956.

Logan, H.A. *Trade Unions in Canada: Their Development and Functioning*. Toronto: Macmillan, 1948.

MacDonald, Lois. *Leadership Dynamics and Trade Union Leaders*. New York: New York University Press, 1959.

MacDonald, Norbert. *Distant Neighbors: A Comparative History of Seattle and Vancouver*. Lincoln: University of Nebraska Press, 1987.

Marks, Gary. *Unions in Politics: Britain, Germany, and the United States in the Nineteenth and Early Twentieth Centuries*. Princeton: Princeton University Press, 1989.

Marx, Karl. *Capital*, vol. 1–3. Moscow: Progress Publishers, 1971.

– *Theories of Surplus Value*, vol. 1–3. Moscow: Progress Publishers, 1972.

– and Fredrich Engels. *Selected Works*, vol. 1–3. Moscow: Progress Publishers, 1976.

– and Fredrich Engels. *Selected Correspondence*. Moscow: Progress Publishers, 1975.

Marshall, Peter. *Demanding the Impossible: A History of Anarchism*. London: Fontana, 1993.

Maximoff, G.P., ed. *The Political Philosophy of Bakunin: Scientific Anarchism*. New York: Free Press, 1964.

McCormack, A. Ross *Reformers, Rebels, and Revolutionaries: The Western Canadian Radical Movement, 1899–1919*. Toronto: University of Toronto Press, 1979.

McDougall, John. *Rural Life in Canada: Its Trends and Tasks*. Toronto: University of Toronto Press, 1973.

McKay, Ian. *The Craft Transformed: An Essay on the Carpenters of Halifax, 1885–1985*. Halifax: Holdfast Press, 1985.

Metcalfe, Alan. *Canada Learns to Play: The Emergence of Organized Sport, 1807–1914*. Toronto: McClelland and Stewart, 1987.

Michels, Robert. *Political Parties: A Sociological Study of the Oligarchical Tendencies of Modern Democracy*. (1915, reprint) Glencoe: Free Press, 1948.

Milband, Ralph. *Divided Societies: Class Struggle in Contemporary Capitalism*. New York: Oxford University Press, 1989.

Mills, C. Wright. *The New Men of Power: America's Labor Leaders*. New York: Harcourt, Brace, 1948.

Mink, Gwendolyn. *Old Labor and New Immigrants in American Political Development: Union, Party, and State, 1875–1920*. Ithaca: Cornell University Press, 1986.

Montgomery, David. *Workers Control in America: Studies in the History of Work, Technology, and Labor Struggles*. Cambridge: Cambridge University Press, 1984.

– *The Fall of the House of Labor: The Workplace, the State, and American Labor Activism, 1865–1925.* Cambridge: Cambridge University Press, 1987.

Moody, Carroll, and Alice Kessler-Harris, eds. *Perspectives on American Labor History: The Problems of Synthesis.* DeKalb, Ill. Northern Illinois University Press, 1989.

Moody, Kim. *An Injury to All: The Decline of American Unionism.* London: Verso, 1988.

Moore, Barrington Jr. *Injustice: The Social Bases of Obedience and Revolt.* White Plains, NY: M.E. Sharpe, 1978.

– *Authority and Inequality under Capitalism and Socialism.* Oxford: Oxford University Press, 1987.

Morley, Alan. *Vancouver: From Milltown to Metropolis.* Vancouver: Mitchell Press, 1961.

Naylor, James. *The New Democracy: Challenging the Social Order in Industrial Ontario, 1914–1925.* Toronto: University of Toronto Press, 1991.

Nelson, Bruce C. *Beyond the Martyrs: A Social History of Chicago's Anarchists, 1870–1900.* New Brunswick: Rutgers University Press, 1988.

Nicol, Eric. *Vancouver.* Toronto: Doubleday, 1970.

Nomad, Max. *A Skeptic's Political Dictionary and Handbook for the Disenchanted.* New York: Bookman, 1953.

Nicolajevsky, Boris, and Otto Maenchen-Helfen. *Karl Marx – Man and Fighter.* London: Penguin, 1983.

Novick, Peter. *That Noble Dream: The 'Objectivity Question' and the American Historical Profession.* Cambridge: Cambridge University Press, 1990.

Nyden, Philip W. *Steelworkers Rank and File: The Political Economy of a Union Reform Movement.* New York: Praeger, 1984.

Oestreicher, Richard. *Solidarity and Fragmentation: Working People and Class Consciousness in Detroit, 1875–1900.* Urbana: University of Illinois Press, 1989.

Oizerman, T.I. *The Making of the Marxist Philosophy.* Moscow: Progress Publishers, 1981.

Ormsby, Margaret. *British Columbia: A History.* Toronto: Macmillan, 1958.

Orwell, George. *Collected Essays, Journalism, and Letters of George Orwell.* Vol. 1. Harmondsworth: Penguin, 1982.

Palmer, Bryan D. *A Culture in Conflict: Skilled Workers and Industrial Capitalism in Hamilton, Ontario, 1860–1914.* Montreal and Kingston: McGill-Queen's University Press, 1979.

– *Solidarity: The Rise and Fall of an Opposition in British Columbia.* Vancouver: New Star Books, 1987.

– *Working-Class Experience: The Rise and Re-Constitution of Canadian Labour, 1800–1980.* Toronto: Butterworth, 1983.

– *Descent into Discourse.* Philadelphia: Temple University Press, 1990.
– *Working Class Experience: Rethinking the History of Canadian Labour, 1800–1991.* Toronto: McClelland and Stewart, 1992.
– ed. *The Character of Class Struggle: Essays in Canadian Working-Class History, 1850–1985.* Toronto: McClelland and Stewart, 1986.
– *Jack Scott: A Communist Life.* St John's, Nfld.: Committee on Canadian Labour History, 1988.
Parkin, Frank. *Marxism and Class Theory: A Bourgeois Critique.* London: Tavistock, 1979.
– *Max Weber.* Chichester: Ellis Horwood, 1982.
Peck, Sidney M. *The Rank and File Leader.* New Haven: College and University Press Services, 1963.
Pelling, Henry. *American Labor.* Chicago: University of Chicago Press, 1960.
– *Popular Politics and Society in Late Victorian Britain.* London: Macmillan, 1968.
Pentland, H. Clare. *Labour and Capital in Canada, 1650–1850.* Toronto: Lorimer, 1981.
Perlman, Mark. *The Machinists: A New Study in American Trade Unionism.* Cambridge: Harvard University Press, 1961.
Perlman, Selig. *A Theory of the Labor Movement.* (1928, reprint) New York: Augustus M. Kelley, 1970.
Petro, Sylvester. *Power Unlimited – The Corruption of Union Leadership.* New York: Ronald Press, 1959.
Phillips, Paul. *No Power Greater: A Century of Labour in British Columbia.* Vancouver: BC Federation of Labour, Boag Foundation, 1967.
– and Erin Phillips. *Women and Work: Inequality in the Labour Market.* Toronto: Lorimer, 1983.
Pollack, Norman. *The Populist Response to Industrial America.* Cambridge: Harvard University Press, 1962.
Price, Richard. *Masters, Unions, and Men: Work Control in Building and the Rise of Labour, 1830–1914.* New York: Cambridge University Press, 1980.
Przeworski, Adam. *Capitalism and Social Democray.* Cambridge: Cambridge University Press, 1985.
Riddell, John, ed. *Lenin's Struggle for a Revolutionary International.* New York: Monad, 1984.
Robin, Martin. *Radical Politics and Canadian Labour, 1880–1930.* Kingston: Industrial Relations Centre, Queen's University, 1968.
– *The Rush for Spoils: The Company Province, 1871–1933.* Toronto: McClelland and Stewart, 1972.
Roy, Patricia E. *Vancouver: An Illustrated History.* Toronto: Lorimer, 1980.

– *A White Man's Province: British Columbia Politicians and Chinese and Japanese Immigrants, 1858–1914.* Vancouver: University of British Columbia Press, 1989.

Rueschemeyer, Dietrich. *Power and the Division of Labour.* Stanford: Stanford University Press, 1986.

Russell, Bertrand. *Power: A New Social Analysis.* (1983, reprint) London: Unwin, 1985.

Saltman, Richard B. *The Social and Political Thought of Michael Bakunin.* Westport, Conn.: Greenwood Press, 1983.

Sangster, Joan. *Dreams of Equality.* Toronto: McClelland and Stewart, 1989.

Sassoon, Anne Showstack. *Gramsci's Politics.* Minneapolis: University of Minnesota Press, 1987.

Saxton, Alexander. *The Indispensable Enemy: Labor and the Anti-Chinese Movement in California.* Berkeley: University of California Press, 1971.

Schorske, Carl E. *German Social Democracy, 1905–1917: The Development of the Great Schism.* Cambridge: Harvard University Press, 1983.

Schwantes, Carlos. *Radical Heritage: Labor, Socialism, and Reform in Washington and British Columbia, 1885–1917.* North Vancouver: Douglas and McIntyre, 1979.

Sennett, Richard. *Authority.* New York: Knopf, 1980.

Shatz, Marshall S. *Jan Waclaw Machajski: A Radical Critic of the Russian Intelligentsia and Socialism.* Pittsburgh: University of Pittsburgh Press, 1989.

– ed. *The Essential Works of Anarchism.* New York: Quadrangle, 1972.

Stanton, John. *Never Say Die! The Life and Times of John Stanton, a Pioneer Labour Lawyer.* Ottawa: Steel Rail Press, 1987.

– *My Past Is Now: Further Memoirs of a Labour Lawyer.* St John's, Nfld.: Canadian Committee on Labour History, 1994.

Stedman-Jones, Gareth. *Languages of Class: Studies in English Working Class History.* Cambridge: Cambridge University Press, 1983.

Steeves, Dorothy. *The Compassionate Rebel: Ernest Winch and the Growth of Socialism in Western Canada.* Vancouver: Boag Foundation, 1977.

Stewart, Mary Lynn. *Women, Work, and the French State.* Montreal and Kingston: McGill-Queen's University Press, 1989.

Swainson, Donald, ed. *Oliver Mowat's Ontario: Papers.* Toronto: Macmillan, 1972.

Thompson, Phillips. *The Politics of Labor.* Toronto: University of Toronto Press, 1975.

Trotsky, Leon. *Terrorism and Communism.* Ann Arbor: University of Michigan Press, 1970.

Tucker, Eric. *Administering Danger in the Workplace: The Law and Politics of Occupational Health and Safety Regulation in Ontario, 1850–1914.* Toronto: University of Toronto Press, 1990.

Tucker, Robert, ed. *The Marx–Engels Reader,* 2nd ed. New York: Norton, 1978.

Valverde, Mariana. *The Age of Light, Soap, and Water: Moral Reform in English Canada, 1885–1925*. Toronto: McClelland and Stewart, 1991.

Van Tine, Warren. *The Making of the Labor Bureaucrat: Union Leadership in the United States, 1870–1920*. Amherst: University of Massachusetts Press, 1973.

Vanneman, Reeve, and Lynne Webber Cannon. *The American Perception of Class*. Philadelphia: Temple University Press, 1987.

Verzuh, Ron. *Radical Rag: The Pioneer Labour Press in Canada*. Ottawa: Steel Rail Publishing, 1988.

Walker, Angus. *Marx: His Theory and Its Context*. London: Rivers Oram Press, 1989.

Walker, Pat, ed. *Between Labor and Capital*. Montreal: Black Rose Books, 1978.

Ward, Peter W. *White Canada Forever: Popular Attitudes and Public Policy toward Orientals in British Columbia*. Montreal and Kingston: McGill-Queen's University Press, 1978.

– and Robert McDonald, eds. *British Columbia: Historical Readings*. Vancouver: Douglas and McIntyre, 1981.

Webster, Daisy. *Growth of the NDP in British Columbia, 1900–70: 81 Political Biographies*. n.p., n.d.

Weibe, R.H. *The Search for Order, 1877–1920*. New York: Hill and Wang, 1967.

Weinstein, James. *The Corporate Ideal in the Liberal State*. Boston: Beacon Press, 1968.

Wilensky, H.L. *Intellectuals in Labor Unions*. Glencoe: Free Press, 1956.

Williams Raymond. *Keywords: A Vocabulary of Culture and Society*. Glasgow: Fontana, 1976.

Wittke, Carl. *The Utopian Communist: A Biography of Wilhelm Weitling, Nineteenth-Century Reformer*. Baton Rouge: Louisiana State University Press, 1950.

Wolfe, Joel D. *Workers, Participation, and Democracy: Internal Politics in the British Union Movement*. Westport, Conn.: Greenwood Press, 1985.

Wood, Ellen Meiksins. *The Retreat from Class: A New 'True' Socialism*. London: Verso, 1986.

Wood, Louis Aubrey. *A History of Farmers' Movements in Canada: The Origins and Development of Agrarian Protest, 1872–1924*. (1924, reprint) Toronto: University of Toronto Press, 1975.

Woodcock, George. *British Columbia: A History of the Province*. Vancouver: Douglas and McIntyre, 1990.

Working Lives Collective. *Working Lives: Vancouver, 1886–1986*. Vancouver: New Star Books, 1985.

Wright, Erik Olin, ed. *The Debate on Classes*. London: Verso, 1989.

Zeitlin, Jonathan, and S. Tolliday, eds. *Shop Floor Bargaining and the State: Historical and Comparative Perspectives*. Cambridge: Cambridge University Press, 1985.

Zerker, Sally. *The Rise and Fall of the Toronto Typographical Union, 1832–1972: A Case of Foreign Domination.* Toronto: Toronto University Press, 1982.

Zerzan, John. *Creation and Its Enemies: 'The Revolt Against Work.'* Rochester: Mutualyst Books, 1977.

II Articles

Adams, Tony. 'Leadership and Oligarchy: British Rail Unions, 1914–1922,' *Studies in History and Politics* 5 (1986), 23–45.

Andras, Hegedus. 'Bureaucracy,' in *A Dictionary of Marxist Thought*, ed. Tom Bottomore, Cambridge, Mass.: Harvard University Press, 1983, 57–9.

Andrews, Margaret. 'Sanitary Conveniences and the Retreat of the Frontier: Vancouver 1886–1926,' *BC Studies* 87 (1990), 3–22.

Arnesen, Eric. 'Crusades against Crisis: A View from the United States on the "Rank and File" Critique,' *International Review of Social History* 35 (1990), 106–27.

Bartlett, Eleanor A. 'Real Wages and the Standard of Living in Vancouver, 1901–1929,' *BC Studies* 51 (1981), 3–62.

Bartley, George. 'Twenty-five Years in the BC Labor Movement,' *BC Federationist*, 27 Dec. 1912.

Beetham, David. 'Michels and His Critics,' *European Journal of Sociology* 22 (1981), 81–99.

Bramble, Thomas. 'Conflict, Coercion, and Co-option: The Role of Full-Time Officials in the South Australian Branch of the Vehicle Builders Employees' Federation, 1967–80,' *Labour History* 63 (1992), 135–54.

Campbell, Marie. 'Sexism in British Columbia Trade Unions,' in *In Her Own Right: Selected Essays on Women's History in BC*, ed. Barbara Latham and Cathy Kess. Victoria: Camosun College, 1980, 167–86.

Clark, John. 'Marx, Bakunin, and the Problem of Social Transformation,' *Telos* 42 (1979–80), 80–97.

Cohen, Lizabeth. 'Reflections on the Making of *Making a New Deal*,' *Labor History* 32 (1991), 592–8.

Cook, Ramsay. 'Tillers and Toilers: The Rise and Fall of Populism in Canada in the 1890s,' *Historical Papers*, 1984, 1–20.

Creese, Gillian. 'Class, Ethnicity, and Conflict: The Case of Chinese and Japanese Immigrants, 1880–1923,' in *Workers, Capital, and the State in British Columbia*, ed. Rennie Warburton and David Coburn. Vancouver: University of British Columbia Press, 1988, 55–85.

Cronin, James E. 'The "Rank and File" and the Social History of the Working Class,' *International Review of Social History* 34 (1989), 78–88.

Darroch, Gordon. 'Class in Nineteenth-Century Central Ontario: A Reassessment of the Crisis and Demise of Small Producers during Early Industrialization, 1861–1871,' in *Class, Gender, and Region: Essays in Canadian Historical Sociology*, ed. G.S. Kealey. St John's, Nfld.: Committee on Canadian Labour History, 1988, 49–72.

Davis, Mike. 'Why the US Working Class is Different,' *New Left Review* 123 (1980), 3–44.

– 'The Barren Marriage of American Labour and the Democratic Party,' *New Left Review* 124 (1980), 43–84.

Dubofsky, Melvyn. 'Lost in a Fog: Labor Historians' Unrequited Search for a Synthesis,' *Labor History* 32 (1991), 295–300.

Foner, Eric. 'Why Is There No Socialism in the United States?' *History Workshop* 17 (1984), 57–80.

Gray, R.Q. 'Styles of Life, the "Labour Aristocracy," and Class Relations in Later Nineteenth-Century Edinburgh,' *International Review of Social History* 18 (1973) 428–451.

Graziosi, Andrea. 'Common Laborers, Unskilled Workers: 1890–1915,' *Labor History* 22 (1981), 512–44.

Hak, Gordon. 'The Socialist and Labourist Impulse in Small-Town British Columbia: Port Alberni and Prince George, 1911–33,' *Canadian Historical Review* 70 (1989), 519–42.

Hann, Russell. 'Brainworkers and the Knights of Labor: E.E. Shepard, Phillips Thompson, and the *Toronto News*, 1883–87,' in *Essays in Canadian Working Class History*, ed. Gregory S. Kealey and Peter Warrian. Toronto: McClelland and Stewart, 1976, 35–57.

Heron, Craig. 'Labourism and the Canadian Working Class,' *Labour / Le Travail* 13 (1984), 45–75.

– 'The Crisis of the Craftsman: Hamilton's Metal Workers in the Early Twentieth Century,' *Labour / Le Travailleur* 6 (1980), 7–48.

Heron, Craig, and Bryan D. Palmer. 'Through the Prism of the Strike: Industrial Conflict in Southern Ontario, 1901–14,' *Canadian Historical Review* 58 (1977), 423–58.

Hobsbawm, Eric. 'Trends in the British Labour Movement,' in *Labouring Men: Studies in the History of Labour*. New York: Anchor, 1967.

– 'Debating the Labour Aristocracy,' in *Worlds of Labour: Further Studies in the History of Labour*. London: Weidenfeld and Nicolson, 1984, 214–26.

– 'The Aristocracy of Labour Reconsidered,' in *Worlds of Labour: Further Studies in the History of Labour*. London: Weidenfeld and Nicolson, 1984, 227–51.

Hyman, Richard. 'The Politics of Workplace Trade Unionism: Recent Tendencies and Some Problems for Theory,' *Capital and Class* 8 (1979), 54–67.

– 'Officialdom and Opposition: Leadership and Rank and File in Trade Unions,' *Bulletin of the Society for the Study of Labour History* 46 (1983), 7.

- 'The Sound of One Hand Clapping: A Comment on the "Rank and Filism" Debate,' *International Review of Social History*, 34 (1989), 309–26.

Jones-Wolf, Elizabeth, and Ken Jones-Wolf. 'Rank-and-File Rebellions and AFL Interference in the Affairs of National Unions: The Gompers' Era,' *Labor History* 35 (1994), 237–59.

Kazin, Michael. 'Struggling with Class Struggle: Marxism and the Search for Synthesis of US Labor History,' *Labor History* 28 (1987), 497–514.

Kealey, G.S. 'Work Control, the Labour Process, and Nineteenth-Century Canadian Printers,' in *On the Job: Confronting the Work Process in Canada*, ed. Craig Heron and Robert Storey. Montreal and Kingston: McGill-Queen's University Press, 1986, 75–101.

Kimeldorf, Howard. 'Bringing Unions Back in (or Why We Need a New Old Labor History),' *Labor History* 32 (1991), 91–129.

Konrad, Gyorgy, and Ivan Szeleny. 'The Intelligentsia and Social Structure,' *Telos* 38 (1978–9), 48–62.

Kulikoff, Allan. 'The Transition to Capitalism in Rural America,' *William and Mary Quarterly*, 3rd series, 46 (1989), 120–44.

Leier, Mark. 'Workers and Intellectuals: The Theory of the New Class and Early Canadian Socialism,' *Journal of History and Politics* 10 (1992), 87–108.

- 'Rethinking Vancouver's Labour Movement: Ethnicity, Urbanism, and the Labour Aristocracy,' *Canadian Historical Review* 74 (1993), 51–34.

Loo, Tina. 'Dan Cranmer's Potlatch: Law as Coercion, Symbol, and Rhetoric in British Columbia, 1884–1951,' *Canadian Historical Review* 73 (1992), 125–65.

Lukes, Steven. 'Power and Authority,' in *A History of Sociological Analysis*, ed. Tom Bottomore and Robert Nisbet. New York: Basic Books, 1978, 633–76.

Lynd, Staughton. 'Trade Unionism in the USA,' *New Left Review* 184 (1990), 76–87.

MacDonald, Norbert. 'The Canadian Pacific Railway and Vancouver's Development to 1900,' in *British Columbia: Historical Readings*, ed. W. Peter Ward and R.A.J. McDonald. Vancouver: Douglas and McIntyre, 1981, 396–425.

McDonald, Robert A.J. 'City Building in the Canadian West: A Case Study of Economic Growth in Early Vancouver, 1886–1893,' *BC Studies* 43 (1979), 3–28.

- 'Victoria, Vancouver, and the Economic Development of British Columbia, 1886–1914,' in *British Columbia: Historical Readings*, ed. W. Peter Ward and R.A.J. McDonald. Vancouver: Douglas, and McIntyre, 1981, ed. 369–95.

- '"Holy Retreat" or "Practical Breathing Spot"? Class Perceptions of Vancouver's Stanley Park, 1910–13,' *Canadian Historical Review* 65 (1984), 127–53.

- 'Working Class Vancouver, 1886–1914 – Urbanism and Class in British Columbia,' *BC Studies* 69–70 (1986), 33–69.

McKay, Ian. 'Capital and Labour in the Halifax Baking and Confectionery Industry during the Last Half of the Nineteenth Century,' *Labour / Le Travailleur* 3 (1978), 63–100.

– 'The Three Faces of Canadian Labour History,' *History Workshop* 24 (1987), 172–8.

McKee, W.C. 'The Vancouver Park System, 1886–1929: A Product of Local Business-men,' *Urban History Review* 3 (1978), 33–49.

Mommsen, Wolfgang J. 'Max Weber and Roberto Michels: An Asymmetrical Part-nership,' *European Journal of Sociology* 22 (1981), 100–16.

Montgomery, David, John Howell Harris, Sanford M. Jacoby, Michael Kazin, Gerald Markowitz, David Rosner, Nell Irvin Painter, and Robert Zieger. 'A Symposium on *The Fall of the House of Labor*,' *Labor History* 30 (1989), 93–137.

Moore, Christopher. 'Men at Work,' *The Beaver* 72 (1992), 60–2.

Mouat, Jeremy. 'The Genesis of Western Exceptionalism: British Columbia's Hard-Rock Miners, 1895–1903,' *Canadian Historical Review* 71 (1990), 317–45.

O'Boyle, Lenore. 'The Image of the Journalist in France, Germany, and England, 1815–1848,' *Comparative Studies in Society and History* 10 (1968), 290–317.

– 'The Problem of an Excess of Educated Men in Western Europe, 1800–1850,' *Journal of Modern History* 42 (1970), 471–95.

Olssen, Erik. 'The Case of the Socialist Party that Failed, or Further Reflections on an American Dream,' *Labor History* 29 (1988), 416–49.

Parkin, Frank. 'Social Stratification,' in *A History of Sociological Analysis*, ed. Tom Bottomore and Robert Nisbet. New York: Basic Books, 1978, 599–632.

Pelling, Henry. 'The Concept of the Labour Aristocracy,' in *Popular Politics and Society in Late Victorian Britain*. London: Macmillan, 1968, 37–61.

Piva, Michael. 'The Aristocracy of the English Working Class: Help for an Historical Debate in Difficulties,' *Histoire Sociale / Social History* 7 (1974), 270–92.

Price, Richard. 'The Segmentation of Work and the Labour Aristocracy,' *Labour / Le Travail* 17 (1986) 267–72.

– '"What's in a Name?" Workplace History and "Rank and Filism,"' *International Review of Social History* 34 (1989), 62–77.

Radosh, Ronald. 'The Corporate Liberal Ideology of American Labor Leaders from Samuel Gompers to Sidney Hillman,' in *For a New America: Essays in History and Politics From 'Studies on the Left,' 1959–1967* ed. James Weinstein and David W. Eakins. New York: Random House, 1970, 125–51.

Roberts, Wayne. 'Toronto Metal Workers and the Second Industrial Revolution, 1889–1914,' *Labour / Le Travailleur* 6 (1980), 49–72.

Rosenthal, Star. 'Union Maids: Organized Women Workers in Vancouver, 1900–1915,' *BC Studies* 41 (1979), 36–55.

Saywell, John T. 'Labour and Socialism in British Columbia: A Survey of Historical Development before 1903,' *British Columbia Historical Review* 15 (1951), 129–50.

Seager, Allen. 'Socialists and Workers: The Western Canadian Coal Miners, 1900–21,' *Labour / Le Travail* 16 (1985), 23–59.
- 'Workers, Class, and Industrial Conflict in New Westminster, 1900–1930,' in *Workers, Capital, and the State in British Columbia,* ed. Rennie Warburton and David Coburn. Vancouver: University of British Columbia Press, 1988, 117–40.
Shortt, S.E.D. 'Social Change and Political Crisis in Rural Ontario: The Patrons of Industry, 1880–1896,' in *Oliver Mowat's Ontario,* ed. Donald Swainson. Toronto: Macmillan, 1972, 211–35.
Thompson, E.P. 'The Peculiarities of the English,' in *The Poverty of Theory and Other Essays.* New York: Monthly Review Press, 1978, 245–302.
Underhill, Frank. 'Political Ideas of the Upper Canadian Reformers, 1867–78,' in *In Search of Canadian Liberalism.* Toronto: Macmillan, 1961, 68–84.
Ward, W. Peter. 'Class and Race in the Social Structure of British Columbia, 1870–1939,' *BC Studies* 45 (1980), 17–35.
Weber, Max. 'Bureaucracy,' in *Critical Studies in Organization and Bureaucracy,* ed. Fischer, Frank, and Carmen Sirianni. Philadelphia: Temple University Press, 1984, 24–39.
Weir, Stan. 'The Conflict in American Unions and the Resistance to Alternative Ideas from the Rank and File,' in *Workers' Struggles, Past and Present: A 'Radical America' Reader,* ed. James Green. Philadelphia: Temple University Press, 1983, 251–68.
Wright, Gavin. 'American Agriculture and the Labor Market: What Happened to Proletarianization?' *Agriculture History* 62 (1988), 182–209.
Zeitlin, Jonathan. 'Trade Unions and Job Control: A Critique of Rank and Filism,' *Bulletin of the Society for the Study of Labour History* 46 (1983), 6–7.
- 'Shop Floor Bargaining and the State: A Contradictory Relationship,' in *Shop Floor Bargaining and the State: Historical and Comparative Perspectives,* ed. Steve Tolliday and Jonathan Zeitlin. Cambridge: Cambridge University Press, 1985, 1–45.
- '"Rank and Filism" in British Labour History: A Critique,' *International Review of Social History* 34 (1989), 42–61.
- '"Rank and Filism" and Labour History: A Rejoinder to Price and Cronin,' *International Review of Social History* 34 (1989), 89–102.

III Unpublished Theses and Papers

Conley, James. 'Class Conflict and Collective Action in the Working Class of Vancouver, British Columbia, 1900–1919,' PhD thesis, Carleton University, 1986.
Darling, David. 'Patterns of Population Mobility in Vancouver, 1891–1931,' MA Extended Essay, Simon Fraser University, 1978.

Grantham, Ronald. 'Some Aspects of the Socialist Movement in British Columbia, 1898–1933,' MA thesis, University of British Columbia, 1942.

Gray, Stephen. 'Woodworkers and Legitimacy: The IWA in Canada, 1937–1957,' PhD thesis, Simon Fraser University, 1989.

Johnson, R.A. 'No Compromise – No Political Trading: The Marxian Socialist Tradition in British Columbia,' PhD thesis, University of British Columbia, 1975.

Loosmore, Thomas R. 'The British Columbia Labour Movement and Political Action, 1879–1900,' MA thesis, University of British Columbia, 1954.

Mouat, Jeremy. 'The Context of Conflict: The Western Federation of Miners in British Columbia, 1895–1903,' paper, University of British Columbia, 1986.

Ralston, J.K. 'The 1900 Strike of Fraser River Sockeye Salmon Fishermen,' MA thesis, University of British Columbia, 1965.

Illustration Credits

Index

Adams, Tony, 31, 32, 34
Adamswaithe, F.W., 47
Alinsky, Saul, 37–8
Amalgamated Society of Carpenters and Joiners, 46, 49, 61, 63, 64, 67, 69, 160, 162, 167. *See also* Carpenters
Amalgamated Society of Engineers, 31, 86, 151
American Federation of Labor (AFL), 20, 46, 50–1, 54–5, 57, 101, 116, 140, 165, 166, 174, 179
American Labor Union, 161, 166
American Railway Union (ARU), 50, 54, 62, 65
Asian exclusion, 46, 53, 96, 126–7, 130, 146–7, 169. *See also* Race
Asiatic Exclusion League, 169

Baker, Colonel James, 76
Bakers, 45, 114
Bakunin, Michael 11, 37–8, 41, 43, 194n53, 194n58
Barbers, 114–15, 164
Barbers Union, 162
Bartenders' Union, 147, 169
Bartley, Connie, 48, 140
Bartley, George, 47, 48–9, 50, 53–4, 57, 59–60, 61, 63, 67–8, 69, 73, 87–8, 90, 97, 99, 105, 116, 118, 119, 120, 123, 127, 128, 140, 143, 145, 151, 155–6, 160, 162, 166, 167, 168, 178, 181, 195n7, 208n26
Bates, Ben, 163, 166
Beer, W.J., 67
Bell-Irving, Henry, 59, 119
Bell-Irving Company, 110
Bishop, F.P., 48, 65, 67, 69, 105, 199n46
Boag, Allan, 144, 152
Boardman, Charles, 50, 168
Bodnar, John, 30
Boilermakers, 50, 61, 164
Boilermakers' Union, 30, 59, 145, 165
Bolshevism, critique of, 25–7, 191n39
Boult, James, 151
Bremner, E.P., 82
Bricklayers, 56, 68, 104, 169, 170, 172
British Columbia Electric Railway, 104, 110, 119
British Columbia Federation of Labour, 6, 179
British Columbia Sugar Refining Company, 127–8
British Columbia Trades Unionist and Label Bulletin, 5, 169, 172–3, 176–7

Brown, J.C., 110
Browne, J.H., 60, 78–9, 140, 156
Bruce, J.T., 84–5
Bryan, William Jennings, 112
Building Laborers' Union, 63
Building trades, 45, 46, 65, 133, 163, 164, 169
Building Trades Council, 86
Bukharin, Nikolai, 25–6
Burns, A.R., 53, 67, 68, 175
Burns, Bertha, 170–1
Burns, Ernest, 144, 150–1, 157, 159, 170–1

Cameron, John, 150–1, 157
Campbell, Marie, 141
Canadian autonomy, 51
Canadian Congress of Labour, 40
Canadian Pacific Railway (CPR), 43, 44–5, 50, 81, 95, 104, 111, 119, 127, 130, 135, 146, 156, 166, 171, 172, 177, 178, 182
Canadian Socialist, 151, 161
Canadian Socialist League, 144–5
Carlyle, Thomas, 14
Carnegie, Andrew, 121
Carpenters, 46, 47, 49, 55, 64, 66–7, 69, 103, 104, 118, 127, 161, 162, 164, 169, 172, 174, 178. See also Amalgamated Society of Carpenters and Joiners; United Brotherhood of Carpenters and Joiners
Carter-Cotton, F., 119
Cigarmakers, 68, 107, 116, 133, 160, 164, 169
Civic employees, 68, 69
Civic Employees Union, 162
Clarke, J.H., 47
Class analysis, 9–11, 21, 210n4, 213n46
Cohen, Lizabeth, 9

Commerford, J., 169
Commons, John, 19
Communist League, 155
Communist Party, 22
Compulsory arbitration, 80–2, 171–2
Congress of Industrial Organizations (CIO), 28, 29, 30, 40, 192n46
Contract labour, 96
Conservatives, 10, 59, 60, 91, 110, 119, 162, 167. See also Politics
Cooks, Waiters and Waitresses Union, 45, 67, 140, 172. See also Waitresses and Waiters Union
Cosgrove, R., 62, 163
Cowan, Harry, 48–9, 50, 53, 59–60, 67, 87–8, 90, 105, 140, 155–6, 175,178
Cross, T.H., 67, 161–2
Crow, John, 68, 160, 161, 162

Dales, George, 151, 156
Darroch, Gordon, 99–100
Deadman's Island, 51, 58–61, 66, 67, 122, 163
Debs, Eugene, 50
DeLeon, Daniel, 88, 143
Dixon, Hugh, 77
Dixon, Joseph, 47, 49–50, 60–1, 67–8, 69, 99, 105, 109, 117, 127, 140, 143–4, 146, 155–6, 160–1, 167, 169, 171, 178, 181
Dobbin, George, 69, 162, 167
Domestic service, 104, 140, 142. See also Gender
Dominion Day, 119–120
Dominion Trades and Labour Congress (DTLC), 6, 50–1, 54–5, 63, 161, 165, 166, 174
Dowler, P.W., 174
Draper, P.M., 51
Drew, Dorothy, 170–1

Dunsmuir, Robert, 135

Edison, Thomas, 152
Edwards, Mrs, 170–1
Engels, Friedrich, 102, 210n4
Ettor, Joe, 179

The Farmers' Sun, 98
Federal Union Number 23, 165, 166
Finances, 62–5, 72–3, 84–6, 109, 111–12,
    113; improprieties involving, 65–6,
    151, 175–6, 199n46
Fishermen, 82, 134, 146, 150, 159
Foley, Chris, 52, 100, 137, 161, 162,
    163–4, 165, 167, 168
Foucault, Michel, 186n10
Franklin, J.L., 118
Freighthandlers, 67, 68, 69, 162
Freight Handlers' Union, 118, 161
Fulton, John, 66

Gagen, George, 54, 66–7
Garden, James, 59
Gender relations, 104, 125, 135–42,
    170–1, 181; and family wage, 138–9;
    and job competition, 141; and sexual
    division of labour, 135–40
George, W., 68, 69, 146, 162
Goldman, Emma, 36
Gompers, Samuel, 20, 51, 60, 88, 146.
    See also American Federation of
    Labor
Gothard, Samuel J., 118, 120, 169,
    176–8
Gouldner, Alvin, 155
Grand Trunk Pacific Railway, 170
Gray, Robert, 106

Hallam, Thomas, 62, 69
Hamilton, L.A., 44

Harpur, Eugene, 162
Harrington, A.N., 52, 67, 162
Harrison, D.C., 54, 84–5, 160
Hawthornthwaite, James, 77, 151–2
Haywood, William D., 168
Hepburn, Walter, 67, 104–5
Heron, Craig, 8, 98, 102
Hexter, J.H., 9
Hill, Joe, 36
Hilton, C.T., 69, 162, 167
Hinton, James, 30–1
Hobsbawm, Eric, 31, 102–3, 106
Hod carriers, 56
Hoffa, Jimmy, 14, 28
Home Club affair, 56–7
Hyman, Richard, 31–3, 34, 37, 40

Incorporation thesis, 29, 32–3, 34
Independence, 99–100
Independent, 5, 48–9, 51, 67, 78–80,
    81, 82–3, 84, 87–91, 93, 94, 96, 98,
    104, 105, 112, 114, 116, 121, 122–3,
    129, 130, 131, 134, 135, 136, 137,
    138, 139, 140, 141, 152, 153, 154–5,
    156, 157, 162, 163, 165, 166, 167,
    168, 176, 178; subscriptions to,
    88–90
Independent Labour Party, 49, 146, 160
Industrial Workers of the World
    (IWW), 8, 13, 22, 149, 161, 168, 179,
    184
International Association of Machin-
    ists, 145, 146, 158–9, 169, 176
International Brotherhood of Electrical
    Workers, 169; Ladies' Auxilliary of,
    171
International Brotherhood of Teamsters,
    13–14
International Typographical Union
    (ITU), 22–3, 46, 48, 53, 54, 66, 67, 68,

69, 78, 87, 90, 104, 114, 118, 120, 127, 140, 175, 176, 177
International Union of Mine, Mill and Smelter Workers, 30
International Woodworkers of America, 30, 192n46
International Workingmen's Association, 102
Iron moulders, 61, 104, 164, 165
Iron Shipbuilders Union, 59
Irvine, George, 47, 69, 72–4, 103, 104, 117

Jackson, J.R., 105
Jameson, David, 47, 48, 69

Kaine, Charles, 67
Kazin, Michael, 72, 106, 126
Kingsley, E.T., 145, 150, 151, 157, 159, 168, 178
Knights of Labor, 46, 47, 53–4, 55, 56–7, 58, 61, 62, 69, 90, 98, 101, 129, 159, 163
Kolko, Gabriel, 29

Laborers' Union, 128
Labour bureaucracy, and authority, 35–6; and culture, 106, 108–24; and knowledge, 38–9; and legality, 73; and socialism, 3–4, 147–9; as ideology, 5–6, 24–5, 180; as power, 8, 26–7, 33–6; consent to and coercion by, 36–8; definition of, 8, 14–16; historiography of, 7–8, 14–42, 102–7, 206n36
Labour Day, 48, 58, 65–6, 73, 108–111, 118, 119, 120, 123, 169
Labourism, 80–1, 147–9; definition of, 92–4; intellectual roots of, 98–100
Labour theory of value, 92–3, 147
Lamrick, W.J., 52, 69, 105, 161, 164, 167

Lang, Alex, 150
Lassalle, Ferdinand, 56
Lathers, 169
Laundry workers, 68, 105
Laundry Workers Union, 170–1
Laurier, Sir Wilfrid, 59
Lawson, W.R., 60, 84–5
Leaper, G.F., 53, 54, 90
Lee, C.N., 68, 105
Lefeaux, Wallis, 152
Lemieux Act, 171
Lenfesty, G.F., 68
Lenin, Vladimir, 24–5, 190n29. See also Bolshevism, critique of
Liberalism, critique of, 23–4
Liberals, 10, 50, 51–2, 59, 60, 82, 105, 120, 131, 146, 160, 161, 162, 163, 164, 165, 175. See also Politics
Liberator, 154
Lib-Labism, 50, 60, 82, 100, 111, 143, 146, 158–9, 163, 164, 168. See also George Maxwell; Ralph Smith
Lilley, J.T., 67, 164
Lipset, Seymour Martin, 22–4; bureaucracy and radicalism, 23; critique of, 22–4, 189n26
Longshoremen, 46, 58, 82, 103–4, 163
Loosmore, Thomas, 98
Ludgate, Theodore, 59

Machinists 45, 47, 67, 107, 171, 178. See also International Association of Machinists
Machinists' Journal, 173
MacClain, William, 69, 134, 144, 146, 158–9, 160
Macdonald, Sir John A., 112
MacLean, M.A., 44
MacPherson, Robert, 52, 160, 162, 163, 165

Madden, R.R., 14
Main, A.D., 130
Mainland Shipmen's Association, 63
Manliness, 139–40; and intellectuals, 152
Marshall, J.C., 67, 160
Martin, Joe, 110
Marx, Karl, 10, 21, 93, 102, 155, 182
Matthews, Thomas, 151
Maxwell, Catherine, 111
Maxwell, George R., 50, 51, 60, 100, 111, 131
McBride, Richard, 118, 119, 162
McCormack, A. Ross, 145, 161, 162, 163, 164
McDonald, Colin, 163
McDonald, Robert A.J., 102, 103
McGuigan, Dr, 119
McKay, Ian, 8
McKinley, William, 112
McRae, Duncan, 47, 48, 49, 111, 127
McVety, James (J.H.), 52, 67–8, 159–60, 168, 170, 171–2, 173–4, 176, 178, 179, 181, 182
Mesher, George, 73
Metal workers, 107
Michels, Robert, 14, 16–19, 22, 23, 24, 26, 32, 34, 40, 53, 103, 180, 182, 188n14, 208n27; oligarchy and reformism, 17–18, 19
Miliband, Ralph, 10
Mill, John Stuart, 14
Mills, C. Wright, 27–8
Miners Magazine, 173
Monck, C.R., 160, 162, 164
Mortimer, John, 156, 159–60, 163, 164, 166, 167
Morton, John, 118, 160
Moyer, Charles, 168

Nanaimo Labor Congress, 64
National Civic Federation, 146
National Union of Railwaymen, 31
Nationalist Party, 50, 100, 117
Natives, 58, 95, 109, 129, 134, 174

O'Brien, J.M., 119
O'Donoghue, Daniel, 78
Ogle, Fred, 151, 156
One Big Union, 179
Oppenheimer, David, 119
Orr, W.J., 105

Painters, 48, 65, 67, 69, 86
Palmer, Bryan D., 8
Parks, 59–60, 121–2
Patrons of Industry, 98, 101
Pearey, John, 59–60, 160
People's Journal, 53
Perkins, J.H., 133
Perlman, Selig, 14, 19–22, 23–4, 25; critique of, 21–2
Pettibone, George, 168
Pettipiece, Parmeter, 52, 100, 150, 151, 156, 157, 168–70, 174–5, 177, 178, 179, 181, 215n19
Pioneer Mixed Alliance, 143
Plasterers, 47, 69, 103
Plasterers Union, 72
Pleming, William, 67, 104, 127–8
Politics, 44–5, 50–2, 58, 60–1, 74–5, 82, 96–7, 112, 113, 116–19, 145–6, 148, 163–5, 168–9, 217n26
Pollay, Mr, 53–4
Populist Party, 159
Postal employees, 67
Postal Employees Union, 161–2
Powell, Mrs, 170–1
Presser, Jackie, 13–14
Price, Richard, 30–1

Printers, 45, 61, 103, 132, 133, 161, 172.
    See also International Typographical
    Union
Prosser, F., 47
Provincial Progressive Party, 61, 166–7
Public ownership, 94–5

Race, 104, 116, 125–35, 142, 169–70,
    181; and job competition, 126–7; and
    skill, 56; and white slavery, 128–9,
    170; of VTLC delegates, 47–50, 52–3
Radek, Karl, 24
Railway carmen, 86
Retail clerks, 45, 69, 116, 140, 164, 166
Retail Clerks International Protective
    Association, 52, 105, 161, 167
Revolutionary Socialist Party of Can-
    ada, 145
Rockefeller, John D., 94
Rogers, B.T., 127–8
Rogers, Frank, 111–12, 134, 144, 146,
    156
Ross, A.W., 59
Rumble, J., 67
Russell, F.J., 68, 69, 118, 161, 162, 164

Saxton, Alexander, 126
Sayer, W.W., 68, 170
Scott, Jack, 30
Shop stewards, 38–41
Smith, Mrs, 170–1
Smith, Ralph, 51, 60, 95, 143–4, 146,
    158–9, 165
Smithe, William, 44
Social Democratic Party (Canada), 6,
    159
Social Democratic Party of Germany
    (SPD), 16–19, 24
Socialist Labor Party (SLP), 143–4, 145,
    146, 158, 168

Socialist Party of America, 22, 144
Socialist Party of British Columbia
    (SPBC), 144, 156, 159, 163, 167, 168
Socialist Party of Canada (SPC), 6, 100,
    151, 159, 168, 170, 179
Socialist Trades and Labor Alliance
    (STLA), 143–4, 146, 214n13
Sombart, Werner, 3
Sons of the British Empire, 110
Soper, A.E., 162, 167
'Southern Cross,' 81
Sports, 121–3
Standard Oil Company, 94
Steamshipmen's Union, 65
Stevedores, 46, 61, 65, 86
Stevedores Union, 163
Stewart, Dan, 104
Stonecutters, 61, 67, 72–3, 104, 164
Streetcar railwaymen, 45, 68, 104, 161,
    164, 172
Streetcar Railwaymen's Union, 159, 160
Strikes, 46–7, 56, 62, 72–3, 81, 140
Suckling, A.E. 'Bones,' 123
Sweeney, C., 119

Tailors, 67, 104, 107, 114, 133, 159
Tailors Union, 178
Tatlow, R.G., 119
Team Drivers Union, 162
Teamsters for a Democratic Union, 13–
    14
Telephone operators, 140, 171
Theodus, C. Sam, 13
Thompson, E.P., 10, 103
Thompson, Sir John, 112
Thompson, Phillips, 100–1, 150
Tisdall, Charles E., 119
Todd, Robert, 118
Trades and Labor Congress of Canada
    (TLC), 40, 100, 101

Union label campaign, 114–16, 123, 133
United Auto Workers, 30
United Brotherhood of Carpenters and Joiners (UBCJ), 46, 47, 48, 49, 54, 83
United Brotherhood of Railway Employees (UBRE), 111–12, 156, 162, 164, 165, 176–7
United Electrical Workers, 30
United Garment Workers Union, 170–1
United Socialist Labor Party, 144, 146, 158

Vancouver, early history of, 43–6
Vancouver Cricket Club, 121–2
Vancouver Electric and Tramway Company, 94
Vancouver Labour Party, 161, 162, 167
Vancouver Trades and Labour Council (VTLC), and business, 110–11, 119–20; and control of labour market, 132–3; and expertise, 79–80; and intellectuals, 149–53; and newspapers, 82–3, 87–91, 176–8; and power (gender and race), 137, 142; and radicalism, 88–90, 120, 143–57; and union hall, 82–7, 175–6; collection of statistics, 62–3, 75–6; eligibility for membership in, 53–4, 165–6; fears of centralization, 54–8, 62; founding of, 46–7; leadership, continuity of, 66–9, 158–79; professionalization, 74, 101, 175, 178; separation from rank and file, 7, 12, 63, 74, 86–7, 91, 143, 157, 171–2, 179, 181–2; socialists' influence in, 158–61, 166, 168–70
Victoria Trades and Labour Council, 127
Von Rhein, A.W., 169–70

Waitresses and Waiters Union, 45, 52, 116, 133, 162, 171. *See also* Cooks, Waiters and Waitresses Union
Waldrop, Joseph, 109
Walker, Mrs, 170–1
Walking delegates, 72–4, 75
Ward, W. Peter, 125, 134, 209n3
Watson, Joseph Henry, 50–2, 59, 60–1, 65, 67, 68, 84–5, 118, 120, 134, 139, 140, 145–9, 155–6, 160, 162, 163, 164–5, 166, 167, 171, 174–5, 178, 202n63
Weber, Max, 15–17, 19, 20, 36, 37, 65, 180
Weinstein, James, 29
Weir, Stan, 28–9, 30, 101
Weitling, Wilhelm, 155
Western Clarion, 100, 170–1
Western Federation of Miners, 168
Western Socialist, 151
Western Socialist Publishing Company, 151, 215n19
Western Wage Earner, 5, 178
Wilks, George, 104
Williams, Francis, 49, 59–60, 67, 84–5, 113, 117, 118, 140, 143–4, 146, 156, 161, 162, 167
Williams, Parker, 77
Woodward, Charles, 59
Working card system, 71–4
Working class, composition of, 45–6, 47, 117, 129, 141–2
World, 109, 111, 119, 128, 137, 140
Wrigley, George Weston, 100, 144, 151, 156, 157

Zeitlin, Jonathan, 14, 30, 31–2, 33, 34, 36; critique of, 33–4
Zinoviev, Gregory, 14